Defence, Security and Development

Defence, Security and Development

Edited by
Saadet Deger and Robert West

St. Martin's Press, New York

First Published in the United States of America in 1987

Printed in Great Britain

Library of Congress Cataloging-in-Publication Data
Defence, security and development.
  Bibliography: p.
  Includes index.
    1. Developing countries—National security—Economic
aspects.   2. Disarmament—Economic aspects—Developing
countries.   3. Munitions—Developing countries.
I. Deger, Saadet, 1950– . II. West, Robert,
1925– .
HC59.72.D4D436   1987   338.4′76234′091724   87-12129
ISBN 0-312-01243-8

Contents

2314506

List of contributors

Nicole Ball is a Senior Analyst at the National Security Archive in Washington D.C., USA, where she specializes in US arms transfers and security assistance. She was formerly Visiting Research Associate of the Swedish Institute of International Affairs. Her most recent book, *Security and Economy in the Third World*, will be published in English by Princeton University Press in 1988 and in Spanish by Fondo de Cultura Economica in 1989.

Michael Brzoska is a Researcher at the Institut für Politische Wissenschaft, Forschungszentrum Kriege, Runstung und Entwicklung, Universität Hamburg, West Germany. He has published widely on arms trade and production including an edited volume on *Arms Production in the Third World* (1986) for SIPRI (together with T. Ohlson). His latest book (co-authored by T. Ohlson), on the arms trade, will also be published by SIPRI in 1987.

Saadet Deger is a Research Fellow at the Department of Economics and Centre for Defence Economics, Birbeck College, University of London, UK. She specializes on the economics of military expenditure in developing countries. Her book, *Military Expenditure in the Third World: The Economic Effects* (Routledge) was published in 1986; the Spanish edition for Latin America, to be published by Sudamericana, Argentina is forthcoming in 1988. Currently she is researching the economic aspects of the arms transfer process and her monograph on the subject will be published by Basil Blackwell in 1988.

Jacques Fontanel is the Deputy Director of the Centre d'Etudes de Défense et Sécurité Internationale, Université de Grenoble, France. He has written numerous papers and books on various aspects of military expenditure both with reference to the French economy as well as comparative analysis with other OECD economies and Third World countries. He has been associated with many United Nations initiatives and programmes on disarmament and development. His book *L'effort économique de défense* jointly written with R. Smith, was published in 1986.

Anthony Humm is a Researcher at the Department of Economics and Centre for Defence Economics, Birkbeck College, University of London, UK.

He specializes in the economic aspects of defence expenditures in the UK as well as OECD countries. He has written papers in the area emphasizing econometric model-building.

Alfred Maizels is a Senior Fellow at the World Institute of Development Economic Research, Helsinki, Finland (part of the United Nations University). Previously, he was an honorary Research Fellow, Department of Economics, University College, London. He is the author of numerous articles on the trade and development problems of developing countries, as well as books on industrial growth and world trade, and exports and economic growth. He is currently preparing a major study on international commodity policy.

Machiko Nissanke is presently a Fellow at Nuffield College, University of Oxford, UK. She is an economist whose current research interest is energy issues and the oil shock. She has also conducted research and published extensively on international trade, East European economies, as well as on defence expenditure in developing countries.

Arcadi Oliveres is Professor of Structural Economics at the Escola Universitaria d'Estudis Empresarials, Universitat Autonoma de Barcelona, Spain. He is also the Director, Institut Victor Seix de Polemologia. He has been engaged in research and written extensively on Spanish defence expenditures as well as on more general aspects of the structure of the Spanish economy.

Robert L. Rothstein Harvey Picker Distinguished Professor of International Relations, is Director of the International Relations Program, Department of Political Science, Colgate University, USA. He has written many articles and books on the politics of the Third World and on international organization, including *The Weak in the World of the Strong* (Colombia University Press, 1977) and *Global Bargaining* (Princeton University Press, 1979).

Somnath Sen lectures at the Department of Economics, University of Birmingham, UK. He specializes in macroeconomics and his book *Protectionism, Exchange Rates and the Macroeconomy* was published in 1985 by Basil Blackwell. He has written widely on defence economics, including specialist reports for the United Nations. He is currently co-writing with Saadet Deger *The Economics of the International Arms Trade*, to be published by Blackwell in 1988.

Ron Smith is Professor of Applied Economics at the Department of Economics and the Director at the Centre for Defence Economics, Birkbeck College, University of London, UK. He has conducted extensive research on many aspects of defence economics and has published numerous papers in major international journals. He has written on the economic causes and effects of defence in the UK, the OECD countries and developing economies. He has contributed academic reports for the House of Commons, and the United Nations. His books *The Economics of Militarism* (Pluto Press), co-authored with Dan Smith, was published in 1983 and *L'effort économique de défense* written with J. Fontanel, also in 1983.

W. Scott Thompson, a member of the Faculty of the Fletcher School of Law and Diplomacy, Tufts University, USA, since 1967, is the author and editor of seven books on foreign policy, including *Ghana's Foreign Policy* (Princeton University Press, 1969) and *The Third World: Premises for U.S. Policy*, which he edited for publication by the Institute of Comtemporary Studies, 1978. He served the Reagan Administration as Associate Director, US Information Agency, and the Ford Administration in the Department of Defense. He is on the board of directors of the US Institute of Peace.

Robert West is Professor of International Economics, The Fletcher School of Law and Diplomacy, Tufts University, USA. He specialises in international resource policy, problems of development finance, and the economics of national security in the Third World. He was formerly a staff member of the United Nations and a Mission Director of the US Agency for International Development. He is co-editor, with Gustav Ranis, of *Comparative Development Perspectives* (Westview Press, 1984).

Herbert Wulf is a Researcher at the Institut für Friedensforschung und Sicherheitspolitik, Universität Hamburg, West Germany. He conducts research on militarization in the Third World, technology transfer and arms production, and the arms trade. He has published numerous papers on these subjects. His book *Runstungsimport als Technologietransfer* was published in 1980. His most recent monograph, in German, on industrial conversion from defence to civilian products will appear in 1987.

Abbreviations

ACDA	US Arms Control and Disarmament Agency
ASEAN	Association of South East Asian Nations
CAT	Conventional Arms Transfer
CES	Constant Elasticity of Substitution
CGE	Central Government Expenditure
CIA	Central Intelligence Agency
DSAA	Defense Security Assistance Agency
EA	East Asia
ELF	Eritrean Liberation Front
ESRC	Economic and Social Research Council
FIDD	Fonds International de Desarmement pour le Developpement (International Disarmament Fund for Development)
ICP	International Comparison Project
IISS	International Institute for Strategic Studies
IME	Industrial Market Economies
IMF	International Monetary Fund
LA	Latin America
LDC	Less Developed Countries
MENA	Middle East and North Africa
MILEX	(Data on) military expenditures
NME	Non-market economies in Europe
NMO	Non-market economies in other regions
OECD	Organization for Economic Cooperation and Development
PPP	Purchasing power parities
SA	South Asia
SEI	Socio-economic index
SIPRI	Stockholm International Peace Research Institute
SSA	Sub-Saharan Africa
UNIDIR	United Nations Institute for Disarmament Research
USAID	United States Agency for International Development
WTO	Warsaw Treaty Organization

Preface

The governments of a hundred developing countries are confronted by a tumult of conflicting demands to provide resources for more rapid development, expanded welfare services and greater national security. For the authorities of these governments, the choices which must be made to reconcile the competing requirements for more national defence and more development are often the touchstone of political survival. In a turbulent era of prevalent violence, the choices made by many Third World governments are described by an exponential rise in arms transfers, a sharp increase in the scale and sophistication of weaponry, and a persisting expansion of military expenditures.

These trends in the growth of Third World military establishments and capabilities have been carefully observed by defence policy analysts. The implications for regional and global security are monitored by students of international political relations. But, until quite recently, the trends have been relatively neglected by both practitioners and analysts in the development community.

Over the decade of the 1970s, the real resources devoted to national defence by the market-orientated Third World countries more than doubled. The growth rates in the budgetary allocations for military expenditure and in the importation of weapons consistently exceeded the rates of growth in national income and external earnings. But throughout this period there was very little investigation by development analysts of the causes for this increasing effort to provide for national security or how it interacted with the pursuit of development goals. The decisions respecting military expenditures and arms imports were generally viewed as being governed by exogenous factors, outside the considerations bearing on allocation of public resources for development and civilian government services, and presented as a kind of budgetary 'Hobson's choice'. The conventional wisdom about the relation of military expenditure to economic performance derived from a very limited, almost casual, base of empirical observation.

The neglect of this subject by development analysts is being redressed in the 1980s. The magnitude of budgetary allocations to national defence and the austerity imposed by severe constraints on the resources available to Third World governments have incited a new interest in accounting for the purposes and the consequences of military expenditures. Donors and lenders abroad, as well as planning authorities and fiscal managers in developing countries, increasingly demand more careful study of defence options and empirical investigation of the interactions between security and economic performance. An expanding research effort, both in Europe and in the United States, has resulted in a substantially enlarged flow of case studies and comparative analyses.

There is, however, little evidence as yet of a consensus with respect to the appropriate weighting of factors in an explanation of the allocation of resources to national defence or in a generally-applicable model of the interactions between security and economic performance. There have been, thus far, few opportunities for direct comparison of research findings and few occasions for exchange of views among the research workers—particularly, between investigators in Europe and the United States. Quite divergent viewpoints are found in different national development-research communities concerning the key questions to be examined and the interpretation of findings; communications among the communities are weak.

This book is the product of an effort to improve those communications by convening a Colloquium of scholars from universities and research institutes of continental Europe, the United Kingdom and the United States, all of whom are engaged in study of security and development in the Third World. The chapters presented here are derived from papers discussed at the Colloquium. They retain the evidence of wide-ranging differences of perspective among the authors and, thereby, accurately disclose the existence of divergent views on these issues in the development research community. But they also reflect the enthusiasm and imagination of progress reports on a contemporary problem of public policy under vigorous investigation.

We thought it inadvisable to impose strict guidelines as to the form or contents of the papers discussed at the Colloquium. In this way we hope that the diversity of basic philosophical points of view would be presented to readers of the book. The papers also reflect the multifarious disciplines that the research community encompasses in the field—international relations, political science, economics and econometrics. We also preferred to maintain the presentational style of the authors to reflect their distinctive approaches to the subject and the languages of their disciplines. It is a measure of the importance of the subject that academics from so many diverse institutions and areas of study could find common ground for discussion and debate.

The Colloquium was conducted at the University of London in March, 1986. Participants included the authors of the chapters in this volume, but we must also note the valuable contributions made by discussants: Dr. Elliot Berg of the World Bank and Washington, D.C.; Dr. Paul Dunne of the University of Cambridge; Dr. Nils Petter Gleditsch of the International Peace Research Institute at Oslo; Dr. Merilee Grindle of Harvard University; Dr. Robert Harkavy of Pennsylvania State University; Dr. Keith Hartley of the University of York; Dr. Huang Su-An of the Beijing Institute for Study of

International Relations; Dr. Robin Luckham of the University of Sussex; Professor Robert Looney of the US Naval Post-Graduate School; Professor Robin Marris of Birkbeck College, University of London; Professor P. N. Mathur of the University College of Wales and University of Birmingham; Professor Robert Meagher of Tufts University; Udayan Mukherjee of the School of Oriental and African Studies; Dr. Stephanie Neuman of Columbia University; Professor Richard Portes of the Centre for Economic Policy Research; Professor Christian Schmidt of the Universite de Paris; Dr. Dennis Snower and Ms. Sue Willett of Birkbeck College. Dr. Luckham and Dr. Grindle also presented papers to sessions of the Colloquium. We are deeply grateful to all the contributors, discussants, and observers who participated in the Colloquium.

The joint sponsors of the Colloquium were Birkbeck College, University of London, and The Fletcher School of Law and Diplomacy, Tufts University. We appreciate greatly the support and assistance provided by Professor Robin Marris, Chairman of the Department of Economics at Birkbeck College, and Professor John Roche, Dean of The Fletcher School.

Financial support for the Colloquium and for a preparatory workshop conducted at The Fletcher School of Law and Diplomacy was provided by a grant awarded by the International Affairs Programs of the Ford Foundation. The sponsors of the Colloquium and the editors are grateful to the Ford Foundation for this generous assistance and to Dr. Enid Schoettle and Mr. Thomas Bayard of the International Affairs Programs for their encouragement and advice.

We would like to acknowledge the help, encouragement and assistance we received from the publishers. In particular, we are grateful to Ms. Mary Harrison for her excellent editing, Ms. Sharon Kelly for technical assistance, and to Ms. Frances Pinter for co-ordinating the whole enterprise.

Dr. Saadet Deger
Birkbeck College, University of London
Professor Robert L. West
Fletcher School of Law and Diplomacy, Tufts University

Introduction: defence expenditure, national security and economic development in the Third World

SAADET DEGER AND ROBERT L. WEST

Basic issues

The last one and a half decades have seen unprecedented global economic turmoil. A rapidly changing international economic order has had to accommodate the transformation of the financial system, including the massive increase in the price of oil, the international debt crisis, major recessions in developed industrial economies, the collapse of commodity prices and large scale famines and deprivation. Yet military expenditure seems to continue to rise in inexorable fashion—one of the unrelenting 'growth' areas of the global system. The decade 1975–85 saw more than a 30 per cent increase in world-wide defence spending in real terms.[1] The poorest countries of the world showed an even greater propensity to spend on armaments and security—a rise of over 50 per cent in defence spending during the same period.[2]

The arms trade also flourished. In 1970, the developing world imported $2.5 billion worth of major weapons (at constant 1975 prices); in 1980 this had increased to over 9 billion dollars—an annual growth rate of nearly 14 per cent for the decade as a whole.[3] New arms exporters entered the market and a period of competitive sales began. Fast technological change led to rapid cost escalation of conventional weapons. Arms purchases by non-oil developing countries also contributed to an increase in international indebtedness.

Within this sombre perspective we need to look carefully at the developmental record of the poor countries of the world. In terms of conventional criteria they had not done too badly in the decade of the 1970s. Growth rates had been reasonably high and recycling of oil revenues helped to finance substantial trade deficits. But when we consider the massive intervention by Third World governments to force growth through planning at any cost, the results look less attractive. Many countries tried to achieve a quick transition from backwardness through direct state intervention. In addition, the extraction of surplus and its distribution to high growth sectors have been carried on relentlessly through taxation, price distortions and state economic enterprises. Given this framework of direct growth inducements, LDC achievements may be judged less than impressive.

When we inspect basic needs and the provision of entitlements to the poorest strata of Third World society, the record is extremely patchy. Even high growth countries have substantial sectors of extreme poverty. It is estimated that 800 million people in the Third World live below a modest poverty line; malnutrition, famine and disease are endemic in this vast population. The infant mortality rate—about 13 in North America—is 69 in Latin America, 122 in Africa and 126 in South Asia. It is believed that half of the world's population do not have access to safe drinking water and three quarters of the developing world has no sanitary facilities. Possibly 200 million are without minimal shelter.

It is tempting to claim that there is a causal link between the growing allocation of resources to defence and the persistence of underdevelopment. After all, military spending is the prototypical 'unproductive expenditure' from a socio-economic point of view. It might be assumed to follow that defence spending must, therefore, reduce growth and endanger development—but the notion is simplistic. Firstly, there is ample evidence that certain aspects of defence spending can be 'productive'. Secondly, it is not obvious that a reduction in the defence burden[4] will automatically lead to an increase in investment and social consumption—a pre-requisite of economic development. Thirdly, the military expenditures may, through the provision of security, foster an environment which encourages increased accumulation and productivity.

There can be little doubt that defence expenditure is often necessary for the preservation of perceived national security. This is particularly true in the developing world, recalling that almost all armed conflicts in the past forty years have been 'Third World Wars'. There are many historical, political and cultural reasons for this to be so. However the central problem remains. In the absence of strategic policy co-ordination, LDCs will continue to play non co-operative games[5] with their neighbours leading to long-term arms races. Coupled with this is the endemic internal dissension and the effects of relying on force for the imposition of legitimacy—a perfect recipe for defence expenditure to rise.

The relationships between national security, military expenditure and economic development are complex. The problems of analysis are compounded by the fact that there may not be unidirectional causality. Thus the model of political economy that tries to encapsulate the essential features of the interrelationship has to accommodate feedbacks and reverse effects. The very simple schematic presentation in Figure 0.1 illustrates the complex structure of the relations; some of the effects shown in the Figure may be either positive or negative, depending on structural characteristics of the country concerned.

Perceived threats to national security may have an internal or external dimension. Both will contribute to higher defence spending, although the external threats will probably lead to a more capital intensive pattern of spending and hence a higher defence burden.

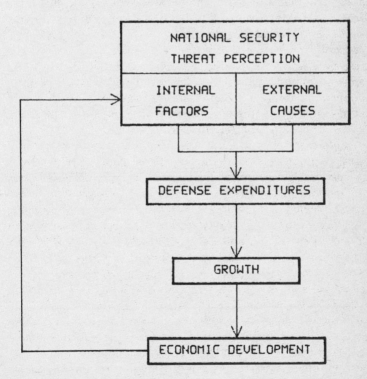

Figure 0.1 Security and development: the linkages

This in turn will have effects on economic growth. As we will demonstrate below, the growth effects of defence spending can be both positive and negative; thus we need to estimate carefully the net impact. Growth may lead, through trickle-down effects, to socio-economic development. In so far as the net effect of defence expenditures may reduce growth, the final effect on development will be adverse. The consequent feedback of development failure on internal dissension (and enhanced threat to the established regime) can induce yet higher defence spending. This establishes a vicious circle.

One approach to investigating the linkages between security, defence and development is to view Third World countries as relatively homogeneous. The search, then, is for common character-istics and general conclusions. The basic features of poverty and backwardness are common enough; these obey no national stereo-types, and may be used to define universal characteristics of developing economies. An alternative approach is to construct classificatory schemes by which it is possible to subdivide the sample of Third World countries and pay closer attention to structural features.

Employing this latter approach, a number of useful hypotheses regarding sub-groups of LDCs can be formulated and tested: for example, do military governments tend to have a higher defence burden than civilian governments? Do resource-constrained nations tend to have a negative causal effect of defence on growth while resource-abundant countries have a positive relation? Do countries with greater international interdependence spend more on the military compared to countries which are relatively isolated? Are newly industrializing countries more prone to arms production than agrarian economies? Are countries with greater arms imports also those with higher domestic spending? These and related questions—while difficult to assess, test and answer—are the subjects of on-going investigation. Some of the chapters in this volume address these specific issues.

Development studies in general, and development economics in particular, have tried to emphasize the importance of 'structure'—the underlying social, political, cultural and economic relations and institutions that shape behaviour in developing countries. Neo-classical theory postulates that human beings ('agents') optimize subject to constraints. As a meta theory encompassing all behaviour, this is a useful assumption. But if the concept of optimization is not to become tautological, its relevance must be bounded. Particularly in poor societies, the underlying structural relations may be crucial in determining the nature of the optimizing function (utility, profit) and the form of the constraints (starvation, indebtedness). It is important, therefore, to assess the structural characteristics of the economy concerned, both in terms of economic linkages and political features, before attempting to specify the role and effect of military expenditure.

Figure 0.2, adapted from Luckham (1978), presents one typology illustrating the different types of security-maintenance functions that the defence establishment may fulfil in developing countries. It links economic structure with forms of political conflict and emphasizes the domestic security role of the military. A similar typology can be constructed by focusing on perceived external threats. The central point is the variety of the interrelationships that bind militarization with the economy and its perceived problems of security.

In the next two sections we will explore the salient features of national security and economic development as they relate to defence expenditures. The fourth section is a résumé of the international dimensions of the problem. The fifth section reviews the chapters of this volume and the last section identifies some policy implications.

National security

For many LDCs, national security is manifestly endangered by external threats. The long running Iran–Iraq war is a vivid demonstration of neighbours engaging in a competitive arms race which finally erupts into war. India and Pakistan, Vietnam and China, Libya and Chad, Israel and the Arab States are additional examples. Even civil uprisings and domestic conflict have often an external dimension which can lead to foreign intervention—witness Bangladesh, Pakistan and India in the early 1970s.

Historical factors frequently have an important role in inter-State wars and defence build-up. The Iran–Iraq conflagration, for example, has been variously attributed to personal animosity (between Ayatollah Khomeni and President Hussain), to the long standing socio-cultural feud between Persians and Arabs, and to the arms build-up nourished by the oil wealth. Whatever its cause, there can be little doubt that defence provision in the face of external threat

	DEVELOPMENT STRATEGIES	CHARACTERISTICS OF ECONOMIC STRUCTURE	ROLE OF THE MILITARY
PRIMARY PRODUCERS; AGRICULTURE AND MINING	(1) Low integration with the international economy.	Small scale production; foreign capital does not play significant role.	Domestic conflicts in a semi-feudal society; military helps national integration; gives it a common identity; military burden low.
	(2) High integration with the international economy.	Enclave production; sophisticated technology; foreign capital crucial; output exported.	Conflict between enclave and rest of economy; military 'protects' enclave; military burden high.
INDUSTRIALISING LDCs	(1) Import substituting industrialisation.	Domestic investment to industrialise; self-sufficiency.	Conflict between labour and capital, industry and agriculture; military provides internal security; active against guerillas, etc.; suppression of organised labour; military burden depends on external threat.
	(2) Export oriented development strategy.	Export promotion; foreign capital crucial; outward-looking policies.	Similar to above, but with greater intensity.

Figure 0.2 Role of the military in domestic conflict Source: R. Luckham (1978).

can be a very expensive business, indeed. In particular, direct costs of modern wars can be astronomical; it is estimated that Israel's twenty-two day war in 1973 cost it the equivalent of a full year's national income. Modern armaments are technologically superior and therefore expensive. In the presence of an external threat, implicit pressure, particularly from the defence establishment, tends to induce the country to equip itself with the latest vintage armaments, quite often bought from the international arms market.

The tacit assumption, in these strategic explanations of weapons systems procurement, is usually that higher military expenditure does actually increase security in developing countries. However, this may not always be true. At least for some LDCs, there may be some connection between ultra-sophistication of strategic plans, excess military spending leading to 'overkill,' and escalation of costs. More sophistication is not necessarily better, particularly for countries with low absorptive capacity and relatively limited technical skills. In addition, if competitive arms races are being fuelled by weapons imports, then imported invention becomes the mother of necessity. Even if a country is unable to task the latest weapons system, there may be pressure to acquire it when an adversary does so.

In the political economy literature, the provision of security is considered a public good with high externalities. Governments are described as duty bound to provide more, to the extent that resource constraints allow. All other social goods, such as education and health services, have their private counterparts. But defence is unique; national security is almost always totally publicly funded. This conception can be used to explain why any increase in wealth is likely, in part, to be channelled toward weapons acquisition. This reasoning may be invoked as a contributory explanation for the very high military spending of major oil exporters in the 1970s (Sivard, 1983).

Perceived threats to internal security are also major factors that may contribute to the growth of militarization and often to a higher military burden. Two concepts are crucial here. The first pertains to the sources of legitimacy enjoyed by Third World regimes. The second relates to expectations, often generated by economic development itself. For many developing countries, given their brief history as modern nation states, it is difficult for any government to establish its legitimacy. It is a commonplace to observe that, in many developing societies, orderly and systematic acquisition and replacement of power by the elite groups are not the traditional norm; the retention of power requires strong government and the capacity to deploy force. Some observers, emphasizing the propensity towards civil strife, see militarization as an entrenched characteristic of political organization in the developing world (Horowitz, 1982).

Economic development and the strains of rapid socio-economic transformation also may be the source of conflict. Economic growth may raise the expectations of the masses. When growth is accompanied by high inequality and very limited trickle-down effects, the situation may become explosive. The larger the difference between the realized and the expected (whether we refer to per capita income or growth or standard of living or basic needs) the greater the potential for political instability.

Given the unstable environment and the traditional reliance on force to confer legitimacy, the military frequently identifies itself as the most suited to claim leadership. The majority of developing countries, in recent years, have seen some form of military government. The military certainly has the power to support and provide the ruling elites; it presents a facade of cohesion which seems to be stronger than the divisive civilian groups; and its identification with 'modernization' often makes it an influential and dynamic part of Third World society. There is, of course, no necessary relation between increased military participation in political life and higher defence burdens. However, repression and emphasis on internal security must have its own costs; this could raise the military burden.

Economic development

The relationships we have identified may be expressed in a syllogism. Internal and external threats need to be met by defence expenditure; in turn, defence spending contributes to perceived national security. Governments feel bound to provide these security services given the 'public good' character of defence, even in circumstances in which added defence spending impacts unfavourably on development. Lack of adequate or equitable development has an adverse feedback on the legitimacy of the ruling elites. This requires additional military expenditures.

The problem is exacerbated and a vicious circle may be established when defence expenditure has a negative effect on growth and indirectly on economic development. It is therefore useful to assess the effects of defence expenditures on the economy. The major question is whether a higher military burden leads to a higher or lower rate of growth. Does increased defence spending increase or reduce economic growth?

Emile Benoit's (1978) startling conclusion, that a higher military burden actually has a positive effect and increases economic growth, has been much discussed in the literature. (See Deger, 1986, for a survey.) There can be little doubt that spin-off effects exist, from the defence sector to the civilian economy, in developing countries. Effective demand creation, R&D diffusion, technological progress, arms industrialization as a leading sector, inter-industrial demand generation, and the creation of employment, are all possible when military spending increases. These are the sources of positive effects.

The negative effects are in terms of allocation and mobilization of resources. From the demand side, military expenditure may crowd out domestic investment and hence lower the rate of growth. It may also displace productive government spending, such as on agricultural improvements or infrastructure. Defence expenditure essentially allocates resources towards the ultimate non-productive consumption. Given supply constraints, which seem to be usual in LDCs, additional defence may mean less of something else which is more productive.

The mobilization effect refers to the supply side, to which little attention has been paid by researchers. Deger (1985) provides some evidence that a higher military burden may affect the national saving ratio itself, thus causing problems for the mobilization of resources for growth. From the government budgetary side, greater defence spending not compensated by increased taxes will mean a lower rate of saving. But even from the private sector point of view, if military spending reduces the provision of other public goods (health, education etc.), then household consumption will rise, thus reducing sectoral saving. Further, if defence-induced inflation fuels a consumption boom (to beat the price rise) and raises inflationary expectations, we have further adverse effects.

Overall, the intuitive sense of the studies thus far conducted is that defence expenditures should in most cases reduce the rate of growth of aggregate output. This is borne out by quite a bit of statistical evidence, much of which is summarized in Deger (1986). In general, the econometric analysis suggests that when all the effects (spin-off, mobilization, allocation and so on) are taken into account, the net effect of defence spending on growth is negative. The result is robust across alternative specifications and seems to hold for large sample sets of LDCs.

Looney and Frederiksen (1985; Looney, 1987) suggest that the developmental homogeneity of developing nations cannot be taken for granted. Thus countries should be sub-divided according to their economic characteristics; the defence–growth relationship should be tested for each sub-group. They find that economies with stringent resource constraints (both domestic and external) tend to show that high military burdens adversely affect growth. On the other hand, countries with less resource constraint (those with greater borrowing capacity, more effective fiscal systems and higher domestic saving) tend to show the positive effects mentioned earlier.

These are useful and suggestive results, complementing the more general findings described above. But the inferences are still tentative. The formal difficulty with sample classification according to characteristics is that, conceptually, numerous divisions are possible and it is difficult to systematize the conflicting empirical evidence that may be produced. Relying on the data alone to establish the characteristics of sub-groups can be criticized on the same grounds as criticisms levelled against atheoretical macro-econometrics in general. We still need to construct better theoretical models which will relate defence burden to growth rates under alternative developmental scenarios.

Economic growth is neither necessary nor sufficient for economic development in the broadest sense of the term. Growth may only benefit certain sections of the economy; in the absence of the rewards of growth 'trickling down' to the masses, there cannot be any development. It is, of course, not easy to quantify the effect of defence on development. There are difficult definitional problems and the choice of a suitable aggregate index to define development is problematic. In the absence of quantification of 'quality of life' it is not easy to have proper empirical tests of the postulated effects. The general suppositions is that defence spending does impact adversely on economic development, and should therefore be costed carefully.

The international dimensions

The existence of an external threat to national security immediately propels a less developed country into the international arena. Superpower involvement tends to exacerbate the problem. Military responses to external strategic threats can be much more expensive, in terms of resource use and economic cost, than domestic security considerations and internal repression. Weapons acquisition, within a competitive arms race, becomes an urgent necessity. In the absence of a well-developed domestic armaments industry, these weapons need to be imported from abroad. Some may come as foreign military aid; others need to be paid for in cash or financed with credit. The foreign exchange costs to the economy now impart an additional burden on growth. Many LDCs have adopted an import-fed growth strategy (rather than an export-led one). This implies that capital formation and output increase depend crucially on intermediate imported goods such as the latest vintage machinery. If additional defence spending on foreign arms reduces the importation of such intermediates, growth suffers.

The arms trade is therefore a crucial link between national security, external threat and economic growth. Foreign exchange constraints make it imperative that unproductive imports (such as armaments) be kept to a minimum. On the other hand, the internationalization of conflicts, with combatants using sophisticated imported arms, demand the economic sacrifice represented by the importation of weapons.

One response to this dilemma is the domestic production of arms. The number of countries, in the developing world, involved in the fabrication of armaments has increased considerably in recent years. Some of them, such as Brazil and Israel, have also entered into export markets.

Two features are of immediate interest and concern. First, the production of arms is neither a necessary nor a sufficient condition for lower imports. Thus India and Israel are simultaneously the largest producers and importers within the Third World. Though domestic output is increased as a response to high foreign exchange costs, there is no guarantee that this will necessarily reduce imports. Once again, it is the external threat and perceived security needs that call the tune. Both Israel and India claim that neighbouring countries pose a grave threat to their national security.

Secondly, there can be an incentive to link weapons imports and exports. Thus, countries may wish to produce and sell certain types of arms abroad in which they have a comparative advantage; the concomitant gain in foreign reserves is then used to import other types of weapons relevant to domestic security needs. This coupling of imports and exports is a growing trend. Even a country such as India, which embarked on domestic production under the broad framework of import-substituting industrialization rather than export promotion, is now seriously considering large scale exports.

The international market is therefore taking on an oligopolistic form where a significant number of countries are competing with each other. Not content with a given downward sloping demand curve and usual price cutting and product differentiation strategies, exporting countries may actively try to shift the demand curve outwards. Thus there will be an incentive to create new markets for weapons—an added threat to world disarmament and peace.

The contents of the volume

The chapters in this volume reflect the concern that analysts and policy-makers feel about the trade-off between national security and economic development that arises from military expenditure. The papers have a wide spectrum but are conveniently divided into four sections which deal with the basic issues: (Part I) measurement and evaluation of the data regarding military spending, its 'share' in government budgets, and the defence burden; (Part II) the inter-relationship between defence and development, both at the national and international levels; (Part III) the causes and determinants of defence expenditures; and (Part IV) the international trade in armaments.

We turn first to a description of what information is available and how it can be evaluated and used. Robert West (Chapter 1) is concerned with the comparison of military spending, share and burden across countries and over time. Given the heterogeneity of LDCs, a classificatory scheme needs to be constructed which will reflect regional groupings and levels of development. West constructs a detailed classification which takes into account the major differences and similarities of developing countries, and therefore provides a useful starting point for data-based discussion of security spending in relation to economic development. But more important, distortions resulting from conversion of local currency data into US dollars by using currency market exchange rates are corrected by conversion using purchasing power parity (PPP) indices. The comparative analysis, summarized in the concluding section of the paper, is revealing. Among oil importing developing economies, the richer countries (upper-middle income) tended to have lower defence burdens, and lower growth rates of defence burdens, relative to the poorest countries (low and lower-middle income). It seems that poverty per se is not sufficient to restrain military spending nor is defence a luxury good whose share (in GDP) is reduced as income falls.

Nicole Ball (Chapter 2) takes a more general perspective on the data by analysing the coverage and procedures of various international reporting agencies, the accuracy and reliability of the information, and the implications that can be drawn from them. The emphasis is on observational validity and descriptive conclusions that may be usefully gleaned from the large data set available.

The third chapter, by Ron Smith, Anthony Humm and Jacques Fontanel, uses a more formal framework to show how econometric analysis can be conducted with the data. They discuss the reliability of statistical procedures, the importance of modelling techniques, and how useful economic and strategic relations can be formulated and tested through econometric methods. Once again the crucial role of measuring the data in term of exchange rate conversions or PPPs becomes central to the conclusions of the formal model. It is clear that, even if the reported data on security spending is reliable, its use, interpretation and analysis require very careful handling.

The second part of the volume is a wide-ranging coverage of three crucial aspects of defence and development. One paper deals wholly with LDCs and domestic economic issues; another looks at the problem from a developed country point of view, specifically that of the United States; the third discusses the international perspective by analysing resource transfer from large armaments spenders among advanced industrial nations to the poorer countries of the Third World—a major practical policy suggestion of how to link disarmament and development at a global level.

Saadet Deger and Somnath Sen (Chapter 4) analyse the intricate relationship between defence spending and economic development within the domestic economy. This is done by using the 'entitlement approach' (Sen, 1983) whereby the state of development is measured by the widest possible indicators of welfare possible—the entitlement to health, nutrition, shelter, education, and basic needs, as well as the standard concept of (per capita) income. The many channels through which military spending can hinder (or help) the poverty-stricken masses of the Third World, to receive their entitlement to a better quality of life, are evaluated. On balance, the authors conclude that military spending must be detrimental to economic well-being, although it does have some positive economic benefits. It is clear that the primary advantages of militarization must come from security and security alone.

W. Scott Thompson (Chapter 5) analyses the links between security and development as seen from the perspective of the United States, particularly at the decision-making level of successive governments. The difficulties of practical policy making and evaluation of Third World problems, at the cutting edge of US governmental agencies, are clearly brought out.

Jacques Fontanel and Ron Smith (Chapter 6) discuss the formation of the International Fund for Disarmament and Development. The Fund will channel international aid by collecting resources from developed countries, who are also the largest arms spenders, and using it for developmental assistance to the poorer countries of the World. This is one of the proposals that have emanated from the recent UN interest in the interrelationships among defence, disarmament and development. The various problems and the attractions of such an institution are carefully discussed.

The causes of military expenditure in LDCs are varied and numerous. But they are crucial in linking the economic and strategic factors that underlie defence provision. Alfred Maizels and Machiko Nissanke (Chapter 7) use an econometric model formally to identify the various determinants of defence burden. They find that political, economic and security-related factors are all important for a large cross section of developing economies. Moreover, national, regional and international linkages need to be differentiated and their respective roles analysed.

Robert Rothstein, in Chapter 8, utilizes the analytical tools of political science to provide a wide ranging review of the major political issues that condition the amount of wealth societies feel obliged to devote to defence. In particular, the legitimacy of the government and the ruling elite provides a framework within which security is measured and defence burden formulated.

Part IV contains three chapters on the arms trade, linking many of the issues mentioned earlier but also adding a new dimension to the problem. Michael Brzoska (Chapter 9) presents a comprehensive survey of recent trends in arms transfers showing how the market for arms continues to undergo fundamental transformations. While Brzoska stresses the overall framework of the international transfer in weapons, Arcadi Oliveres (Chapter 10) reviews the prospects and policies for arms exports of an individual country. Spain is important since it is in transition from a developing to a developed economy and its experience appears to have wide application for the many Newly Industrializing Countries that are preparing to enter the oligopolistic arms market.

Chapter 11 marks the movement from description to policy formulation. Herbert Wulf analyses in some detail the feasibility of controlling arms transfers and suggests major policy measures which might reduce the obvious burden on poor economies without jeopardizing their national security.

In essence, the chapters in this volume discuss four major questions: what do we know about the military expenditure process and how can we interpret the information? What is the relation between defence and development in the Third World, both from the point of view of LDCs themselves as well as from the perspective of the superpowers? What causes defence expenditure and arms imports to rise in spite of obvious economic constraints and widespread poverty? What can be done, at the national as well as the international level, to safeguard security and to foster development, particularly when significant trade-offs exist?

Conclusion

The authors of this volume clearly indicate the close interconnection between national security and economic development. Defence expenditure is needed to safeguard the former. But military spending may have a detrimental effect on growth and will, in all probability, reduce the level of development. Thus a basic trade-off exists between expenditures in the military sector and civilian sectors. Defence spending may exacerbate the 'poverty trap'; but in its absence the 'security dilemma' is heightened.[6] The choices are difficult.

All of the contributors to this volume assume that governments, and societies or elites they represent, need to optimize. The authorities will, therefore, seek to equate marginal costs and benefits, even though this may be done only implicitly. Two conditions need to be satisfied for optimization. The first requires adequate information gathering—knowing exactly how much is being spent in terms of domestic purchasing power (West, 1987). The second requires an integration of economic and strategic planning—a form of policy coordination. We should note some of the broad policy implications which the contributors to this volume identify as instances of the needed policy coordination.

At the international level, arms control negotiation should be widened to include weapons transfers to the Third World. The United Nations and other dispute-resolution instruments should be strengthened and given more support to deal with explosive inter-State conflict situations. Development can be accelerated through wealth transfers via such institutions as the International Fund for Disarmament and Development.

With reference to the management of international tensions, development per se may not be the panacea of all ills. As discussed earlier, there may be disequilibrium adjustments as development produces rising expectations which cannot be satisfied. To address sources of domestic security threats, the political process needs to be strengthened and democratic institutions established. If people know that a particular government is not going to last forever, they will have less incentive to use violence to change it.

The problems are complex; the solutions are not clear-cut. The basic idea behind this book, and the colloquium which preceded it, is that we must clarify the intellectual ground rules for analysis and discussion. We hope that the ideas generated here will, in particular, provide the foundation for case studies of individual countries. The problems facing the Third World, to reconcile the conflicting objectives of security and development, are massive in their complexity. We hope that the present volume helps in some ways to clarify the fundamentals and contributes modestly to our understanding of useful defence, the prospects for disarmament and attainable development.

Notes

1. Calculated from SIPRI data (SIPRI, 1986).
2. These are countries with 1982 per capita GNP of less than US $440, as reported by the World Bank.
3. The figures exclude Vietnam. Data from SIPRI register of the arms trade with Third World countries (SIPRI, 1986).
4. Defence burden is defence expenditure as a proportion of national income or GDP.
5. We use the language of game theory, which we find apposite to explain the responses to external threats.
6. See Chapter 8, by Robert Rothstein, in this volume.

PART I
Interpreting Information on Defence Expenditures

1

Improved measures of the defence burden in developing countries

ROBERT L. WEST

An important part of the information used to describe the national defence activities of developing countries is derived from the fiscal reports by governments on the scale and content of their expenditures for national security. Data on military expenditures (MILEX) are frequently employed by analysts to evaluate national defence policies and their effects in the Third World. It is also a familiar convention to compare MILEX with total expenditures by the central government (CGE) and with gross national product (GNP); these ratios are used as indicators of the effort by a government to provide for national security. The MILEX:GNP ratio is commonly designated the 'defence burden'.

For their discussion of many of the subjects addressed in this volume—in more than half of the chapters—the authors have adopted these widely-used conventions. They employ estimates of military expenditures assembled from government fiscal documents by the three major international reporting agencies: the International Institute for Strategic Studies (IISS), the Stockholm International Peace Research Institute (SIPRI), and the US Arms Control and Disarmament Agency (ACDA).

The growing use of MILEX estimates by analysts is attributable, in large measure, to the diligent commitment of these three reporting agencies to the task of assembling, editing, and publishing data for a large number of nations. Nearly two decades of sustained effort has produced a highly useful body of information. It remains the case, however, that precautions must be observed to derive reliable inferences from these data about national security activities in the Third World—particularly so when the data are used to make comparisons among countries or to compute trends.

Part I of this volume contains an introduction to the published information about military expenditures in the Third World; a discussion of reasons why caution is required for accurate interpretation of the data; and an explanation of the measures taken to improve the reliability of inferences drawn from these data about the structure and trend of national defence efforts by developing countries.

In Chapter 2, Nicole Ball compares the coverage and procedures of the three international reporting agencies. In the present chapter, we introduce the information published by ACDA, the agency which provides the most comprehensive coverage of military expenditures. The first two sections of this chapter present the data available on world-wide military spending; inspect its distribution across geographic regions and political–security alliances; and recast the estimates into more homogeneous groupings of countries, useful for analysing the national security behaviour of Third World governments.

The third section explores the important sources of bias in the ACDA-reported information, resulting in distortions which compromise the usefulness of the published data for making inter-country comparisons or estimating trends. The subjects of reporting precision and accuracy of observations are addressed by Nicole Ball in Chapter 2; the focus in this chapter is on the requirement to correct the reported expenditures for distortions attributable to intercountry differences in the structure of prices and to changes through time in national and sectoral price levels.

This source of bias in the published information is corrected in the section on 'Estimates of the real defence burden' where, purchasing power parity estimates of the ACDA expenditures data are introduced. These improved measures of real expenditures are employed to identify different patterns in the efforts made by groups of developing countries to provide for their national defence.

In the section on 'Evolution of defence burdens 1969–81' we present evidence that countries within groupings—differentiated by size, income level and resource endowment—have engaged, over the span of nearly fifteen years, in quite similar efforts to provide for their national security. By contrast, there are clear between-group differences in the scale and trend of the national defence efforts of these Third World countries. The evidence respecting different patterns of behaviour in management of their national defence burdens by Third World countries is summarized in the conclusion.

Sources of data

For the past sixteen years the United States Arms Control and Disarmament Agency has assembled and published information on international arms transfers and military spending by governments; the data bank maintained by ACDA contains estimates for 145 countries and territories, providing virtually world-wide coverage. Revisions and adjustments are made on a continuous basis to improve the accuracy of the data and to make entries more nearly comparable. Generally consistent estimates for the years since 1969 are now available for a very large sample of countries—including more than 100 developing countries and territories. A description of the coverage and definition of reported series appears in ACDA, *World Military Expenditures and Arms Transfers* (1985: 139–45). Table 1.1 summarizes the ACDA estimates (as at July 1985) of MILEX, CGE and GNP for the year 1975, the mid-year of the period discussed in this chapter.

The primary sources of information underlying these data and the methods of estimation are fundamentally different for the non-market economies as contrasted with the sources and methods used for countries with market-orientated economies. Estimates for the seventeen non-market countries are not evaluated in this chapter. The following description of the ACDA series applies to the 128 market-economy countries and territories.

MILEX consists of expenditures by each country's ministry of defence, net of known costs of internal security. For some countries it omits some capital expenditures, including external arms purchases. The quality of these data varies among countries, largely because of differences in accounting and reporting practices, but also due to intentional under-reporting. These deficiencies of the reporting system are assessed by Nicole Ball in Chapter 2 (see also, Ball 1984). The sources of error impart a downward bias and the series should be interpreted as a minimum or underestimate. It is not yet established if there are other systematic distortions in the MILEX data reported for the market-economy countries other than the bias deriving from currency conversion procedures, discussed below.

Central Government Expenditures (CGE) consists of current and capital expenditures plus net lending to public enterprises by central government. Gross National Product (GNP) is the familiar national accounts aggregate representing total output of goods and services produced by nationals and valued at market prices. For the 128

Table 1.1 Military Expenditures, Central Government Expenditures and
Gross National Product: 145 ACDA WMEAT countries (in
billions of ACDA 1982 dollars)

	N	TMILEX	TCGE	TGNP
ACDA groups by region and organization				
ACDA 'Developed'	28	489.8	2,263.1	8,204.6
ACDA 'Developing'	117	129.1	582.0	2,089.5
OECD	24	256.8	1,736.9	6,328.7
Warsaw Pact	7	243.3	583.5	2,100.9
Other Non-Market	10	38.8	105.5	328.5
OPEC	13	40.8	179.6	474.7
Other 'Developing'	91	39.2	239.6	1,061.2
World Totals	145	618.9	2,845.1	10,294.0
Revised country groups				
Less All Non-Market	17	282.1	689.0	2,429.4
All Market Economies	128	336.7	2,156.1	7.864.7
Less Industrial (IME)	27	261.5	1,756.8	6,362.2
All Market Developing	101	75.3	399.3	1,502.5
Less ICP Data Missing	7	0.5	2.5	10.7
Less High Income Oil-exporters	7	14.4	50.7	125.5
Developing ICP	87	60.3	346.1	1,366.4
World Totals	145	618.9	2,845.1	10,294.0

Notes

1. IME: OECD less Turkey; Cyprus, Malta, Israel, South Africa.

2. ICP Data Missing: Cape Verde, Equit. Guinea, Guinea-Bissau, Lebanon, São Tomé and Pr., Yemen (Aden), Yemen (Sanaa).

3. High Income Oil-exporters: Bahrain, Kuwait, Libya, Oman, Qatar, Saudi Arabia, United Arab Emirates.

Source: US Arms Control and Disarmament Agency, *World Military Expenditures and Arms Transfers* (1985 Issue). Data for 1975.

market economies, with a very few exceptions, the CGE and GNP data reported by ACDA correspond to the (local currency) estimates of the World Bank data bank.

The primary estimates of MILEX, CGE and GNP are denominated in each country's local currency at current year prices. However, ACDA does not publish these local currency estimates. In its annual publication, ACDA presents the estimates converted into US dollars. The currency conversion method used by ACDA is the same for all three series. Data expressed in local currency at current prices are deflated by the national implicit GNP deflator and converted to US dollars at the 1982 annual average par/market exchange rate. Where this method of presenting data in constant dollars applies to series shown in this chapter, it is indicated by the term 'in ACDA 1982 dollars'. Where we reproduce the MILEX, CGE and GNP estimates in the form reported by ACDA, this is indicated by a prefix 'T', such as in Table 1.1.

The selection of developing countries

ACDA publishes estimates for each of the 145 countries and for groups of countries classified by geographical region, alliance membership, and a distinction between 'developed' and 'developing'—as shown in the upper panel of Table 1.1. Except for the alliance classes, the ACDA groupings contain both market-oriented and non-market economies with a resultant mixture of different sources and estimation procedures. For example, the 'developed' category consists of six Warsaw Pact members, sixteen Western European market economies, Australia, Canada, Japan, New Zealand, South Africa and the United States. The balance of the reported world, 117 entities, is classified as 'developing'.

It is useful for our purposes to segregate the cases of non-market economies and adopt a system of classification for groups of countries with more homogeneous membership. The major categories of the World Bank's World Development Report are adopted here for the 128 market-oriented countries. Two analytical advantages of this classification system are that (1) a wide variety of social and economic indicators are reported by the World Bank and others for these groups; and (2) the boundaries of these groupings roughly define differences among countries in access to sources and terms of international financing. (The classification system is described in the World Development Indicators annex, World Bank 1985: 168–73, 230 ff.)

The lower panel of Table 1.1 shows the distribution of the 145 ACDA countries and territories among the primary World Bank categories. The total 145 includes seventeen non-market economies and twenty-seven industrial market economies (IME); the IME category contains the OECD members plus Cyprus, Malta, Israel and South Africa, but Turkey is classified among the developing countries. This results in a total developing market economies list of 101 countries and territories. Of these, seven are omitted from discussion in this chapter because critical information is lacking. Another seven High Income Oil Exporters are evaluated separately from the population of eighty-seven developing International Comparison Project (ICP) Countries for which comparisons of defence-burden indicators are presented in this chapter. Table 1.1 shows the distribution of MILEX, CGE and GNP, as reported by ACDA, among these primary groups of non-market, industrialized (IME), and developing countries. The World Bank further classifies developing countries by real per capita income levels and by relative resource endowments—the latter distinguishing oil-importing from oil-exporting economies. It also differentiates between large and small economies, chiefly by reference to population size. This system of classification has roots in economic theory and reflects the results of empirical investigations to identify the key distinctions among national economies which define different paths of development and patterns of accumulation and allocation (Chenery and Syrquin 1975; Chenery 1979, Part I). Employing these World Bank categories, we will observe that there are significant differences in the allocation of resources for national defence purposes among the groups of developing countries classified by real income level, resource endowment and size. This observation is not unexpected in view of the origin of the classification system: it is intended to reveal the distinctive patterns of accumulation and allocation attributed to the country-members of these groups.

The World Bank income and resource-endowment classes consist of Low Income Economies (less than $400 per capita income in 1983 as estimated by the World Bank), all of which are net oil-importing countries; Lower-Middle Income (between $400 and $1,600 per capita income in 1983) Oil-Importing Economies; Upper-Middle Income (more than $1,600 per capita income in 1983) Oil-Importing Economies; the corresponding Lower-Middle and Upper-Middle Oil-Exporting Economies; Industrialized Market Economies; and two classes of Non-Market Economies, in Europe (NME) and in other geographic regions (NMO).

The Appendix of this chapter lists the 145 ACDA countries, and shows their membership in these World Bank groups. The Appendix also identifies the ACDA countries by World Bank regional groupings for Sub-Saharan Africa (SSA); Middle East and North Africa (MENA); East Asia (EA); South Asia (SA); and Latin America (LA). All IME countries are assigned to one class, regardless of geography.

Table 1.2 shows the distribution of MILEX, CGE and GNP for the

Table 1.2 Military Expenditures, Central Government Expenditures and
Gross National Product: 145 ACDA WMEAT countries in World
Bank groups (in billions of ACDA 1982 dollars)

	N	TMILEX	TCGE	TGNP
World Bank income groups				
Low Income/M	35	8.0	49.7	260.0
Low-Mid Income/M	30	8.5	45.3	225.7
Upper-Mid Income/M	11	7.6	74.8	346.6
Low-Mid Income/X	9	12.0	54.5	180.7
Upper-Mid Income/X	9	24.6	124.2	364.0
High Income/X	7	14.4	50.7	125.5
Industrial (IME)	27	261.5	1,756.8	6,362.2
Non-Market Europe	9	246.0	597.7	2,148.3
Non-Market other	8	36.2	91.3	281.1
Total	145	618.9	2,845.1	10,294.0
World Bank regional groups				
Sub-Saharan Africa	42	6.8	53.7	185.4
Mid. East.–N. Africa	20	45.1	156.0	387.6
East Asia	17	44.5	122.7	468.6
South Asia	5	5.9	29.4	167.5
Latin America	25	9.2	128.9	574.5
Industrial (IME)	27	261.5	1,756.8	6,362.2
Non-Market Europe	9	246.0	597.7	2,148.3
Total	145	618.9	2,845.1	10,294.0

Notes

1. See Appendix for country-membership of World Bank groups.

2. /M indicates group consists of net oil-importing countries; /X indicates group
consists of net oil-exporting countries.

3. Data for 1975.

year 1975, in ACDA 1982 dollars, for the 145 ACDA countries
classified by the World Bank categories.

Purchasing power parity conversion

It has long been recognized that the conversion of local currency
values into a numeraire currency, such as US dollars, by use of
exchange rates results in statistics which are far from satisfactory for
making intercountry comparisons of real income or real product.

The same deficiency of exchange rate conversion methods obtains for making comparisons of real income and product through time, for groups of countries or for one country. The structure of prices for goods and services differs widely among countries, and the changes which occur in these structures through time are quite different across countries. Exchange rates do not adequately reflect these international differences in price levels and structures (Marris 1983: 37-8 references cited).

ACDA, together with many others, recognizes that the practice of converting primary data in local currencies into 'dollars' by use of exchange rates is a serious source of distortion in its published estimates, where the purpose is to aggregate the expenditures by groups of countries or to compare expenditures across countries and through time. In the current issue of its annual publication ACDA notes that its use of a single, base-year (1982) exchange rate avoids the distorting effect which can result from changes in exchange rates over the span of years for which it reports expenditures. But, ACDA observes, this method does not correct for a number of other factors:

One [factor] is that any within-country differences between the price indices for military or central government expenditures and GNP are not taken into account. . . . Another and probably more serious factor is that exchange rates in many cases do not adequately reflect the relative purchasing power of currencies. This has been demonstrated by a detailed study of purchasing power parities (PPPs) for the GNPs of a large number of countries. . . . This study found that the greater the disparity in the per capita income of countries, the greater the tendency for exchange rates to understate the value of the poorer country's product, and that the understatement can be very large, reaching as much as threefold in some cases. (ACDA 1985: 144.)

The study of purchasing power parities cited by ACDA is the Phase III Report of the International Comparison Project, a long-term cooperative undertaking coordinated by the Statistical Office of the United Nations to improve the comparability of real income and real product aggregates for a large number of countries (Kravis, Heston, Summers 1982). The ICP studies have demonstrated that there are even greater international variations in the price levels for government expenditures than for GNP as a whole; where exchange rates are used to convert government expenditures, the understatement in comparing outlays of central governments in poor with rich countries sometimes exceeds four to one.

There seems little doubt that conversion by use of exchange rates is by far the most important source of bias in the published data on military and other government expenditures, and very seriously compromises use of these data to make intercountry comparisons or to estimate trends through time. As ACDA acknowledges, reliable cross-section or time-series comparisons require expenditures data expressed in purchasing power parity values.

Purchasing power parities, as computed by the International Comparison Project (ICP), are based on measured indices of the local price levels for expenditures aggregates (such as GNP or government final consumption expenditures). Using intercountry PPP ratios to convert expenditures aggregates—which are denominated in local currencies at current local prices—provides values in a numeraire currency: 'PPP dollars'. These values accurately measure the real quantities of goods and services corresponding to the expenditures recorded in each country and each year.

The 'PPP dollar' expenditure aggregate in each country is the equivalent of the real quantity of goods and services purchased at a common, world-wide set of PPP dollar prices—where the same set of PPP dollar prices obtains for expenditures in all countries in that year. Expenditures expressed in PPP dollars can be aggregated for groups of countries, compared across countries, and compared through time. In all these cases, the aggregates and comparisons correspond to real quantities of goods and services. These cross-country and inter-temporal comparisons are not subject to the distortions which result from currency conversion by use of exchange rates (Summers and Heston 1984; Kravis, Heston and Summers 1982).

In principle, PPPs can be computed for any expenditure aggregate for which sufficient information is assembled to measure the price indices for detailed categories of goods and services purchased. A United Nations expert group has been engaged for a number of years in the effort to compute PPPs and price indices for military expenditures by some UN members. This work proceeds slowly, in large part due to incomplete reporting, especially on prices of military equipment (Ball 1983: 19–30; ACDA 1985: 144).

The submissions made to the UN experts of disaggregated expenditures information tend to reinforce information obtained from case studies of military budgets in developing countries. These show a very high proportion of personnel outlays and relatively modest construction and procurement expenditures; only price levels of the latter, it may be noted, are likely to deviate significantly from the already-known prices of civil government expenditures. In fact, the composition of military expenditures appears to be quite similar to total government spending. It seems unlikely that the developing country price levels for military expenditures, which may ultimately be reported by the UN experts, will be found to differ greatly from the price levels for central government total expenditures, civil and military. Unfortunately, ACDA and the other international reporting agencies apparently are resolved to await the appearance of specific military PPPs to substitute for exchange rates—and the practice continues of reporting data in exchange rate conversion values.

From one perspective it can be argued that price levels specific to military expenditures or arms purchases are not needed—indeed, they would not be of any direct use—to make comparisons of the military burdens assumed by different countries or to study the trend of such burdens through time. The most evident concept of a military burden is the social opportunity cost of the military expenditures—that is, the alternatives foregone as a result of the expenditures made for military or other national security purposes. It conforms with this concept of a military burden to compute the real value of the alternative bundle of goods and services sacrificed by the residents of a nation (that is, the real value of the purchases which are not made) as a result of the decision to spend the amount of local currency devoted to military expenditures. For this purpose we need indices of prices for the alternative purchases foregone; these will enable estimation of the appropriate indicators for comparing the real military burdens assumed by different countries, and their trend through time.

Estimates of the real defence burden

How can we identify the goods and services foregone as a result of a nation's military expenditures, that is, what would have been purchased if the country had not made the military expenditures actually observed? We cannot know the counterfactual, but we can make reasonable assumptions. Military expenditures represent public use of resources and money expended for public purposes is fungible. In the period of years addressed in this chapter, and for the selection of developing countries, civil governmental expenditures were expanding rapidly. We assume that the alternative foregone as a result of a given country's military outlays is additional spending on the actual mix of goods and services purchased by the government in its civil expenditures during that year. We measure the real value of the opportunity cost of military expenditures as the reported military spending in local currency converted at the PPP coefficient for general government final consumption expenditures.

Sectoral price level indices for government final consumption expenditures are computed by the International Comparison Project. The sectoral and GNP price level indices and PPPs for conversion of local currency expenditures have been reported by the ICP for 114 market-orientated economies, covering the period from before 1969 through to 1981 (Summers and Heston 1984). The country coverage closely corresponds to that of the World Bank market-economy countries and territories discussed above and consists of the twenty-seven IME countries and the eighty-seven Developing ICP countries, as listed in the Appendix. Comparable PPPs are not available for members of the High Income Oil Exporting countries class. The problem of measuring real income and product for the seven capital-surplus oil exporters, in a manner comparable with other developing countries, has not been solved.

Estimates of real military burdens can be made for eighty-seven developing countries for the years 1969–81. The data which are presented in the tables of this chapter have been computed by use of the ICP 1969–81 PPP coefficients (from the Penn World Table Mark III Computer Tape) and the ACDA local currency expenditures estimates (from the WMEAT 1985 computer tape).

The local currency data base used by the ICP to compute PPP coefficients is that of the United Nations Statistical Office while, as already noted, the ACDA series for market-oriented economies uses estimates from the World Bank data bank. There are differences in the estimates for individual countries and some differences in the national accounting concepts. There is no final equivalency attainable, but a substantial effort has been made to reconcile the differences in reported estimates on a country-by-country basis. The ICP PPPs have been used, for this study, in conjunction with the World Bank local currency estimates for central government expenditures (although the PPP coefficients were computed from the United Nations estimates of general government final consumption expenditures), and in conjunction with the World Bank values for Gross National Product (although the PPP coefficients were computed by the ICP from the United Nations data on Gross Domestic Product).

Table 1.3 Military Expenditures, Central Government Expenditures and
Gross National Product: 114 ICP Countries in World Bank
groups (in billions of ACDA 1982 dollars)

	N	TMILEX	TCGE	TGNP
World Bank income groups				
Low Income/M	31	8.0	49.6	259.7
Low-Mid Income/M	27	8.1	42.9	215.4
Upper-Mid Income/M	11	7.6	74.8	346.6
Low-Mid Income/X	9	12.0	54.5	180.7
Upper-Mid Income/X	9	24.6	124.2	364.0
Industrial (IME)	27	261.5	1,756.8	6,362.2
Total	114	321.8	2,102.9	7,728.5
World Bank regional groups				
Sub-Saharan Africa	38	6.8	53.6	185.1
Mid East.–N. Africa	10	30.2	102.8	251.8
East Asia	10	8.9	41.9	205.0
South Asia	5	5.9	29.4	167.5
Latin America	24	8.5	118.4	557.0
Industrial (IME)	27	261.5	1,756.8	6,362.2
Total	114	321.8	2,102.9	7,728.5

Notes

1. See Appendix for country-membership of World Bank groups.

2. /M indicates group consists of net oil-importing countries; /X indicates group
consists of net oil-exporting countries.

3. Data for 1975.

Table 1.3 shows the 1975 MILEX, CGE and GNP for the 114 ICP
countries in World Bank classes, in ACDA 1982 dollars. Table 1.4
shows the same series for the same countries and classes in PPP
dollars at current year (1975) international prices. Table 1.5 contains
the same information as Table 1.4, but for the eighty-seven ICP
Developing Countries, only; expenditures and GNP for members of
World Bank income classes are shown separately for the eighteen
large and sixty-nine small developing countries in Table 1.5. The
prefix 'CY' in Tables 1.4 and 1.5 indicates that the estimates of
MILEX, CGE, and GNP are all computed on the basis of Current Year
International Prices (CYIP) for the reported year, 1975.

The PPP dollar estimates of Table 1.4 measure the real quantities
of the expenditures (and the real quantity of gross national product)

Table 1.4 Military Expenditures, Central Government Expenditures and
Gross National Product: 114 ICP countries in World Bank groups
(in billions of PPP dollars at current year international prices)

	N	CYMILEX	CYCGE	CYGNP
World Bank income groups				
Low-Income/M	31	31.2	175.1	485.8
Low-Mid Income/M	27	17.2	94.1	307.3
Upper-Mid Income/M	11	11.7	115.8	362.6
Low-Mid Income/X	9	28.0	118.7	236.3
Upper-Mid Income/X	9	25.1	133.2	367.4
Industrial (IME)	27	143.3	980.9	4,106.9
Total	114	256.6	1,617.7	5,866.3
World Bank regional groups				
Sub-Saharan Africa	38	12.6	93.3	205.4
Mid. East.–N. Africa	10	43.2	146.2	300.6
East Asia	10	17.8	85.6	270.2
South Asia	5	26.5	139.3	374.2
Latin America	24	13.2	172.4	609.0
Industrial (IME)	27	143.3	980.9	4,106.9
Total	114	256.6	1,617.7	5,866.3

Notes
1. See Appendix for country-membership of World Bank groups.
2. /M indicates group consists of net oil-importing countries; /X indicates group consists of net oil-exporting countries.
3. Data for 1975.

in each country, valued at a common set of international prices of 1975 applied to all countries. This provides a reliable basis for cross-country comparisons of real expenditures and product in the year 1975.

The contrast in the relative distribution of TMILEX and CYMILEX (in Tables 1.3 and 1.4) among groups of developing countries—and for the eighty-seven developing countries compared with the twenty-seven IME countries—illustrates the distortion attributable to conversion by use of exchange rates. The ACDA exchange rate and PPP estimates of MILEX and GNP for groups of developing countries with estimates for the IME countries are compared in Table 1.6.

The MILEX outlays by developing countries are seriously under-estimated by exchange rate conversion. The PPP estimate of military expenditures by the eighty-seven developing countries in 1975 is 79 per cent of defence expenditures by the twenty-seven IME countries rather than 23 per cent as indicated by values converted at the 1982 exchange rates. Real MILEX of oil-importing developing countries in 1975 was 42 per cent of military expenditures by IME countries, but the exchange rate estimate is 9.1 per cent. Similar distortions are

Table 1.5 Military Expenditures, Central Government Expenditures and Gross National Product: 87 ICP countries in World Bank groups (in billions of PPP dollars at current year international prices)

	N	CYMILEX	CYCGE	CYGNP
Population greater than twenty million				
Low-Income/M	6	27.8	141.1	389.7
Low-Mid Income/M	4	10.6	51.1	188.0
Upper-Mid Income/M	3	9.2	99.0	324.8
Low-Mid Income/X	3	25.4	101.9	178.5
Upper-Mid Income/X	2	14.3	66.7	237.0
Total	18	87.3	459.8	1,318.0
Population less than twenty million				
Low-Income/M	25	3.4	34.0	96.1
Low-Mid Income/M	23	6.6	42.9	119.3
Upper-Mid Income/M	8	2.5	16.8	37.8
Low-Mid Income/X	6	2.6	16.8	57.8
Upper-Mid Income/X	7	10.8	66.5	130.4
Total	69	26.0	177.0	441.4

Notes

1. See Appendix for country-membership of World Bank groups.

2. /M indicates group consists of net oil-importing countries; /X indicates group consists of net oil-exporting countries.

3. Data for 1975.

Table 1.6

	TMILEX	CYMILEX	CYCGE	CYGNP
27 IME countries	100.0	100.0	100.0	100.0
87 ICP developing	23.1	79.1	21.5	42.8
18 oil-exporting	14.0	39.0	8.5	14.7
69 oil-importing	9.1	42.0	12.9	28.1

found in comparing the Tables 1.3 and 1.4 distributions of relative military spending by groups of developing countries in all the different income classes and regions.

It is conventional practice to compare military expenditures with gross national product and with total government expenditures, as two ratios reflecting the scale of effort to provide for national security. For an individual nation, only the MILEX:GNP ratio is corrected for intra-country differences of sectoral price levels by the use of PPPs rather than exchange rates. But the distortion of real comparisons which is attributable to exchange rate conversion is neither uniformly nor randomly distributed among countries; there is a systematic bias such that there is far greater distortion for poor countries when compared with all others. When the data are aggregated for groups of countries, both the government expenditure 'share' devoted to military outlays and the ratio of military expenditures to GNP are affected by the method of conversion from local currency values. This result can be seen by comparing the ratios of estimates in Tables 1.3 and 1.4. The 'share' (MILEX:CGE) and the military burden (MILEX:GNP) for the lower income country groups are most significantly affected by the distortion which adheres to the exchange rate estimates set out in Table 1.7.

When comparisons are made through time, to observe trends or inter-temporal variation, the effect of changes in the general level of prices from year to year must be removed to permit comparison of real magnitudes. This is the conventional role of deflators. Correction for changes in the general level of prices through time produces the 'constant-currency' estimates, in ordinary usage for inter-temporal comparisons where conversion of different currencies does not intrude. The corresponding correction for magnitudes denominated in different currencies is provided by use of another set of

Table 1.7

Ratio:	TMILEX / TCGE	CYMILEX / CYCGE	TMILEX / TGNP	CYMILEX / CYGNP
Low-Income	16.1	17.8	3.1	6.4
Low-Mid Income	20.6	21.3	5.1	8.3
Upper-Mid Income	16.2	14.8	4.5	5.0
IME	14.9	14.6	4.1	3.5

price level and PPP estimates to compute values expressed in purchasing power parities for a single base-year set of international prices. For the data presented in this chapter, the base year is 1975. Unlike the CYIP values, for which a different set of international prices is adopted in each different year, Purchasing Power Parities in 1975 International Prices are used to compute real values which can be compared through time, using the same set of (base-year 1975) international prices in all years of the period.

Tables 1.8 and 1.9 present the MILEX, CGE and GNP series for the year 1975 (in Purchasing Power Parity dollars at the 1975 Inter-

Table 1.8 Military Expenditures, Central Government Expenditures and Gross National Product: 1975 levels and 1969–81 growth rates of 87 ICP developing countries in World Bank income groups (in billions of PPP dollars at 1975 international prices)

	Data for 1975			1969–81 growth rates (%)		
	PMILEX	PCGE	PGNP	PMILEX	PCGE	PGNP
World Bank income groups						
LYC/M	28.5	159.9	474.1	3.90	5.72	4.11
MYL/M	15.7	86.1	303.4	11.13	11.17	6.17
MYU/M	10.7	106.0	360.0	6.42	11.72	7.41
MYL/X	25.6	108.5	232.4	7.49	14.43	7.51
MYU/X	23.0	121.8	363.9	13.73	14.48	6.41
Total	103.6	582.3	1,733.9	7.79	10.35	6.04
World Bank regional groups						
SSA	11.5	85.4	201.8	6.34	9.98	5.05
MENA	39.5	133.7	296.1	13.73	15.31	7.10
EA	16.2	78.3	267.0	8.31	11.52	7.05
SA	24.2	127.2	364.9	3.39	5.66	4.26
LA	12.1	157.7	604.1	5.13	11.17	6.14
Total	103.6	582.3	1,733.9	7.79	10.35	6.04
N.B. IME	131.1	897.3	4,070.6	−0.33**	4.56	3.08

Notes

1. See Appendix for country-membership of World Bank groups.

2. /M indicates group consists of net oil-importing countries; /X indicates group consists of net oil-exporting countries.

3. ** not significantly different from zero at the 5% level.

national Prices used for inter-temporal comparisons) for the World Bank income and regional groups of eighty-seven developing countries. For the World Bank income classification, countries of different population size are shown separately in Table 1.9. To differentiate these estimates from ACDA 1982 dollars, and from CYIP PPP dollars, the prefix 'P' is used. For other than the base year (1975 in this chapter), the cross-country or inter-group comparisons of 1975 International Price estimates are subject to the usual index number problem associated with use of any deflator. But these data can be used to compute growth rates and measure trends through time.

Table 1.9 Military Expenditures, Central Government Expenditures and Gross National Product: 1975 levels and 1969–81 growth rates 87 ICP developing countries in World Bank income groups (in billions of PPP dollars at 1975 international prices)

	Data for 1975			1969–81 growth rates (%)		
	PMILEX	PCGE	PGNP	PMILEX	PCGE	PGNP
Eighteen large countries: population greater than twenty million						
LYC/M	25.4	128.8	380.0	3.47	5.67	4.29
MYL/M	9.7	46.8	185.7	12.85	12.08	6.40
MYU/M	8.4	90.6	322.9	6.46	12.72	7.93
MYL/X	23.2	93.1	175.6	7.03	16.56	8.76
MYU/X	13.1	61.0	234.8	8.47*	12.60	6.11
Total	79.8	420.3	1,299.0	6.48	10.44	6.36
Sixty-nine small countries: population less than twenty million						
LYC/M	3.1	31.1	94.1	7.00	5.95	3.42
MYL/M	6.0	39.3	117.7	8.84	9.85	5.82
MYU/M	2.3	15.4	37.1	6.38	6.56	4.07
MYL/X	2.4	15.4	56.8	10.01	6.92	3.98
MYU/X	9.9	60.8	129.2	16.57	16.08	6.91
Total	23.8	162.0	434.9	11.16	10.13	5.17

Notes

1. See Appendix for country-membership of World Bank groups.

2. /M indicates group consists of net oil-importing countries; /X indicates group consists of net oil-exporting countries.

3. * not significantly different from zero at the 1% level, but significant at the 5% level.

Tables 1.8 and 1.9 show the exponential growth rates for 1969–81 of each series, for each of the World Bank income and regional country groups. In these tables, and in Tables 1.10 and 1.11, a growth rate estimate with a double asterisk (**) indicates it is not significantly different from 0 at the 5 per cent level of confidence; a single asterisk (*) indicates it is significant at the 5 per cent level but not at the 1 per cent level. All other annual growth rates are significant at the 1 per cent level.

Caution should be exercised in interpreting growth rates for groups in which a very large country predominates. Any group containing India is an example; the Indian experience is likely to swamp the recorded growth performance of other countries with which it is classified. The most important case of this kind is for the regional classification of Sub-Saharan Africa; where Nigeria is included, it disguises the performance of other African economies. For 1969–81, the growth rates of SSA excluding Nigeria are: PMILEX 8.69 per cent, PCGE 6.84 per cent, GNP 3.62 per cent—a pattern quite different from the rates for the SSA region in Table 1.8.

A few of the World Bank classification cells contain a small number of countries with sharply different growth rates, attributable to identifiable differences of international or domestic experience over the past decade and a half. A cross-classification table is provided in the Appendix showing the number of countries in each group. It may be helpful to observe that the two large countries in the 'MYU:X' category are Mexico and Iran. This is a case where the classification system disguises more than it reveals, aggregating the significantly lower growth performance of Mexico with growth of other oil-exporting countries.

Interpretation of the Table 1.8 and 1.9 growth rates may also be aided by observing the location of countries which have experienced civil war, international armed hostilities, occupation or colonial hegemony during the period. We may note that the four large country members of the 'MYL:M' category are Colombia, the Philippines, Thailand and Turkey—all countries which confronted major insurgencies and perimeter security problems in the 1969–81 period.

When account is taken of the modest growth performance of Mexico, the World Bank income groups for the eighty-seven developing countries and the eighteen large countries appear in Tables 1.8 and 1.9 in ascending order of GNP growth rates. For the 1969–81 period, higher per capita incomes and oil-exporting status were associated with higher rates of growth of GNP, CGE and MILEX among the large developing countries. The exceptionally high growth of military expenditures by the four 'insurgency' countries is a clearly visible deviation.

The regularities of this large-country pattern do not obtain for the small-population developing countries and there is a very different relationship between the relative growth rates of MILEX and GNP for large and small countries in each income group. For each World Bank income category, the GNP growth rates of large countries were higher than those of small developing countries; but the MILEX growth rates of small countries were generally higher than those of large developing countries (the exception being the large 'insurgency' countries already noted). The growth rates of MILEX relative to growth of GNP and CGE are significantly higher for most categories of small countries than for the corresponding groups of large developing countries. These differences will be found to result in distinctly different large and small country patterns of change in the military 'shares' and defence burdens over the 1969–81 period.

Evolution of defence burdens 1969–81

The real growth rate of military spending for the high-income, industrialized (IME) countries was zero from 1969 to 1981. Real central government expenditures increased at an exponential rate of more than 4.5 per cent and real GNP rose at an average annual rate of slightly less than 3.1 per cent. There were two distinct eras. Real military spending by the IME countries fell absolutely from 1969 to 1976. In this period, the military 'share' of government spending fell and the defence burden (MILEX:GNP) also declined sharply. From 1976 to 1981 (and continuing to the present), real military spending rose at the same rate of growth as total government expenditures— there has been no substitution of military for civil spending, or vice versa, for the IME countries in this period. Over the full span of thirteen years, the 'share' of military expenditures in total central government spending has fallen at an exponential rate of 4.7 per cent, government spending as a ratio to GNP has grown at the rate of 1.4 per cent, and the defence burden has declined by an average 3.3 per cent annually.

Over the same thirteen years, the armed forces of the IME countries combined fell at an average annual rate of 1.7 per cent while population grew at a rate of slightly more than 0.8 per cent.

This is not cited as an international standard, but to provide a point for perspective. Inspection of the real growth rates shown in Tables 1.8 and 1.9 make it quite clear that no World Bank category of developing countries shared the pattern of trends in the IME countries. Overall for the eighty-seven countries, for most groups, and for most countries the defence burden rose. For most, but not all groups of developing countries the growth of total government expenditures increased more rapidly than military spending—the 'share' of military expenditures fell as compared with government civil spending. For all groups in both income and regional classifi- cations of developing countries, real government spending increased more rapidly than GNP and generally at a real rate of growth much above that of the IME countries.

The pattern of trends for large countries is different from that for smaller countries. For large countries, the defence burden increased only in the four 'insurgency' countries and in Iran. The defence burden of all categories of smaller developing countries rose. Size of the developing country cannot be rejected as an influence on the spending decisions which led to increased military burdens over the 1969–81 period. But it apparently was not the group of large developing countries—containing the nations generally cited as emergent regional powers—which was prepared to bear increased defence burdens. For the groups of countries shown in Tables 1.8 and 1.9, the growth rates of real military spending are substantially higher than growth in numbers of armed personnel—a general trend toward more capital-intensive military establishments.

Tables 1.10 and 1.11 show more detail for selected groups of market-orientated countries. The two upper panels of Table 1.10 compare the twenty-seven IME countries with all eighty-seven developing countries. As already noted, from 1969 to 1981 the defence burden of the former fell while the defence burden of the latter rose. In the terms of alternatives foregone, the MILEX:GNP ratio for the group of developing countries as a whole was greater than for the industrialized countries throughout the span of thirteen years—a burden 85 per cent greater at the end of the period, and still rising.

As shown in the bottom panel of Table 1.10, growth of the government sector was particularly marked for the oil-exporting countries. For most of the smaller oil exporters, but apparently not for the larger countries, both the military 'share' and the military burden rose sharply. Because of the great disparity in size of populations and economies among these eighteen oil-exporters, the declining military 'share' of the larger members dominates in the category containing all oil exporters. There is no single pattern of rising or falling defence burden among the oil exporting countries. In general, the relatively lower income members of this group experienced declines in defence burdens, while relatively higher income oil-exporters adopted higher defence burdens. We should recall, however, that these data do not incorporate the seven high income capital-surplus oil exporters of the Gulf and North Africa. For these seven countries, defence burdens rose, probably even more sharply than for the oil-exporting group shown in Table 1.10.

Table 1.11 shows three groups of oil-importing developing countries. The members of each group have generally similar growth rates, shares, and burdens. But a comparison of the patterns shown in the three panels of Table 1.11 reveals significant differences between the groups.

For the eleven Upper-Middle Income countries, the growth of total central government expenditures was much more rapid than the growth of military expenditures. The civilian share of government spending rose more rapidly than the government share of GNP. The defence burden declined very little or remained stable over the 1969–81 period; it was at a relatively low level at the beginning of the period and was low at the end.

The ten large countries in Low and Lower-Middle Income categories experienced substantially lower rates of growth than the Upper-Middle Income countries in this period. The civilian government expenditures increased more rapidly than those of the military, but the growth rate of the civilian share of total central government expenditures was lower than the growth rate of government share of GNP. The military burden for this group of large countries rose at a very moderate rate. The military burden was relatively high in 1969 and was still higher in 1981.

The forty-eight small countries in the Low and Lower-Middle Income categories generally maintained the same military share of total government expenditures throughout the period, but the government share of GNP rose rapidly. The full effect of the growth of the public sector share of GNP was reflected in the growth rate of the military burden. The GNP growth rate of these small, poor countries was below that of the large and higher-income countries, but the growth of the military burden in the small, poor countries

Table 1.10 Military Expenditures, Central Government Expenditures and Gross National Product: levels, shares and growth rates 1969–81 (in billions of PPP dollars at 1975 international prices)

		1969	1981	1969–1981 growth rate %
Twenty-seven industrialized market economies				
MILEX	PPP $	156.7	148.9	−0.33**
CGE	PPP $	625.9	1,112.5	4.56
GNP	PPP $	3,405.0	4,842.9	3.08
MILEX/CGE 'share'	%	25.04	13.39	−4.68
CGE/GNP 'share'	%	18.38	22.97	1.44
MILEX/GNP 'burden'	%	4.60	3.08	−3.31
Eighty-seven ICP developing countries				
MILEX	PPP $	56.0	130.0	7.79
CGE	PPP $	290.4	886.3	10.35
GNP	PPP $	1,167.6	2,288.6	6.04
MILEX/CGE 'share'	%	19.29	14.67	−2.32
CGE/GNP 'share'	%	24.87	38.73	4.06
MILEX/GNP 'burden'	%	4.80	5.68	1.65
Eighteen oil-exporting developing countries				
MILEX	PPP $	17.9	50.7	10.40
CGE	PPP $	72.7	308.5	14.49
GNP	PPP $	352.1	772.6	6.85
MILEX/CGE 'share'	%	24.55	16.42	−3.57
CGE/GNP 'share'	%	20.65	39.93	7.15
MILEX/GNP 'burden'	%	5.07	6.56	3.32*

Notes

1. See Appendix for country-membership of World Bank groups.

2. * not significantly different from zero at the 1% level, but significant at the 5% level.

3. ** not significantly different from zero at 5% level.

was much higher than for other oil-importing nations. The level of the military burden in 1969 was relatively low, below that of the IME countries. By 1981, however, although still below the level of the larger poor countries, it substantially exceeded the level of the IME countries.

While this pattern of growth rates is generally shared by countries

Table 1.11 Military Expenditures, Central Government Expenditures and Gross National Product: levels, shares and growth rates 1969–81 (in billions of PPP dollars at 1975 international prices)

		1969	1981	1969–1981 growth rate %
Eleven upper-middle income oil-importing countries				
MILEX	PPP $	7.7	15.0	6.42
CGE	PPP $	37.8	178.0	11.72
GNP	PPP $	222.6	474.0	7.42
MILEX/CGE 'share'	%	20.36	8.44	−4.74
CGE/GNP 'share'	%	16.98	37.57	4.01
MILEX/GNP 'burden'	%	3.46	3.17	−0.92*
Ten large, low and lower-middle income oil-importing countries				
MILEX	PPP $	24.3	49.1	5.90
CGE	PPP $	135.6	293.7	7.44
GNP	PPP $	428.7	755.1	4.97
MILEX/CGE 'share'	%	17.91	16.72	−1.43
CGE/GNP 'share'	%	31.63	38.90	2.35
MILEX/GNP 'burden'	%	5.67	6.51	0.88
Forty-eight small, low and lower-middle income oil-importing countries				
MILEX	PPP $	6.2	15.2	8.21
CGE	PPP $	44.3	106.1	8.03
GNP	PPP $	164.2	287.0	4.70
MILEX/CGE 'share'	%	13.96	14.33	0.16**
CGE/GNP 'share'	%	26.95	36.96	3.19
MILEX/GNP 'burden'	%	3.76	5.30	3.35

Notes
1. See Appendix for country-membership of World Bank groups.
2. * not significantly different from zero at the 1% level, but significant at the 5% level.
3. ** not significantly different from zero at 5% level.

in both the Lower-Middle and Low Income groupings, it is accentuated in the latter group. For the poorest of the poor developing
countries, military outlays appear to have displaced civilian government expenditures and constituted a higher share of total government use of resources in 1981 than in 1969. The rate of growth of
real military spending was more than double the real GNP growth
rate in 1969–81 period for the small Low-Income countries.

Conclusions

In this chapter we have surveyed the body of information on military
expenditures published by one of the major international reporting
agencies. The information assembled by ACDA has very broad
coverage; for a large number of countries, it records defence
spending over more than a decade. It is a highly valued resource for
investigation of the national security activities of developing countries.

To draw reliable inferences from this body of information, some
caution is warranted and refinement of the published data is
required. Nicole Ball, in Chapter 2 of this volume, explores key
questions about the observational accuracy of the data. In this
chapter we have demonstrated several procedures to refine the data,
designed to increase our confidence in drawing inferences about the
evolution of defence burdens in developing countries. We have:

1. Assigned the military expenditures, central government total
   expenditures and gross national product of eighty-seven developing countries to World Bank income and regional categories.
2. Corrected the most important source of systematic bias in the
   published data, to permit real comparisons across countries and
   through time.
3. Computed indicators of the real military burden, defined as the
   real alternatives foregone, for the World Bank groups of developing countries in the base year 1975, and estimated the trend
   growth rates of the military 'share' and defence burden for
   1969–81.
4. Shown that there appear to be statistically significant differences
   (in the growth rates of the military 'share' and burden) among the
   groups of countries attributable to differences of size, real per
   capita income, and resource endowment (that is, differences
   among oil-importing and oil-exporting countries).

Our inspection of these improved military expenditures data and indicators of national defence effort for a large number of developing countries confirms that, for groups of Third World countries, there were quite different patterns of resource allocation for national security in the 1969–81 period. There is evidence of distinctly different behaviour in the management of national defence burdens by oil-exporting countries, by relatively high-income countries, by large lower-income countries and by small lower-income countries.

For the oil-exporting countries, the defence burden increased rapidly in the period but the military share of total government expenditures declined. At the end of the period, in 1981, the real defence burden was at a higher level than for other groups of developing or industrialized countries.

The three other groups consist of oil-importing countries.

For the Upper-Middle Income countries, the defence burden was unchanged in the period but the military share of total government expenditures fell sharply. At the end of the period, the defence burden was at a lower level than for other groups of developing countries—at about the same real level as the industrialized countries.

For the large Low and Lower-Middle Income countries, the defence burden was unchanged in the period but the military share of total government expenditures fell moderately. The military share of government expenditures, in 1981, was at a higher level than for other groups and the defence burden was at a higher level than found in any group of developing or industrialized countries.

For the small Low and Lower-Middle Income countries, the defence burden rose rapidly in the 1969–81 period while the military share of total government expenditures was unchanged. The growth rate of the real defence burden was higher than for any other group of oil-importing countries. These characteristics were accentuated for the small Low Income countries; for the poorest category of developing countries, the growth rate of the real defence burden was higher than any other group, including the oil-exporters.

Very broadly, these patterns describe the differing intensity of efforts made in the recent past by governments of the Third World to provide for their national security. The relation of these efforts to national development and the determinants of this behaviour are explored in Parts II and III of this volume.

Table 1.12 Distribution of eighty-seven ICP developing countries by World Bank income and regional groups

	SSA	MENA	EA	SA	LA	Total
All eighty-seven ICP developing countries						
LYC/M	23	1	1	5	1	31
MYL/M	10	2	4	—	11	27
MYU/M	—	1	3	—	7	11
MYL/X	4	2	1	—	2	9
MYU/X	1	4	1	—	3	9
Total	38	10	10	5	24	87
Large countries: population greater than twenty million						
LYC/M	2	—	1	3	—	6
MYL/M	—	—	3	—	1	4
MYU/M	—	—	1	—	2	3
MYL/X	1	1	1	—	—	3
MYU/X	—	1	—	—	1	2
Total	3	2	6	3	4	18
Small countries: population less than twenty million						
LYC/M	21	1	—	2	1	25
MYL/M	10	2	1	—	10	23
MYU/M	—	1	2	—	5	8
MYL/X	3	1	—	—	2	6
MYU/X	1	3	1	—	2	7
Total	35	8	4	2	20	69

Notes See Appendix for country-membership of World Bank groups.

Appendix: ACDA listing of 145 countries in World Bank groups

	Country Sample[1]	Bank Region[2]	Mil. Expen. 1975	
			TMILEX[3]	CYMILEX[3]
Low Income Oil-Importing (LYC/M)				
Afghanistan	Small[4]	MENA	59	391
Bangladesh	Large[4]	SA	64	1,016
Benin	Small	SSA	8	32
Burma	Large	EA	140	690
Burundi	Small	SSA	19	49

Cape Verde	n/a	SSA	2	n/a
Central African	Small	SSA	13	24
Chad	Small	SSA	34	149
Equator. Guinea	Small	SSA	3	n/a
Ethiopia	Large	SSA	139	511
Gambia, The	Small	SSA	0	0
Ghana	Small	SSA	592	251
Guinea	Small	SSA	17	81
Guinea-Bissau	n/a	SSA	2	n/a
Haiti	Small	LA	18	59
India	Large	SA	4,443	20,678
Kenya	Small	SSA	71	109
Madagascar	Small	SSA	48	107
Malawi	Small	SSA	17	59
Mali	Small	SSA	24	81
Mozambique	Small	SSA	42	101
Nepal	Small	SA	12	109
Niger	Small	SSA	9	27
Pakistan	Large	SA	1,318	4,318
Rwanda	Small	SSA	17	39
São Tomé & Prín	Small	SSA	0	n/a
Sierra Leone	Small	SSA	12	32
Somalia	Small	SSA	30	74
Sri Lanka	Small	SA	53	373
Sudan	Small	SSA	176	408
Tanzania	Small	SSA	163	387
Togo	Small	SSA	12	40
Uganda	Small	SSA	161	312
Upper Volta	Small	SSA	25	102
Zaire	Large	SSA	271	558

Lower Middle Income Oil-Importing (MYL/M)

Bolivia	Small	LA	113	175
Botswana	Small	SSA	0	0
Colombia	Large	LA	343	602
Costa Rica	Small	LA	13	29
Dominican Rep.	Small	LA	91	265
El Salvador	Small	LA	47	82
Guatemala	Small	LA	82	201
Guyana	Small	LA	37	87
Honduras	Small	LA	38	84
Ivory Coast	Small	SSA	60	129
Jamaica	Small	LA	26	33
Lebanon	Small	MENA	306	n/a

Lesotho	Small	SSA	0	0
Liberia	Small	SSA	8	19
Mauritania	Small	SSA	11	26
Mauritius	Small	SSA	1	3
Morocco	Small	MENA	500	1,259
Nicaragua	Small	LA	51	98
Papua New Guinea	Small	EA	9	17
Paraguay	Small	LA	48	136
Philippines	Large	EA	847	2,651
Paraguay	Small	LA	48	136
Phillipines	Large	EA	847	2,651
Senegal	Small	SSA	36	101
Swaziland	Small	SSA	2	4
Taiwan	Small	EA	1,907	2,855
Thailand	Large	EA	608	1,343
Turkey	Large	MENA	2,446	6,021
Yemen (Aden)	n/a	MENA	56	n/a
Yemen (Sanaa)	n/a	MENA	128	n/a
Zambia	Small	SSA	615	735
Zimbabwe	Small	SSA	113	251

Upper Middle Income Oil-Importing (MYR/M)

Argentina	Large	LA	1,272	2,350
Barbados	Small	LA	1	1
Brazil	Large	LA	2,274	3,511
Chile	Small	LA	852	990
Fiji	Small	EA	3	5
Jordan	Small	MENA	515	711
Korea, Rep. of	Large	EA	2,043	3,298
Panama	Small	LA	24	36
Singapore	Small	EA	416	454
Surinam	Small	LA	13	14
Uruguay	Small	LA	218	327

Lower Middle Income Oil-Exporting (MYL/X)

Angola	Small	SSA	243	248
Cameroon	Small	SSA	65	150
Congo, Peop. Rep	Small	SSA	52	87
Ecuador	Small	LA	204	311
Egypt, Arab Rep	Large	MENA	4,703	12,661
Indonesia	Large	EA	2,218	5,487
Nigeria	Large	SSA	3,688	7,250
Peru	Small	LA	778	1,645
Tunisia	Small	MENA	87	188

Upper Middle Income Oil-Exporting (MYU/X)

Algeria	Small	MENA	768	1,065
Gabon	Small	SSA	35	22
Iran	Large	MENA	15,576	13,180
Iraq	Small	MENA	3,953	5,607
Malaysia	Small	EA	727	964
Mexico	Small	EA	727	964
Syrian Arab Rep	Small	MENA	1,544	2,121
Trinidad & Tobago	Small	LA	12	11
Venezuela	Small	LA	1,134	1,031

High Income Oil-Exporting (HYO/X)

Bahrain	MENA	26
Kuwait	MENA	1,160
Libya	MENA	1,313
Oman	MENA	1,155
Qatar	MENA	140
Saudi Arabia	MENA	10,588
United Arab Em.	MENA	56

Industrial Market Economies (IME)

Australia	IME	3,069	1,351
Austria	IME	613	386
Belgium	IME	2,271	1,159
Canada	IME	4,698	1,935
Cyprus	IME	34	42
Denmark	IME	1,190	596
Finland	IME	592	304
France	IME	17,274	9,928
Germany, Fed. Rep	IME	20,412	9,867
Greece	IME	2,129	2,309
Iceland	IME	0	0
Ireland	IME	252	175
Israel	IME	4,958	3,472
Italy	IME	7,099	4,881
Japan	IME	6,917	3,975
Luxembourg	IME	29	14
Malta	IME	11	15
Netherlands	IME	3,975	1,579
New Zealand	IME	1,429	571
Norway	IME	1,429	571
Portugal	IME	919	1,455
S. Africa	IME	2,175	2,974

Spain	IME	4,342	3,480
Sweden	IME	3,024	1,285
Switzerland	IME	1,778	589
United Kingdom	IME	21,484	14,318
United States	EA	150,427	76,468

Non-Market Economies: Europe (NME)

Albania	NME	216
Bulgaria	NME	3,605
Czechoslovakia	NME	6,139
Germany, East	NME	7,745
Hungary	NME	3,020
Poland	NME	10,689
Romania	NME	4,713
Soviet Union	NME	207,426

Non-Market Economies: Other (NMO)

China Mainland	EA	31,425
Cuba	LA	650
Kampuchea	EA	111
Korea, North	EA	1,786
Laos	EA	1
Mongolia	EA	1
Vietnam	EA	1,450
Vietnam, So.	EA	759

[1] '87 ICP Developing Countries' are those with an entry in Column 2, '87 Country sample'.

[2] World Bank Regions are: Sub-Saharan Africa (SSA); Middle East and North Africa (MENA); South Asia (SA); East Asia (EA); Latin America (LA).

[3] TMILEX in millions of ACDA 1982 dollars; CYMILEX in millions of PPP dollars at Current Year International Prices.

[4] Large countries have population greater than 20 million; small countries have population less than 20 million.

2

Security expenditure: measurement and trends

NICOLE BALL

Introduction

All countries do not place equal value on the collection and dissemination of data. Many Third World countries are less well-
equipped for these activities than Western industrialized ones and
do not accord the improvement of their statistical services high
priority. In addition, some developing countries have opted for what
might be termed the 'East bloc' pattern of data dissemination: the
fewer data published, the better. Security-expenditure data are
particularly problematic since the question of how much of its
resources a country devotes to security-related activities is often
considered sensitive and subject to secrecy on the part of governments.[1] Restricting the availability of such data is one way of
reducing the information to which other governments have access.
Just as important, it is also a means of preventing the general public
from learning too much about their own security sector.

Researchers examining the relationship between the allocation of
resources to the security sector and development in the Third World
are thus confronted with a number of obstacles when collecting
security-expenditure data. In the first place, the desire on the part of
many governments to make public as little information as possible
hampers efforts to collect data and many of the data available are of
dubious accuracy. Second, although some developing-country
governments do publish reasonably detailed security budgets, it can
be difficult for individuals outside those countries to obtain the
relevant documents. As a result, publications which provide
statistical information on the security-related outlays of a large
number of Third World countries are widely used in the research
community. It is only, however, since the late 1960s that such data
have been published on a regular basis.

There are now three groups which provide information solely on
the security-related component of government expenditure. These
are the United States Arms Control and Disarmament Agency

(ACDA, *World Military Expenditures and Arms Transfers*), the Stockholm International Peace Research Institute (SIPRI, *World Armaments and Disarmament: SIPRI Yearbook*), and the International Institute of Strategic Studies (IISS, *The Military Balance*). A fourth major source is the International Monetary Fund (IMF) which publishes functional breakdowns of government expenditures that, for most countries, include outlays on the security sector (*Government Finance Statistics Yearbook*).

Trends

Although these sources are often in disagreement about the precise amount of resources devoted to the armed forces in individual countries, a number of general statements about security expenditure in the Third World during the last thirty-five years can be made based on the data they provide. The first is that Third World security spending has increased sharply in real terms over the last three decades. Figure 2.1 shows that, according to data published by ACDA, Third World security expenditure (measured in 1982 US dollars) tripled between 1963 and 1983.[2] A second general point is that the Third World's share in global security expenditure has also increased significantly. Figure 2.2 and Table 2.1 show that the Third World's share (as reported by SIPRI) has nearly tripled since the early 1950s and more than doubled since 1970.

Much of the increase in Third World security expenditure can be attributed to external conflicts, the protection of domestic ruling elites, the growing influence of the armed forces in the political system and the rising costs of weapon procurement. Quite apart from these factors, however, there are several reasons why the Third World should have been expected to account for a somewhat larger share of global security expenditure over the years. First of all, the number of independent countries has approximately tripled since 1950. Second, many developing countries, particularly those in Africa, had virtually no indigenous armed forces when they became independent. If each newly independent country created even just a small army, the Third World's share in global security spending would have had to rise. This is evident from the figures presented for Africa in Table 2.1. During the 1960s, the decade of decolonization in Africa, that continent's share of global security expenditure increased by more than 300 per cent. A third factor that would have affected the regional shares of global security spending was the

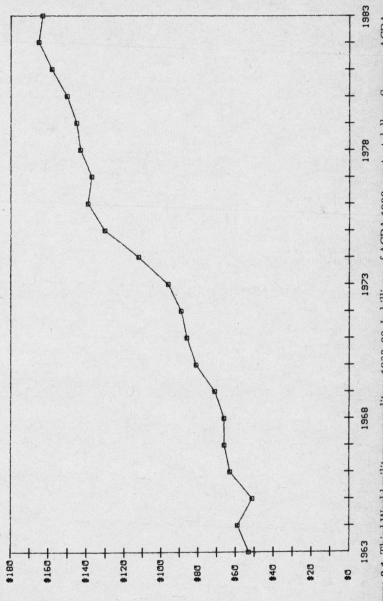

Figure 2.1 Third World military expenditure 1953–83. In billions of ACDA 1982 constant dollars. *Source*: ACDA, *World Military Expenditures and Arms Transfers*, various issues.

Table 2.1 Third World regional shares of military expenditure, 1950–84
(in percent of world total)

Region	1950	1955	1960	1965	1970	1975	1980	1984
Middle East	0.5	0.5	0.9	1.2	2.5	6.9	7.3	7.1
Far East	2.0	0.8	1.3	1.6	1.8	2.1	3.0	3.1
South Asia	1.2	0.7	0.7	1.2	1.0	1.0	1.2	1.3
Africa	0.1	0.1	0.2	0.7	0.9	2.3	2.5	1.7
South America	1.3	1.0	1.1	1.1	1.1	1.7	1.8	2.0
Central America	0.5	0.2	0.3	0.3	0.3	0.3	0.4	0.5
Total LDC	5.6	3.3	4.5	6.1	7.6	14.3	16.2	15.7
LDC without Middle East	5.1	2.8	3.6	4.9	5.1	7.4	8.9	8.6

Notes
  Middle East includes Egypt; Far East excludes People's Republic of China; and
Africa excludes Egypt.
  Sources: SIPRI Yearbooks, 1972, 1974, 1979, 1985.

decline in military-related grant assistance which began in the mid-
to late 1960s. A number of Third World countries with relatively
large armed forces were required to begin using more of their own
resources to purchase weapons.

A third general statement that can be made is that the increase in
security expenditure has not been distributed evenly among the
developing countries. As Figure 2.2 and Table 2.1 demonstrate,
Middle Eastern countries have been responsible for a disproportionately large share of the growth in security expenditure recorded by
the developing world. Indeed, if one subtracts the Middle East's
share of global security outlays from that of the Third World as a
whole, one finds that the remaining countries have increased their
share by less than 70 per cent since 1950. This is considerably less
than the 180 per cent increase obtained when all developing
countries are considered as a group. It has already been pointed out
that the growth in Africa's share can in part be attributed to
decolonization and the creation of national armed forces where none
existed previously. In the Middle East, the various unresolved
conflicts among the countries in the region and the rise in the price
of petroleum in 1973, and again in 1979, have played an important

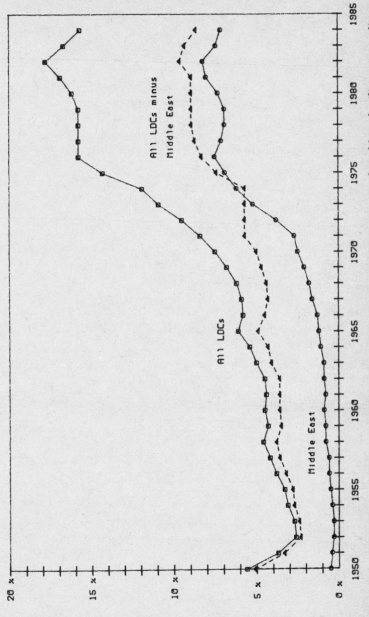

Figure 2.2 Third World share in world military expenditure 1950–84.In percentage of world total military expenditure.
Source: SIPRI Yearbooks (1972, 1974, 1979, 1985).

role in determining the amount of resources devoted to the security
sector.

The increase in security expenditure has not only been distributed
unequally among the different regions in the Third World, it has also
occurred unevenly within regions. This is particularly clear in Africa
where much of the increase since the beginning of the 1970s can be
attributed to a relatively limited number of countries. SIPRI lists
fourteen African countries for which security expenditures more
than tripled in real terms between 1970 and 1980, several of which
derive a large proportion of their income from exports of petroleum
(Algeria, Libya, Gabon and Tunisia) and several of which have been
engaged in serious domestic or external conflicts (Morocco,
Zimbabwe, South Africa, Ethiopia and Tanzania) (SIPRI 1985: 298).

A fourth characteristic of Third World security expenditure which
emerges from an examination of the various sources is the way in
which it is influenced by general economic conditions. Figure 2.2
shows the effect of the increase in petroleum prices on expenditure
in the Middle East, which is in turn reflected in the overall
expenditure figures portrayed in Figure 2.1. Similarly, the impact of
the recessions in 1974–5 and in 1980–2 are visible in both Figure 2.1
and Figure 2.2. The latter, which was a longer and more serious
recession, caused a sharper and more prolonged decline in Third
World security expenditures than the 1974–5 economic downturn.
The decline in expenditure was particularly marked in Africa as
might have been expected given the serious economic problems
confronting most of the countries on that continent.

Finally, figures published by ACDA in various issues of *World
Military Expenditures and Arms Transfers* suggest that, as a group,
the Third World countries now allocate a larger proportion of their
gross products to the security sector than they did in the 1960s while
the share of national budgets devoted to security expenditure has
declined markedly over the last twenty years. This indicates that
governments have gained control over an increasingly large portion
of their gross products. They have thus been able to increase their
expenditure in the non-military sectors of the economy without
necessarily having to cut back on the total amount of resources
available to the armed forces. In many cases, the security sector's
share in total budget outlays has declined at the same time as expenditure on the armed forces has increased in real terms.[3] This has been
facilitated by the substantial increase that occurred in at least some
developing countries' gross products (particularly prior to the 1980s).

Measurement

When assessing the effects of security expenditure on the economies of Third World countries and when negotiating arms control agreements, it is necessary to have data which are as accurate as possible. It was noted above that there are often differences among the major sources in the values they assign to the security expenditure of individual countries. It was also pointed out that primary data can be difficult to obtain and are frequently of uncertain quality when available. Researchers thus more often than not find it convenient or necessary to rely on the data collected by the IMF, ACDA, SIPRI and the IISS. It is therefore important to determine how accurate and reliable the data presented by these sources are and whether any of them can be considered more accurate or reliable than the others. This is far from an easy undertaking, in part because of the way in which the data are presented.

Since none of the major sources provide disaggregated expenditure data, it is not immediately evident if funds allocated to the security forces have been omitted from the figures they publish or if non-military expenditures have been included. Both are distinct possibilities because there is no universally agreed-upon definition of security expenditure to which all countries adhere and countries arrange their budgets in different ways. Some countries record part of their security-related expenditures outside that portion of the budget clearly identified as 'military'. Items such as military pension, debt incurred through the procurement of weapons, military-related construction and outlays on paramilitary forces frequently appear as sub-headings in ministries other than the Ministry of Defence.

Other countries list civilian-type activities in the defence budget. For example, civil aviation in Pakistan and Saudi Arabia, and the non-paramilitary youth organization, National Service in Guyana are included in the respective countries' military budgets because they are the responsibility of the Minister of Defence. Still other countries complicate the situation even further by moving portions of their security expenditure from one budget category to another over a period of years. Expenditure on the Iranian Gendarmerie and the Central African Republic's Garde Republicaine, both of which are classified as paramilitary forces, has been included under the Ministry of Defence in some years and under the Ministry of the Interior in others. Any source which simply took the expenditure listed under Ministry of Defence for either of these countries would produce an expenditure series which, over the years, would have serious internal inconsistencies.

A second presentational characteristic which renders the comparison of expenditure data from the major sources more difficult is ACDA's policy of publishing its statistics only in US dollars. While both SIPRI and the IISS also publish figures converted into US dollars, differences in methods of conversion and in base years employed to construct constant dollar series make comparisons next to impossible. Furthermore, when evaluating the effect that expenditure in the security sector has on individual economies, it is more useful to have data in local currencies.[4] The local currency data on which most of ACDA's dollar figures for Third World countries were based (at least up to the 1985 edition of *World Military Expenditures and Arms Transfers*) have, in most years, been available only in an annual report to the US Congress which was not sold by the US Government Printing Office, making it difficult to obtain.[5]

All this points up the need for a unified definition of security expenditure and the presentation of data in a disaggregated form. None of the major sources has ever attempted to produce disaggregated security-expenditure data and while the definitions employed by the IMF, SIPRI and ACDA are not too dissimilar, it is really only the IMF that makes a serious attempt to adhere to its definition when collecting data. A recent United Nations effort aimed at institutionalizing the collection of security-expenditure data according to a common definition and in disaggregated form appears to have failed.

Definitions

The IISS has no detailed definition of what constitutes security expenditure and accepts whatever figure national sources provide for security outlays. ACDA and SIPRI have definitions which, although slightly different from each other, are both based on the NATO definition of military expenditure. In estimating the security spending of Third World countries, they both make some effort to bring the figures collected into conformity with each other. In accordance with its definition, ACDA attempts to exclude expenditure on 'internal security' (that is, paramilitary forces) whereas SIPRI, in line with its definition, attempts to include it. ACDA has also recently begun to make adjustments to the figures reported by a few countries suspected of grossly understating their security-related outlays. This involves adding the estimated value of arms imported during the year in question to the expenditure reported for that year. Given the way in which arms are actually paid for—in instalments—and the uncertainty surrounding the true cost of weapons for the purchaser, this method produces a figure of dubious accuracy. It has, however, been employed for only a few countries and these are clearly marked in the 1985 edition of *World Military Expenditures and Arms Transfers*.

The IMF has its own definition of defence expenditure which is quite detailed and similar to the one employed by NATO. IMF members are directed to use it as a guideline when supplying data to the Government Finance Division. Since IMF security-expenditure data are supposed to include all items listed in the definition, how a country chooses to arrange its budget is, in theory, irrelevant for those who use IMF statistics. Iran and the Central African Republic should always report expenditure on the Gendarmerie and the Garde Republicaine. Saudi Arabia and Pakistan should never report the portion of their defence budgets allocated to civil aviation. The IMF is probably the most reliable of the available sources and its data are frequently reproduced in both ACDA and SIPRI publications. Since SIPRI publishes a local currency series, it is possible to determine when the IMF has been made use of and when it has not. For ACDA, it is not possible to see when the IMF has been used as a source unless one has access to the Congressional report prepared by USAID (United States Agency for International Development) which contains the local currency data on which ACDA has based many of the statistics found in the various volumes of *World Military Expenditures and Arms Transfers*.

Table 2.2 compares the security-expenditure figures for Guyana published by the IMF and SIPRI and those prepared by USAID for ACDA with expenditure data derived from the Guyanese national budget. Guyana was chosen because figures for actual outlays were available for most of the years surveyed and Guyanese security expenditure is, as far as can be determined, concentrated in the Ministry of Defence's budget, making it unlikely that one or the other of the sources would omit important expenditure categories.

For the years 1967–73, the IMF would appear to have reported total outlays on the military forces. Between 1974 and 1977, there are considerable differences between Guyanese data published in the budgetary documents and those reported to the IMF and it is only in

Table 2.2 Comparison of Guyanese security expenditure estimates for total security expenditure (in millions of Guyanese dollars)

	USAID/ ACDA	IMF	SIPRI	Guyana government estimates total security expenditure		
				Total	OPER.	CAP.
1967	NA	4.1	4.8	11.2	9.6	1.6
1968	NA	4.0	4.0	11.1	10.2	0.9
1969	NA	4.5	4.5	12.8	12.5	0.3
1970	NA	6.7	6.7	15.5	15.2	0.3
1971	NA	6.2	6.1	15.3	14.7	0.6
1972	7.0	7.5	7.5	17.4	17.0	0.4
1973	9.0	10.6	22.5	22.7	21.0	1.7
1974	16.0	24.8	38.1	32.9	30.0	2.9
1975	25.0	76.4	78.9	49.6	40.3	9.3
1976	87.0	86.7	120.0	99.9	76.3	23.6
1977	61.0	61.9	77.5	67.0	58.0	9.0
1978[c]	44.0	44.2	65.0[d]	67.0	65.8	1.2
1979[e]	44.0	43.8	95.0[d]	67.1	65.4	1.7

Notes

OPER. = Operating costs (personnel, operations, maintenance).
CAP = Capital costs (procurement and construction).
c   = Guyanese government figures are revised estimates.
d   = SIPRI estimates.
e   = Guyanese government figures are first estimates.
Sources: USAID/ACDA Data: USAID, *Implementation of Section 620(s)*, *Report to Congress*, various years. IMF data 1967–72: World Bank, *World Tables 1976*; IMF data 1973–9: IMF, *Government Finance Statistics Yearbook*, Vol. 9. SIPRI data: SIPRI Yearbook, 1979, 1983, 1985. Guyana government data: *Estimates. . . . as Passed by the National Assembly*, various years.

1977 that the two series are very close to each other. In 1978 and 1979, the IMF would again appear to be reporting total expenditure on military forces. The problem with the data for 1967–73 and 1978–9 is that the IMF definition includes expenditure on paramilitary forces and the expenditure reported by the Guyanese government on the police force (right-hand three columns in Table 2.3) should have been added in.

SIPRI seems to have reported total expenditure on military forces between 1967 and 1972 and to have used the IMF as a source in 1968–70 and 1972. After 1972, the IMF has clearly not been used as a

Table 2.3 Comparison of Guyanese security expenditure estimates for military and police forces (in millions of Guyanese dollars)

	Guyana government estimates military forces			Guyana government estimates police/paramilitary		
	Total	OPER.	CAP.	Total	OPER.	CAP.
1967	4.3	3.1	1.2	6.9	6.5	0.4
1968	4.1	3.4	0.7	7.0	6.8	0.2
1969	4.7	4.5	0.2	8.1	8.0	0.1
1970	6.7	6.5	0.2	8.8	8.6	0.2
1971	6.1	6.0	0.1	9.2	8.7	0.5
1972	7.1	7.0	0.1	10.3	10.0	0.3
1973	10.1	8.8	1.3	12.6	12.3	0.3
1974	17.9	15.9	2.0	15.0	14.1	0.9
1975	32.7	24.5	8.2	16.9	15.8	1.1
1976	70.0	48.3	21.7	29.9	28.0	1.9
1977	47.5	38.7	8.8	19.5	19.3	0.2
1978[c]	43.8	42.8	1.0	23.2	23.0	0.2
1979[e]	40.7	39.7	1.0	26.4	25.7	0.7

Notes
OPER. = Operating costs (personnel, operations, maintenance).
CAP = Capital costs (procurement and construction).
c   = Guyanese government figures are revised estimates.
e   = Guyanese government figures are first estimates.
Sources: Guyana government data: *Estimates. . . . as Passed by the National Assembly*, various years.

source, although for the year 1975 the two sources are not that far apart in their estimates. In 1973 SIPRI would appear to have reported total expenditure on both the military forces and the police force and, in 1978, it may be reporting operating costs for the military forces and the police force. For the remaining years, SIPRI data diverge considerably from any others shown in Table 2.2.

In 1972, 1973 and 1975, USAID reported the operating costs portion of expenditure on the military forces. In 1974 and 1978, it reported total expenditure on the military forces. In 1976, 1977 and 1979, it appears to have reported IMF figures which, at least during 1976 and 1977, probably included some expenditures on the Guyanese police force.

Each of the sources has reported incomplete expenditure figures according to its own definition (the IMF and SIPRI by excluding outlays on the police force in various years and ACDA by omitting the capital outlays of the military forces during three years). They have also published expenditure series which are not internally consistent. ACDA would seem to be particularly prone to this latter problem: its definition of security expenditure excludes outlays on paramilitary forces, but it is increasing its reliance on the IMF as a source of data. The IMF, of course, includes paramilitary expenditures in its definition of security spending. The USAID office which used to prepare so much of ACDA's data made an effort to collect primary budget materials and exclude paramilitary expenditure whenever possible, but ACDA itself is not known to collect such primary documents. Thus, even if ACDA suspects that expenditure on paramilitary forces is included in the IMF data that it uses, it cannot determine what portion of the IMF's figure should be eliminated in any given year.

Disaggregated data

Disaggregation and the major sources

Table 2.2 demonstrates the importance of access to disaggregated, primary data in determining the reliability and accuracy of security-expenditure figures published by the major sources. As mentioned above, none of the major sources has ever attempted to collect data that are in any way broken down into their component parts, not even in terms of recurrent and capital expenditure.[6] Neither the IISS nor SIPRI works primarily with national budgetary documents, which would be the only means of compiling more detailed statistics. The USAID office which until recently prepared so much of ACDA's Third World security-expenditure data did collect some budgetary materials but rarely used these to do anything beyond ensuring that paramilitary expenditures were excluded from its statistics.

IMF staff members argue that if they were to ask member governments to provide anything beyond the single figure that is currently requested for outlays on the security sector, many would cease to make any information whatsoever available. While the IMF makes no attempt to check the data provided by governments against budgetary documents, they do believe that the figures reported to them are fairly accurate as far as the operating costs portion is concerned. It is with weapon procurement that problems arise. As a rule of thumb, therefore, one can say that the fewer weapons a country imports, the more accurate the data provided to the IMF are likely to be. As far as expenditures for weapon procurement are concerned, IMF staff members suggest that, at least in some Latin American countries, payments that do not appear in the budget itself would probably appear in extra-budgetary accounts. For all countries, they should appear in the balance of payments. How one is to gain access to the relevant extra-budgetary accounts or to balance of payments statistics that are sufficiently detailed to enable weapon procurement to be identified is another question.

The United Nations unified reporting system

The United Nations has made the only attempt to date to institutionalize the collection of disaggregated security-expenditure data by developing a reporting system which requires data to be presented in a very detailed form. This system was devised as part of an effort to reduce the military expenditure of the major powers and to make some portion of the savings realized available to developing countries. An expert group examining the possibilities of reducing military expenditure reported to the UN Secretary General that 'a prerequisite for negotiating the reduction of military expenditures was agreement on the scope and content of such expenditures'.[7] In an effort to obtain expenditure figures that would be mutually agreeable to all parties involved in expenditure reduction exercises, a unified reporting system was worked out by the Ad Hoc Panel on Military Budgeting. The first test of this system in 1978–9 was deemed sufficiently successful to warrant the continued use of the reporting mechanism.

One purpose of the entire exercise was, of course, to obtain somewhat more accurate data on the security expenditures of the Soviet Union and other Warsaw Treaty Organization members than are presently available. In that respect, it has failed, since only one WTO member, Romania, presented any data during the first six years of the system's existence and it participated only in the most recent year, 1985. The United States government has now seemingly decided that the Soviet Union will never accept the reporting system and ceased to supply information itself in 1985 (after having participated between 1980 and 1984). Other governments seem to have reached a similar conclusion and the number of countries reporting to the United Nations during 1985 was much lower than in any of the preceding five years.

This is regrettable because although the focus was on East–West disarmament negotiations, such a system, if institutionalized, could have provided useful information on the security outlays of Third World countries. As it is, only fifteen developing countries reported to the UN at one time or another and none participated for the entire 1980–5 period.[8] Some of these countries provided quite detailed information; others presented the bare minimum. The matrix which UN members are asked to complete requires 588 separate pieces of information if it is to be filled in entirely.[9] When the UN first began developing the reporting system, there were suggestions that the proposed matrix might be too complex for the accounting system of many member governments, particularly those in the Third World. Governments were thus urged 'not to refrain from participating in the test but to present their figures on the level of aggregation that they find appropriate'.[10] Even to have accurate data at the first level of disaggregation would be a considerable step forward as far as most Third World countries are concerned.

There is reason to believe that most countries could provide at least that bare minimum of information, and probably a good deal more. Only one of the fourteen countries taking part in the preliminary test of the UN reporting system provided no information at all at the third, sub-subheading level. That country was France. The two Third World countries that participated, Mexico and Indonesia, presented very detailed breakdowns of their security expenditures. It might be argued that the Mexican and Indonesian statistical bureaus are more highly developed than those in other Third World countries, and there is certainly some truth in that contention. None the less, an examination of the data provided by more than fifty developing countries in their own budgetary documents demonstrates quite clearly that large numbers of them could very easily provide information at the first level of disaggregation and that for many of them the second and third levels would pose no very great difficulty either.[11]

The real obstacle to the participation of larger numbers of Third World countries (and of course industrialized countries as well) in the UN reporting system is political. Governments do not want to provide information or to undertake meaningful negotiations to reduce security expenditure. They would be quite happy to see their neighbours disarm, but they are unwilling to contemplate doing the same themselves. The unwillingness of governments to provide even a small amount of detail about their security-related outlays makes it difficult to believe that they can be serious about any arms limitation or arms reduction proposals they might make or about finding peaceful solutions to conflicts. The disclosure of disaggregated security-expenditure data might be seen as a first step, albeit a very small one, in dismantling the wall of secrecy behind which so much security-related information is hidden.

Disaggregated data, security expenditure and economic growth

Disaggregated security-expenditure data are important not only as input to arms control negotiations; they are also helpful in assessing the economic effects of security expenditure in individual countries. It is important to know not only what proportion of state or national resources the armed forces have at their disposal when evaluating the interaction between security expenditure and growth but also what the armed forces are buying with their money. In common with other forms of public expenditure, outlays on the security sector can both promote and hinder economic growth. They will tend to encourage it, for example, if they bring into use resources that were previously idle or if the balance between consumption and investment is altered in favour of the latter. They will tend to hinder growth if they compete with more productive government outlays or if they contribute to excessive inflation or indebtedness. Which effect security expenditure will have in any given country depends in part on the composition of its security budget.

'What the armed forces are buying' can be divided into salaries, operations and maintenance material, weapons, construction, and research and development. The payment of salaries might increase the demand for locally produced goods or, because of training received in the armed services, it might expand the available pool of skilled labour or management personnel available to the civil sector, both of which would promote growth. Alternatively, military personnel might be trained at the expense of civil sector employees or the training received might not be transferable to the civil sector and growth would thus be hindered. Similarly, the domestic procurement of weapons, operations and maintenance and construction materials might cause investment to increase in such a way as to benefit the civil sector or it might lead to investment in techniques and processes that are unsuited to the civil sector. Procurement of weapons and other items for the armed forces from abroad can impose an intolerable burden on an economy which is short of foreign exchange, but may be acceptable for an economy which is not faced with such a shortage.

It is extremely difficult to generalize about the effect that security expenditure in the abstract will have on economic growth in the abstract. The economic situation in Third World countries, although similar in many respects, can vary considerably from one country to another and this means that security expenditure (which will also vary in composition among countries) will work its way through economies differently. It is therefore necessary to look at countries individually if one wishes to obtain a clear picture of how expenditure in the security sector has influenced economic growth.

There is one characteristic that is common to many Third World defence budgets: a much larger proportion tends to be allocated to operating costs than in the industrialized world, with salaries alone often accounting for over 50 per cent of total outlays in any given year. Table 2.4 demonstrates that even in some of the wealthier Third World countries, operating costs absorbed between 70 and 90 per cent of reported security outlays at the end of the 1970s. This means that less than 30 per cent of the budget was allocated to procurement, construction and R&D. There are, of course, good reasons for believing that security budgets in many countries do not reflect the true weapon procurement costs (Ball 1984: 15–19). Yet even if one assumed that procurement costs were underestimated by as much as 100–200 per cent each year, operating costs would still account for more than three-quarters of all outlays on the security forces in most of the countries listed in Table 2.4. While it would be unwise to draw any hard-and-fast conclusions based on such a small sample, the data in this table do suggest that—contrary to popular conception—weapon procurement accounts for a relatively small proportion of total security expenditure in a large number of the countries in Asia, Africa and Latin America.

When one looks at the composition of these operating costs, one finds not only that a large proportion is devoted to salaries and wages, much of which will be spent in the local economy, but also that a sizeable share of the remainder is spent on items such as food and clothing for the troops, office and barrack furniture and other office supplies, all of which are often produced domestically. Thus, for countries with this pattern of expenditure, outlays on the armed forces can be expected to stimulate economic growth, especially if there is excess capacity in consumer industries. Econometric studies

Table 2.4 Proportion of operating costs in total security budgets[a] (in per cent of total security expenditure)

Country	1951	1955	1960	1965	1970	1975	1979
India[b]	93.5	91.0	84.6	82.3[c]	79.8[c]	82.3[c]	81.6[c]
Iran[d,e]	NA	NA	NA	82.4	48.1	29.6	NA
Malaysia[b]	NA	NA	NA	80.3	76.1	84.3	NA
Pakistan[d]	53.6	79.1	86.1	—[f]	—[f]	—[f]	—[f]
Phillipines[b]	99.7	99.6	94.6	99.6	98.3	90.8	NA
Sri Lanka[d]	76.5	72.6	77.5	95.1	85.2	84.9	90.9
Ghana[d]	NA	NA	68.1	60.5	82.9	70.2	NA
Liberia[g]	NA	98.6	98.5	94.3	NA	92.1	91.9
Malgasy Rep.[g]	NA	NA	NA	97.5	99.1	98.1	84.1
Morocco[h]	NA	NA	90.0	96.9[i]	97.3	71.3	67.5
Nigeria[b]	NA	NA	91.6	55.3	78.7	66.4	46.2[j]
Sierra Leone[b]	NA	NA	97.6[k]	94.1	92.6[d]	96.5[d]	NA
Argentina[b]	67.4	66.4	82.5	87.8	84.3	67.8	67.5[d]
Brazil[g]	NA	NA	NA	NA	83.7[l]	84.3	85.0
Chile[b]	—[f]	—[f]	94.4[k]	96.8	98.9	92.3	95.7
Colombia[h]	95.8	74.0	93.2	97.8	85.6	NA	NA
Guyana[b]	NA	NA	NA	85.1[i]	97.6	81.2	97.4[g]
Nicaragua[g]	NA	74.5[m]	94.6	96.3	96.1[n]	92.1	100.0
Trinidad[b]	NA	NA	NA	90.2	89.9	NA	NA
Venezuela[g]	NA	NA	93.2[k]	94.7	92.2	NA	NA

Notes

NA = Budget data not available.

a = Total security expenditure includes outlays on police and paramilitary forces.

b = Based on actual expenditure.

c = These values are slightly underestimated because it was impossible to disaggregate police/paramilitary expenditure.

d = Based on a combination of actual and estimated expenditure.

e = Outlays of the Ministry of Defence only.

f = No disaggregation of data possible.

g = Based on estimated expenditure.

h = Based on approved estimates.

i = Data for 1966.

j = Based on provisional expenditure.

k = Data for 1961.

l = Data for 1971.

m = Data for 1956.

n = Data for 1969.

Sources: Ball (1984a), *Third-World Security Expenditure*: Derived from country budgets collected by the author. Data for security expenditure in local currencies disaggregated to show operating, capital and R&D costs for military forces, police/paramilitary forces, and military industries.

of India and Morocco, for example, indicate that, all things being equal, security expenditure—just like any other form of public spending—can stimulate growth. In the case of India, this result is not at all surprising in light of the suggestion from Indian economists that limited domestic demand has been an important constraint on Indian economic growth.[12]

If, however, some portion of these operating expenditures leak abroad, then their growth-inducing effects will be correspondingly reduced. There are several reasons to anticipate that such leakage might occur. Domestic production of some of the goods purchased either by individual soldiers with their wages or by the armed forces for operations and maintenance purposes may not exist, or there may be no excess capacity in some industries necessitating imports, at least in the short to medium term. Alternatively, some of the industries from which purchases are made may be highly dependent on imported inputs. Increased demand for their goods would increase demand for imports. In Iran during the 1970s, for example, foreign technical personnel tended to command high salaries from the Iranian armed forces and to consume imported products. The same pattern of consumption might be anticipated for domestic military elites in many Third World countries. Fuel to operate military vehicles, aircraft and naval vessels and spare parts for weapons are classified as operating expenses and frequently must be purchased from abroad.

Conclusion

While there are considerable difficulties associated with collecting accurate information on the security-related expenditures of developing countries, it is important for researchers not merely to rely on the major sources but to attempt to generate their own data which can then be compared with those published by the major sources. It is also important that these data be as detailed as possible, both in order to ascertain whether large categories of expenditure have been omitted or under-reported, and in order to evaluate all the ramifications of the allocation of resources to the security sector on development in the Third World.

Notes

1. The terms 'security sector' and 'security expenditure' are used in preference to the more commonly employed 'military sector' and 'military expenditure' to indicate the inclusion of paramilitary forces in the discussion. This usage also reflects the fact that Third World governments frequently use their armed forces to maintain themselves in power, that is, to promote regime security.

2. SIPRI data (measured in 1973 US dollars) show that between 1958 and 1978 Third World security expenditure (excluding that of China) grew from about $7 billion to just over $38 billion, an increase by a factor of five and a half (SIPRI Yearbook 1979: 34–57).

3. A notable exception to these trends is Brazil where security expenditure as a proportion of both gross product and central government outlays has steadily declined since the beginning of the 1970s and where, according to some measures, it has also declined in real terms over the last decade or so. Different volumes of ACDA's *World Military Expenditures and Arms Transfers* show different trends for 'constant US dollars' expenditure, presumably because of the different base years employed. SIPRI data show a generally declining trend from about 1973 onward.

4. Although the IISS does publish data in local currencies, the figures refer to estimated rather than actual outlays. SIPRI and the IMF both up-date their local currency series and are thus more reliable than the IISS.

5. See US Agency for International Development (1983). In December 1980 this report was published by Congress in a form that makes it available for purchase. The 1980 report contains data for the years 1974 to 1978. See US Congress, House, Committee on Foreign Affairs (1980).

6. The *Europa Yearbook* does occasionally publish security- expenditure figures broken into their recurrent and capital portions but this source is of unknown reliability.

7. United Nations, Centre for Disarmament (1981: 1). A brief history of the development of the reporting system is contained in pages 1–5 of this document.

8. Although a member of NATO, Turkey is classified here as a developing country. The thirty-five countries referred to in this paragraph do not include countries which responded to the UN request for information by explaining that they could not provide data. In 1985, for example, the government of Lesotho informed the UN that 'Lesotho has no army, but a para-military force, and for security reasons the Government of Lesotho is unable to provide the data requested.' United Nations, General Assembly (1985).

9. Information is requested on three main types of resource costs (operating costs, procurement and construction, and research and development) which are, in turn, subdivided into six main subheadings

and thirty-two sub-subheadings for thirteen separate force group categories, only one of which—strategic forces—is (theoretically, at least) not applicable to any of the developing countries.

10. United Nations, General Assembly (1985: 35). The UN matrix is reproduced on pp. 32–4.

11. Data for forty-eight of these, disaggregated according to the UN matrix but published in a less detailed form, are found in Ball (1984).

12. The Moroccan case is discussed by Jacques Fontanel; he concludes that '. . . it is possible to say that in the absence of any other action, increased military expenditure may lead to a slight increase in gross domestic product, but public action would be better justified, at the strictly economic level, if it were aimed at other items of public expenditure (education, health, etc.)' (Fontanel 1980: 31–2). On India, see Peter Terhal (1981: 2001) and Emile Benoit (1973: 18–19). C. T. Kurien (1978: 1264) has observed that '. . . paradoxical as it may appear, the major constricting factor in the development of the Indian economy along the path that it has been taking so far is the limitation of the domestic market.' According to Ajit Singh (1979: 598–9) it was 'clearly the lack of demand which is holding back industrial expansion' from about 1978 onward. He is not certain, however, what has caused the general deceleration in the rate of growth of industrial output in India since 1965. One of the explanations of this phenomenon has centred around insufficient demand from the domestic market.

3

Capital–labour substitution in defence provision

RON SMITH, ANTHONY HUMM AND JACQUES FONTANEL

Econometric studies of military expenditure have tended to emphasize either its economic consequence (for example, Chan 1985) or its
determination (for example, Maizels and Nissanke in this volume).
The military supply side by which factor inputs—such as armed
forces weapon systems and logistic facilities—produce output has
not been the subject of such econometric attention, though it is, of
course, the focus of military science. This chapter presents some
preliminary estimates of one aspect of the military supply side: the
labour-intensity of defence provision.

Macro-statistical econometric procedures remain controversial in
the analysis of military topics. Thus it seems useful to try to
illuminate the advantages and limitations of these techniques, by
also including a fuller discussion of the methodological issues
involved in their application than is usual. This will be done in terms
of the framework set out in Pesaran and Smith (1985). That paper
proposed that econometric models should be evaluated in terms of
three criteria: relevance to the required purpose, consistency within
a theoretical framework, and adequacy at representing a particular
sample of data.

The first section of this chapter discusses the purpose of the
enquiry which is to obtain an estimate of the elasticity of substitution between military labour and capital, and explains why such
an estimate is relevant to important military questions. To obtain an
estimate of the elasticity of substitution requires an explicit model of
the military production process: this is set out in the second section,
which also discusses the role of formal models in ensuring the
consistency of the analysis. The third section examines the statistical
adequacy of the proposed model when it is estimated on data using
both market exchange rates and Purchasing Power Parity (PPP)
rates. The fourth section draws some general conclusions.

Purpose

The international analysis of military expenditure raises a range of questions in which knowledge of the extent to which military manpower is substituted for equipment plays an important role. For instance, in order to estimate Soviet military expenditure the CIA counts numbers of weapons and forces, then aggregates these components by valuing them at US prices and wages. The bias in this estimate will depend, in part, on the extent to which military technology allows substitution between personnel and equipment in response to different relative costs. It can be argued that the Soviets have larger armed forces, relative to the United States, because labour is a relatively cheap factor. In this case pricing Soviet forces at US wage rates is misleading. On the other hand, if the scope for substitution is small, the bias will be less, since the balance between personnel and equipment will be relatively insensitive to the difference in relative costs. Holzman (1980) discusses this index number problem in the measurement of Soviet military expenditure.

The extent to which substitution is possible can be measured by the elasticity of substitution—the percentage change in the personnel–equipment ratio in response to a percentage change in their relative cost. If the elasticity of substitution is zero—one pilot is required for each plane, for instance—changes in relative costs will have no effect on the labour intensity of defence provision. If the elasticity of substitution is unity, the share of personnel costs in total expenditure will remain constant, increases in factor cost being exactly balanced by reductions in factor use.

A second problem which involves some judgement about the extent of substitution arises in comparing defence budgets between countries with and without conscription. Given that the difference in wage rate between a conscript and volunteer is known there are two natural ways to correct the figures for the country with conscription. One is to assume that the size of forces would be constant, and calculate the budget which would result if volunteer rates were paid. The other is to assume that the personnel budget would be constant and calculate the size of forces that would result if volunteer rates were paid. Aben and Smith (1985, 1986) use both methods, conscript-corrected budgets and conscript-corrected forces, to compare British and French defence structures. The first method corresponds to assuming that the elasticity of substitution is zero, the second method to assuming that it is unity. To provide a single estimate requires a value for the elasticity of substitution, which we might expect to lie somewhere between zero and unity.

The final problem involves the evaluation of the reliability of published numbers on military expenditure for Less Developed Countries (LDCs). A useful check is to see whether the implied proportion of the budget spent on personnel is reasonable. What is reasonable depends on the elasticity of substitution. If this is constant across countries, there should be a linear relationship between the logarithms of the share of personnel costs in the budget and the real wage, with a slope of one minus the elasticity of substitution. The very high shares of personnel costs in many LDCs, then suggest either that the elasticity of substitution is considerably greater than unity, that there are systematic shifts in the production function or that these countries are under-reporting their imported equipment purchases, as has been suspected. Deciding between these hypotheses requires estimates of the elasticity of substitution.

There are thus a range of important problems in the international analysis of military expenditure in which it would be useful to have an estimate of the elasticity of substitution between personnel and equipment, or military labour and capital, which could be used for comparisons between countries. The purpose of this chapter is to discuss estimates of the elasticity of substitution obtained from a cross-section of countries for which fairly good data are available. Were this to produce clear results, we might have some confidence in extrapolating to cases where the data are less good.

The model

Any process of estimation and testing requires the use of a theoretical model. In much applied work the model is implicit, taken for granted, and hardly even noticed. However, even the simplest regression requires choice of dependent and explanatory variables, specification of appropriate measures and functional form, and a set of stochastic assumptions that make a particular technique, such as Least Squares, an appropriate estimator. There are advantages, however, in using an explicit formal model. The assumptions are set out more fully, allowing them to be evaluated. The model suggests important variables, allows the interpretation of parameters, organizes the analysis and defines the limits of application. It is a deliberately simplified representation of reality designed to provide a framework for thought, within which the data can be organized and questions of interest posed.

Implicit in the discussion of substitution between personnel and equipment is the notion of some underlying production function, which describes how the output of military services, denoted by M, is produced from factor inputs. We shall measure this output in the usual way by total expenditure. Military output is conceptually distinct from power or security, which are relative concepts. The inputs will be summarized as the services of military labour, S, measured by the number of armed service personnel, and the services of military capital, E, which is an aggregate of equipment, logistic infrastructure and civilian personnel. The Production Function will be represented in a Constant Elasticity of Substitution (CES) form:

$$M = \gamma \left\{(1 - \delta)E^{-\varrho} + S^{-\varrho}\right\}^{-\nu/\varrho} \tag{1}$$

Optimization then requires that the authorities equate the marginal product of service personnel to the real military wage, W. Taking logarithms of the first order condition gives

$$\ln(M/S) = \sigma \ln W + \sigma\varrho \left((\nu - 1)/\nu\right) \ln M$$
$$+ (\sigma\varrho/\nu) \ln \gamma - \sigma \ln \delta - \sigma \ln \nu \tag{2}$$

It was the constant returns to scale version of this equation that Arrow, Chenery, Minhas and Solow (1961) estimated from cross-country industry data. Derivations and discussion of estimation and inference for this model can be found in Wallis (1979).

The elasticity of substitution in this equation is given by $\sigma = 1/(1 + \varrho)$. The other parameters also have meanings which provide a way to interpret the results. The returns to scale are given by ν, constant returns to scale implying $\nu = 1$. The labour intensity of the process as described by δ and γ is an efficiency parameter which describes the relation of output to weighted inputs.

It is clear that a model of this sort cannot be regarded as a literal representation of the true process. It provides what McCloskey (1983) calls a metaphor, a useful instrument for organizing thought and evidence; a window through which to view the data. The formal presentation also provokes a range of questions in a way that a vaguer formulation would not. For instance, making the assumptions about optimization, aggregation and common parameters explicit, immediately makes one examine their applicability.

If we look at the individual assumptions, it is immediately clear that aggregating all the other inputs but the armed forces into a single index E is not plausible. In particular the degree of substitution between military personnel and weapons, civilian personnel, and the other elements of E would differ. However, E does not appear directly in (2), the equation which will be used for estimation. Thus, choice of a measure for E does not play an operational role and the violation of the assumption may only have second order effects.

The assumption of optimization, which is used in the derivation, is very strong and it may be argued that the evidence of military inefficiency and the lack of incentives for the military to minimize cost suggests that it is inappropriate. In the absence of optimization, the estimated elasticity will reflect both technological substitution and behavioural substitution: the extent to which decision makers respond to relative prices and budget constraints. There will also be lags in response and slow adjustment, but these are likely to average out over an international cross-section.

The assumption of a common production function is less constraining than it appears, since we can relax it by allowing each of the parameters to be functions of other variables which might shift the production function. In particular, the production technology associated with land, air and sea forces is likely to differ, with land forces in general involving less equipment relative to the others. This lower capital intensity can be represented by making δ, which represents labour intensity, a function of A, the proportion of land forces in total personnel.

$$\delta = A^{\delta_1} \tag{3}$$

A number of experiments were carried out making γ a function of membership of alliances, possession of nuclear weapons, and other strategic factors, but none of these variables proved significant. Thus, for the moment, the efficiency parameter will be regarded as constant.

To move from the theoretical model to the estimated econometric model, we have to choose observable proxies for the variables. One particular difficulty is that suitable comparative cross-section data on military wage rates are not available. However, apart from conscription it might be expected that across countries the market wage will be proportional to per capita income, and that the military wage would be depressed below this level by conscription. Therefore the military wage can be represented as

$$W = \beta \, Y \, R^{\alpha} \tag{4}$$

Y is GDP per capita, which is being used as a proxy for the relative cost of labour. R is the proportion of regular volunteer troops in the armed forces. Equations (2), (3) and (4) provide the basic elements of the model. If they are combined, the following estimating equation is obtained.

$$f = A0 + A1\,y + A2\,m + A3\,r + A4\,a + u \tag{5}$$

f 　is the productivity measure, the logarithm of military expenditure per member of the armed forces, $\ln(M/S)$;

y 　is the logarithm of per capita income;

r 　is the logarithm of the per centage of volunteers in the total armed forces;

a 　is the logarithm of the percentage of land forces in the total;

m 　is the logarithm of military expenditure;

u 　is a disturbance term, which is assumed to be independent normal with zero mean and constant variance.

The assumptions of normality and constant variance will be tested below.

　The estimated coefficients are related to the structural parameters:

$$A0 = -\,\sigma \ln \nu + (\varrho\sigma/\nu) \ln \gamma + \sigma \ln \beta$$

$$A1 = \sigma$$

$$A2 = \varrho\sigma \, ((\nu - 1)/\nu)$$

$$A3 = \sigma\alpha$$

$$A4 = -\,\sigma\delta_1$$

The parameters α, δ_1, ν and σ (ϱ) are just identified, in that we can solve for them uniquely from the estimated coefficients.

　Equation (5) will treated as a 'reduced form' for the structural model described by equations (1) to (4). There are two aspects of this treatment that should be noted. Firstly, the right hand side regressors are regarded as exogenous, in that the disturbance is independent of them. However, since it is possible that M may be determined jointly with S, while R and A both are calculated from ratios to S, the exogeneity assumption may not hold. If other variables known to be exogenous were available this assumption could be tested. As it is we have to rely on a theoretical derivation which suggests that countries determine their force structure in terms of proportions of volunteers and land forces and a level of military expenditure which can be regarded as predetermined. A possible process for the autonomous determination of military expenditure is described in Smith (1980).

The second aspect of the treatment of (5) as a reduced form for this structure arises because a similar equation, involving the same variables, might be generated by a quite different structural theory. Under our structure the coefficient of income measures the elasticity of substitution. Under an alternative structure, it might have a quite different interpretation. Alternative interpretations are discussed below. Another consequence of the possible consistency of this reduced form with other theories is that the adequacy of the estimated equation does not necessarily validate the structural model.

Estimates

The first set of estimates use data for M and Y in US dollars converted at market exchange rates. S is measured by full-time military personnel; allowing for reserves did not improve the explanation. Sample selection was largely determined by availability and reliability of data, omitting countries involved in costly wars or with a history of military involvement in domestic politics. The sample was: Australia, Austria, Belgium, Britain, Canada, Denmark, Eire, Finland, France, West Germany, Greece, Italy, Japan, Malaysia, Netherlands, New Zealand, Norway, Portugal, Singapore, Spain, Sweden, Turkey, United States. The source of the data is IISS (1976–7).

The cross-section results for this sample of twenty-three countries for 1976 is given in column A of Table 3.1. The fit of the equation is reasonable for an international cross-section. The estimate of the elasticity of substitution at 0.6 is significantly different from zero and accords with our prior expectations. The hypothesis of constant returns to scale can be accepted, since the coefficient of m is not significantly different from zero. This also suggests that the endogeneity of m is not a problem. Military expenditure per member of the armed services is reduced both by a higher proportion of conscripts and of land forces. The hypothesis that the

Table 3.1 Regression results for three models

Dependent variable:	Model A m − s	Model B mp − s	Model C mp − s
y	0.604* (0.099)		
yp		0.273 (0.154)	−0.192 (0.285)
m	0.065 (0.044)		
mp		0.086 (0.038)	0.112* (0.041)
r	0.296* (0.132)	0.296* (0.117)	0.339* (0.112)
a	−0.780* (0.313)	−0.928* (0.289)	−1.002* (0.273)
d			−0.666 (0.352)
int	−0.638 (2.209)	2.687 (2.473)	6.518* (3.073)
SER	0.272	0.244	0.288
J–B	1.439	4.470	9.0156*
$\check{R}^2$	0.837	0.784	0.8118

Notes
   n = 23, t = 1976.
Standard errors of coefficients in parentheses.
* indicates significantly different from zero at the 5% level.
SER is Standard Error of Regression.
J–B is the Jarque–Bera Asymptotic LM normality test, Chi Squared with 2 degrees of freedom.

residuals are normally distributed can be accepted, while other diagnostic tests did not indicate that the functional form was misspecified. The results do not seem sensitive to variations in the sample, and very similar estimates were obtained on a 1982 cross-section. Inspection of the residuals suggested that the presence of a domestic arms industry might have a positive effect on military expenditure per member of the armed forces, but suitable data were not available to test this statistically.

Fuller details of the results obtained using income at market exchange rates, together with further discussion, can be found in Fontanel, Smith and Humm (1985). In general, our conclusion in this earlier paper was that the model appeared successful. It gives a well determined relationship between military expenditure per member of the armed forces and per capita income. The estimates imply a value of the elasticity of substitution and an effect of force structure which accords with prior expectations. The model passes a range of diagnostic tests, and appears to be stable over time. However, we noted that there have been a variety of criticisms of the use of per capita income at market exchange rates, and the sensitivity of the results to the measurement of income needed to be investigated.

The two main problems with per capita income data converted at market exchange rates are that they exhibit variance and bias. The large variance arises because market exchange rates fluctuate widely from year to year. If this is treated as a traditional measurement error problem, it would suggest that the income coefficient in column A would tend to be underestimated. The bias arises because market exchange rates deviate systematically from the real purchasing power of the currency, because of price differences between countries. In particular, low income low wage countries have lower prices than high income countries. As a result, market exchange rate estimates of GDP are biased downward. This problem can be dealt with by valuing the quantities of goods and services produced in each country at common 'international' prices to give real or PPP estimates of national product. Kravis (1984) and Marris (1984) provide a survey and discussion of the issues involved in this calculation.

In terms of the theoretical model introduced above, it is not clear that PPP income is the more appropriate variable. Income is acting as a proxy for relative labour costs and by valuing output at international prices, the PPP income measure strips out a lot of the variation in labour costs across countries. The bias in market exchange rate income as a measure of real product arises partly because non-traded goods, such as services, tend to be relatively labour intensive and thus relatively cheaper in poor countries. The PPP measure removes this effect. Since the PPP measure is a poorer proxy for the theoretical variable we might expect it to have a lower coefficient.

Estimates of real GDP per capita, adjusted for the terms of trade, measured in 1975 international dollars were taken from Summers and Heston (1984), the series they call RGDP. Call this PPP estimate of real per capita income YP and the market exchange rate estimate Y. The ratio $D = YP/Y$ measures the exchange deviation, the divergence between the market and PPP exchange rate. This ratio takes the value unity for the US and greater than unity for other countries, the deviation being larger for lower income countries. An estimate for real military expenditure can then be obtained by multiplying nominal military expenditure by the exchange deviation, that is $MP = D M$. It should be noted that this procedure only corrects for the overall deviation between market and PPP rates. It does not allow for the fact that the relative price of M to Y differs between countries.

Using lower case letters for logarithms, the model is then:

$$mp - f = B0 + B1\,yp + B2\,mp + B3\,r + B4\,a \qquad (6)$$

The results are shown in the second column of Table 3.1. The use of PPP rather than market exchange rate figures has led to a reduction in the standard error of the regression, though the R squared is also smaller, since the variance of mp is considerably less than the variance of m. The main feature of the results is that the coefficient of income is now much smaller, and the estimated elasticity of substitution is not significantly different from zero.

The models in columns A and B are not nested, and so cannot be directly tested against each other. However, noting that $mp = m + d$ and $yp = y + d$ they can both be nested within a model of the form:

$$(m + d) - f = C0 + C1(y + d) + C2(m + d) + C3r + C4a + C5d \quad (7)$$

The results for this are given in column C of Table 3.1. The restriction $C5 = 0$ has a t statistic of -1.89, so we can just accept model B against model C at the 5 per cent level. Model A can be obtained from model C, by the restriction $C5 = 1 - C1 - C2$. The t statistic for this restriction is 2.92 which rejects model A against model C. Model C is an artificial model merely designed to nest models A and B. It has no obvious theoretical basis or interpretation given the negative coefficient on income. It is possible that the exchange deviation variable d, which has a negative sign, may be acting as a proxy for relative labour costs. Low labour cost countries tend to have a large exchange deviation and lower military expenditure per member of the armed forces.

These results are rather unsatisfactory. Model A, using market exchange rates, has coefficients that accord with prior expectations, but is rejected by the data. Model B, using PPPs, is not rejected by the data but implies an implausibly low estimate of the elasticity of substitution. Of course, one might expect the PPP estimate to be low if one accepts the argument that it is a worse proxy for the relevant variable, relative labour costs. However, if it is a worse proxy it should also fit less well, whereas in fact it fits better.

These results might lead us to reconsider the specification. One possibility, within the framework that we have been using is that the efficiency of military production is related to the general level of productivity in the society. This would suggest that the efficiency parameter is a function of per capita income. Suppose it is assumed that:

$$\gamma = \gamma_\phi \, Y^{\gamma_1} \qquad (8)$$

The coefficient of per capita income, which up to now has been interpreted as the elasticity of substitution, is then given by $\sigma + \gamma_1$ ($\varrho\sigma/\nu$), which is a mixture of both substitution and technical change effects.

The effect of this can be seen if we write the first order condition for the CES production function in the form:

$$\ln(WS/M) = A + (1 - \sigma)\ln W + (\sigma - 1)\ln \gamma \qquad (9)$$

If we assume that the elasticity of substitution lies between zero and unity, this equation says that the share of personnel costs in military expenditure is a positive function of the wage, and a negative function of the efficiency parameter. The relationship between the share of personnel costs and per capita income, then depends on how wages and efficiency change with income.

Conclusion

The econometric approach adopted in this paper was justified by three arguments. These are that estimates of the elasticity of substitution between military labour and capital are relevant to a number of interesting military questions; that formal theoretical models enable us to analyse the available data within a consistent framework; and that statistical techniques allow us to evaluate the adequacy with which the proposed model represents the data. It is not claimed that the procedure guarantees satisfactory results or necessarily produces unambiguous answers, and it has not done so in this case.

The results discussed above would not lead one to revise a prior belief that the elasticity of substitution between military labour and capital probably lay between zero and one. However, the results do suggest that the specification of the model is unsatisfactory in a number of ways. The most effective way of improving the specification would be to evaluate and extend the model using more informative data which could distinguish between competing interpretations of the results. The estimates obtained from the data available on this single cross-section do not allow us to decide whether the variance introduced by fluctuations in market exchange rates contaminates the results, whether market rate or PPP measures of national income are better proxies for labour costs, or whether there are income-related shifts in efficiency.

There are a number of obvious ways to extend the data. Rather than use a single cross-section, time-series for a sample of countries could be pooled. Measures of military capital could be constructed from the available data on holdings of different types of equipment and used to test the concept of an underlying production function. The relative prices for disaggregated components of GNP could be used to examine substitution responses directly. These are all possibilities for future research within an econometric framework.

PART II
Relation of Defence and Development

4

Defence, entitlement and development

SAADET DEGER AND SOMNATH SEN

Basic concepts

Theories of economic development have traditionally emphasized growth of total and per capita income as important objectives in analysing the economic conditions of Less Developed Countries (LDCs). Recent analysis have also emphasized income distribution as well as related specialized concepts such as extreme inequality, basic needs and poverty. The latter concerns have often been linked with growth, either emphasizing the interrelationships or stressing the conflicts that may arise in the pursuit of possible mutually conflicting objectives.

Growth theory, in its linkages with economic development, concentrates on the basic concepts of capital planning; the choice of the optimal rate of saving; the allocation of that saving into alternative sectoral investments; and finally, the choice of suitable techniques of production in labour surplus economies. For small open economies these issues have been supplemented by analogous problems emanating from the external sector: foreign saving, trade strategies for investment (import substituting or export promoting industrialization) and the use of international technology.

After two to three decades of intensive growth orientated policies many Less Developed Countries have failed to raise substantially per capita growth rates; thus average incomes have increased less than anticipated. More important, large segments of the population do not enjoy even the basic necessities, such as adequate food, required to achieve a better quality of life. Early optimism, regarding the possibility of raising the rate of growth of per capita income and the efficacy of high growth leading to a marked improvement in the standard of living, at least in the medium term, was ill founded. Concern therefore has shifted to an analysis of distribution for its own sake, eradication of inequality, improving the economic well-being of the vast majority of the population rather than a select few, a direct attack on poverty instead of the long awaited trickle down effect, and finally the provision of basic needs to all, in preference to a sophisticated economic sub-structure superimposed on the backward 'dual' economy.

Dissatisfaction with growth has lead analysts to move to the other extreme; in the eradication of backwardness, growth matters very little, except perhaps in the very long run; and in the long run we are dead in any case! This nihilism is based on a profound mis-conception. The end or objective of economic development was never meant to be growth *per se*; development was expected to improve the physical and social quality of life; growth was the means towards that end. In that respect its performance has not been as bad as its critics would have us believe, though there are major exceptions. But, as we shall see later, the record, of growth with socio-economic development in the wider sense of the term, is often patchy; it is necessary to widen the theoretical framework of traditional theory pertaining to developing countries. An analysis of growth must also be supplemented by noting the advancement made by the particular society in, for example, the reduction of infant mortality, as well as increases in life expectancy, literacy, education, health and nutrition.

Amartya Sen has recently argued for a shift in emphasis from a study of growth of national income to an analysis of 'entitlements' of individuals and groups of people in developing countries, as well as the 'capabilities' that these entitlements can produce. We can do no better than quote him: 'Entitlement refers to the set of alternative commodity bundles that a person can command in a society using the totality of rights and opportunities that he or she faces.' Sen (1983: 754–5) continues:

On the basis of this entitlement, a person can acquire some capabilities, i.e. the ability to do this or that (e.g. be well nourished), and fail to acquire some other capabilities. The process of economic development can be seen as a process of expanding the capabilities of people. Given the functional relation between entitlements of persons over goods and their capabilities, a useful—though derivative—characterisation of economic development is in terms of expansion of entitlements.

The entitlement set in general consists of an individual's endow-ment vector (the goods and services she owns), and whatever goods and services are available by utilising the possibilities of exchange open to her. Exchange can be of many types; it can be with 'nature', the use of technology, capital and the production frontier to acquire more goods; it can be through the market, using relative prices to determine the amount of goods it is possible to get; it can be through non-market transactions, own consumption, social security, government expenditure on public goods; and finally one can include non-economic entitlements, such as security, justice, status, freedom, human rights—difficult to quantify, but nevertheless important for their own sakes as well as their effect on economic variables.

Within this broader framework, the emphasis of traditional development theory on growth, income and its egalitarian distribution can be linked to the endowment vector of society as a whole as well as of individual members in it. Thus high growth, leading to a high per capita income, implies that society as a whole has more endowments. But this does not necessarily mean that the entitlements enjoyed by people are higher. Emphasizing entitlements therefore leads us on to a wider and in a sense more worthwhile concept of development.

Table 4.1 gives comparative data for 1980, on five countries regarding the level of per capita income (the traditional focus and end-product of growth), as well as indices of a broad set of empirical criteria that may stand proxy for entitlements. It also provides information on growth rates per head. Brazil and South Korea are examples of high growth countries, while Nigeria is oil-rich and relatively prosperous within the African context. On the other hand Sri Lanka and Tanzania have low per capita income as well as moderate growth. Even a cursory glance will show that these two countries, in spite of having very poor economies in the conventional sense, have done rather well in terms of entitlements for its citizens. Compare ˙Tanzania and Nigeria, both major African countries. The former's GNP per head is a quarter of the latter, yet it has a far better record in terms of health, mortality, sanitation, and possibly womens' rights. Similar comments are applicable to Sri Lanka as compared to South Korea and Brazil. Sri Lanka has a GNP per head of about one-fifth that of South Korea, yet it has a better record in terms of woman going for higher education, provision of hospital beds and life expectancy. Sri Lanka's literacy rate, infant mortality rate and life expectancy are superior to Brazil's, yet the per capita income is about one-eighth of Brazil's. By conventional criteria Sri Lanka and Tanzania are 'less developed' than South Korea, Nigeria and Brazil, but given the wider definition, we can not be sure.

It should be noted that it is also possible to have conflicts between

Table 4.1 Income, growth the entitlements

	Sri Lanka	South Korea	Brazil	Tanzania	Nigeria
GNP per capita in US$	279	1388	2002	264	1035
Growth rate per head 1960–80 (%)	2.4	7.0	5.1	0.8*	1.9*
Women in total university enrolment (%)	42	22	38	20	16
Literacy rate (%)	85	94	76	70	34
Population per hospital bed	343	608	250	482	1251
Infant mortality rate	40	34	77	103	135
Life expectancy in years	66	65	63	52	48
Calorie per capita	2251	2926	2513	2028	2337
Population with safe water (%)	22	79	63	39	28

Note
* values for 1970–81.
Source: Sivard (1983); World Bank, World Development Report (1982); World Bank, World Tables (1983).

the two components of the concept of entitlement—endowment and exchange entitlements. Thus increasing the endowment vector of society and enlarging the degree of entitlements may not be compatible. If for example, infant mortality drops, birth rate rises, famines are eradicated, health care is improved, safe water provided for, public services made available, then population may increase. Higher growth of population may reduce the growth of per capita income and pull down endowments available to each member of society. Bauer (1965: 16) gives an early exposition of this:

Economic progress is usually measured by the growth of real income per head. This procedure implies various judgments which are generally covert and unrecognised. The increase in population in underdeveloped countries has been brought about by the fall in death rate (especially, but not only, among children) and this implies a longer expectation of life. The position of those who have failed to die has certainly improved as has the situation of those whose children continue to live. Thus there is here an obvious and real psychic income. Its reality is clear from people's readiness to pay for the satisfaction of the postponement of death. Thus the usual way of drawing conclusions from income per head obscures important conceptual problems of the defined and measured income.

One of the most important characteristics of entitlement enhancement is the strongly positive role that government policy and public action can play. Country studies almost inevitably show that the fastest way to increase the quality of life of the masses in developing countries is through state action and direct or indirect government intervention. Countries like Sri Lanka and Tanzania have achieved a state of socio-economic development far in excess of that warranted by growth and income simply because of vigorous action by the authorities in providing public services, cheap basic needs and highly subsidized food to the majority of the population. Government intervention in favour of greater entitlements to a better quality of life may be a sufficient condition to tip the balance.

The role of military expenditure in particular and militarization in general is important in analysing growth and development specifically in the context of government policy. Defence is, in many senses, a unique 'good': it is the classic example of a 'pure' public good, its characteristics and security-related output can be enjoyed by everyone independent of payment towards its maintenance; it is also always publicly funded, even military industries in LDCs are owned by the state. On the other hand the various facilities for education, health and so on, that increase entitlements can be partly (or wholly) provided by the private sector. For the advantages that defence spending can bring there is therefore an implicit compulsion to give a greater priority to military spending by LDC governments. There entails a trade-off therefore between extra military expenditure and the provision of facilities, goods and services that the state can provide for social and economic entitlements. One of the major intentions of this chapter is to explore this potential negative effect of defence expenditures.

It should be emphasized clearly that the 'entitlement approach' and its relation to defence spending has a much wider applicability than that pertaining to Less Developed Countries alone. For example famines occur and people starve in LDCs not *necessarily* because of a decline in food output or that national income is low; rather the lack of an entitlement to famine relief may be the chief cause of famine deaths. Even in the absence of explicit famine some people may suffer from malnutrition not because the country has insufficient food, but due to a lack of individual purchasing power or societal aid in buying relatively over-priced food. Again, absence of the right to receive subsistence consumption, independent of one's own income, over long periods of time may be the major contributory reason for malnutrition. In similar vein, individuals do not starve in a developed country not because per capita income is high or there is an abundance of necessities; it is simply due to the fact that society acknowledges the right to basic needs for everyone and sets up a social security system to honour the relevant entitlements (Sen 1980).

In developed countries therefore the 'social wage', in terms of publicly funded opportunities for education, health, pensions, old age provisions, unemployment benefits and so on, is a major conduit through which the entitlement set is widened to bring in large groups of people who might have suffered great deprivation in the (invisible) hands of the market mechanism. In the allocation of the national 'cake' if the military burden competes against the share of social wage in aggregate output then there will be a direct trade-off between defence and entitlements even in a rich country. It is of course possible that the sheer size of the cake will make the implicit conflict less obvious; but its presence must be felt. Smith (1977; 1980) has shown that, until the 1970s for major OECD countries there seemed to be no essential conflict between these shares; an increase in military burden was exactly compensated by an almost one-to-one reduction of the proportion of investment in GDP. Thus defence, at least in this form, did not reduce the right of society to receive minimal acceptable levels of various goods and services which constitute a relatively decent quality of life. However, the policies of the present UK government, in raising real defence spending in the early 1980s at the expense of social goods, is possibly a good example of the postulated trade-off.

The purpose of this chapter is to provide a framework to study the complex interrelationships between defence expenditure, growth and entitlements in developing countries. The next section analyses, in some detail, the various linkages and considers the effect that increased military spending may have on quality of life and economic entitlements. Section three emphasizes a slightly different, though major, topic in the area: the relation between military spending (including that during wars) and famines. Independent interest focuses on this question due to the seminal application of the 'entitlement approach' to famines in LDCs applied by Amartya Sen (1981).

Defence, entitlement and growth

It should be stressed right at the beginning that defence expenditure can provide a major form of entitlement—that of security defined in the broadest sense of the term. The appropriateness of that security has, however, sometimes been questioned: for example, the effectiveness of a given amount of military expenditure (MILEX) in the provision of protection from threats is debated; the form in which LDCs spend on defence is often a matter of concern; and finally, there have been ˙discussions as to whether, in developing countries regional arms races, supply (of militarization) is creating its own demand, rather than the more desirable opposite case. Nevertheless, we accept for the purposes of this chapter that military expenditure provides sufficient and appropriate security, an important entitlement. We are more interested in socio-economic entitlements, goods and services which increase the quality of life directly; our main purpose is to see whether, in a macroeconomic framework, such services and their products are substitutes for, or complements of, military spending.

There are both direct as well as indirect relations between these variables. We deal with each in turn. Figure 4.1 shows a few of the major interconnections broadly true for most countries. We choose to emphasize developmental similarities rather than discuss country specificity. The analysis, at this stage, lays the foundations of the applicability of the 'entitlement approach' to the LDC MILEX problem; country studies may build on this.

It must also be pointed out that both for the theoretical analysis as well as the empirical model we take defence spending as exogenously determined, principally influenced by external considerations of security and threat (implicit, as in the Richardson model). We can therefore discuss such questions as the possible effect of military burden on growth and entitlements; the framework also allows us to analyse counterfactual situations such as a possible Third World reduction of their collective defence burden by a certain amount and its effects on their economies. It can be argued that the causation should be the other way around. In effect low entitlements to a proper quality of life causes widespread misery and revolt against the ruling classes; this needs to be suppressed and increases in MILEX are necessary to impose 'law and order'.

There are basically three reasons why this view may be misplaced. First, the theoretical models of arms expenditures tend to emphasize action–reaction mechanisms whereby MILEX or defence burden in one country is intricately bound with the MILEX (burden) in the opposition's country. Such models are relevant for LDCs, witness the arms races between say Iran–Iraq, Greece–Turkey, India–Pakistan and so on. Econometric tests for such cases also demonstrate that defence expenditures are explained well by external factors. Second, heuristic country evidence show that low entitlements do not lead, necessarily, to high defence spending; observe for example countries like Brazil (there are many other Latin American examples). Finally, empirical estimates trying to explain military burden by suitable indices of entitlements do not give significant coefficients. From the points of view of theory, country study and econometrics it is preferable to take military spending or burden as autonomous. (See Deger (1986) for a more detailed discussion.)

The direct effects of defence burden on socio-economic entitle-

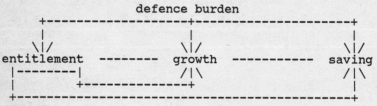

Figure 4.1

ments may be classified under three groups: (a) the allocation effect, through government budgets and public (sector) expenditures; (b) the militarization effect; (c) the spill-over effect whereby military spending may affect the quality of life through intangible channels which are not related specifically to either security or entitlements.

It has been shown that the most effective means of providing entitlements to the people is through public action and government spending on health, sanitation, nutrition (food subsidy), education and so forth (Sen 1981). The market may also provide these, but only in the very long run when high growth has raised per capita income at such levels as to make it possible for the majority to buy the relevant services. The availability of private sector facilities, at a price, is not a sufficient condition for their utilization by everybody: effective demand is crucial. National income has to be disproportionately high before appropriate provisions of these facilities can be utilized. Even when market-orientated growth is adequate its form is extremely important; here government strategy in redirecting growth towards specific forms may also be vital. An economy, using labour intensive technology and geared to maintaining full employment of the labour force, aided and abetted by the government, is in a much better position to provide higher entitlements through the market, compared to one where capital intensive modes of production with high productivity are being used. If we contrast South Korea and Brazil, both countries with high growth and per capita incomes, we observe that the form of industrialization and the role of the state is rather different. Employment generating industrialization has helped the former to provide its citizens with a higher level of entitlements, within the market system, relative to the latter. The role of the government in fostering such a development is well documented (Sen 1981; Datta-Chaudhuri 1979).

Whatever may be the attitude of the state towards the provision of a better quality of life in the short run, all governments are intimately concerned with providing security. Defence is the perfect paradigm of a pure public good. In most LDCs it is totally public funded/ provided; even defence industries are owned by the government. Thus the authorities have a special concern for military activities since they believe that they are the only and unique agencies which can provide these:

LDC governments have extremely strong commitments to military expenditure to bolster security and counter threats. Aggregate defence expenditure is almost always state-induced, and the consumption of scarce resources to support the military machine as well as reallocation of valuable inputs into armaments production must generally be provided for in national budgets. (Deger 1986: 113)

On the other hand all entitlement-enhancing measures can be provided in principle by the private sector. As we have noted earlier, governments may find it easier to subsidize these activities; but it is by no means the sole agency in any society, however poor, for the provision of social services and welfare (the constituents of the development budget). Thus a 'natural' trade-off occurs whereby the first casualty of enhanced military burden is the reduction of state spending on health, education, and so on, as a share of GDP. This allocation effect could be the most potent adverse consequence of defence on entitlement.

The other two postulated effects could work in either direction. Higher military burden may lead to greater militarization though the link is occasionally tenuous. Latin America provides the pertinent counter-examples. The 1970s showed many countries in Latin America with dominant military institutions, but with low defence shares in GDP. It is not easy to define militarism or militarization. Some of the operational characteristics, in its extreme form, are identified by Sivard (1983: 11) as ' . . . key political leadership by military officers; existence of a state of martial law; extra-judicial authority exercised by security forces; lack of central political control over large sections of the country where official or unofficial security forces rule; control by military forces.' In the early 1980s it was claimed that out of 114 developing countries 56 were under military control as defined above; the situation has changed recently but the magnitude of the problem remains. This can have two contradictory effects on entitlements. It can either produce a repressive regime which can impose strict authoritarian and anti-democratic rules with scant respect for human rights. Repression can hurt the attempt to provide basic needs and greater entitlements. Or the opposite could be true. By providing domestic and external stability as well as the framework in which socio-economic change can be implemented, militarization may make it easier for society to acquire a better quality of life. The Turkish military administration, in the early 1980s, increased the literacy rate to almost one hundred per cent in about a year; this was done by forcibly sending all adults without education to literacy classes and making avoidance a punishable offence. Entitlement to literacy was enhanced substantially.

The primary function of defence spending is to increase security and to protect the country from threats. The way it is done however has repercussions and spill-overs. If the military engages in civic-action orientated programmes, uses its skills to build and maintain hospitals and schools, disseminates technology, and so forth, it can contribute significantly and positively to development. Benoit (1973:277) gives a clear exposition:

Defence programs of most countries make tangible contributions to the civilian economies by (1) feeding, clothing, and housing a number of people who would otherwise have to be fed, housed, and clothed by the civilian economy—and sometimes doing so, especially in LDCs, in ways that involve sharply raising their nutritional and other consumption standards and expectations; (2) providing education and medical care . . . that may have high civilian utility; (3) engaging in a variety of public works . . . that may in part serve civilian uses.

This optimistic scenario can of course be negated by numerous counter-examples of the military having the opposite effects. A general conclusion needs empirical evidence; specific examples can be provided both for and against these hypotheses.

Turning now to the indirect relationships, the most important is that between military burden, growth and entitlements. There has been an extensive theoretical and econometric debate, starting with the seminal work by Benoit (1973), on whether defence burden increases or decreases growth rates in developing countries. See in particular Deger (1986), Deger and Sen (1983), Deger and Smith (1983), Faini, Arnez and Taylor (1984), Frederikson and Looney (1983). The empirical evidence, mostly using cross-section data, seems to imply that there are definite positive effects of military expenditures, in developing countries, in the enhancement of growth rates. However, when all the direct and indirect effects are taken together the net result is a negative trade-off shown, in particular, in a simultaneous equation econometric system usually giving a negative multiplier when estimating the growth effects of defence (burden). The military has a positive spin-off in terms of technology absorption, R&D, modernization and so on, but it allocates investible resources away from more productive invest-ments and thus reduces growth. In addition there may be an adverse reaction on resource mobilization, a pernicious effect not much discussed in the literature. (See Deger (1985) for single equation empirical evidence and Deger (1986) for a simultaneous equation econometric model.)

The negative effect of defence on growth through the previously mentioned mobilization channel is even more important in the context of entitlements. Empirical tests show that an increase in the defence burden usually reduces the national savings ratio; this is due to inflation induced by spending on the military, lowering the level of government saving in an attempt to finance additional spending, and increases in private sector consumption to supplement the possible reduction of the social wage as a direct trade-off with the military. The last effect already shows a potential problem with entitlements. But there are more complicated interconnections. Specifically, saving may itself be affected by the level of entitlements. For example, a more egalitarian distribution of income will reduce the saving–income ratio. An export-orientated agrarian policy (production of cash crops, say) may simultaneously reduce entitlements (to, for example, adequate food) and increase the propensity to save via an adverse distribution of wealth among rich and poor farmers.

Finally, the relation between growth and entitlements remains. This works both ways. High growth, by raising income and producing a trickle-down effect, might increase the quality of life. On the other hand greater entitlements might act as a sort of 'efficiency wage', a productivity enhancing feature which raises absorptive capacity and thus growth. A well-nourished, well-fed, educated and healthy workforce is expected to produce higher growth of aggregate output.

It is quite clear that the interrelationships are quite complex; in addition there are extensive simultaneities between the various channels. The effects work either way. Theoretically, it is not possible to say whether defence spending or burden increases or decreases entitlements. The final answers can only be given by looking at the data.

The first empirical problem is to construct a measure that will reflect economic entitlements of society. Two indicators are important: inequality of income distribution gives a good indication of relative deprivation; the physical quality of life measured by socio-economic welfare is also crucial. Table 4.2 gives data on these measures in the form of *ranks*, which avoids the problems of wide disparity of non-comparable units. Information is provided for ten countries. In column 1 we have a ranking of these countries based on their performance in an aggregate socio-economic index (SEI). The SEI is constructed from the following information, taken from

Table 4.2 Rank order for socio-economic index, income distribution, military burden and growth of real income per capita.

Countries	(1) SEI	(2) Income distribution	(3) Military burden	(4) Growth of p.c. GDP
Argentina	1	3	5	10
Costa Rica	2	5	10	7
Venezuela	3	7	6	8
South Korea	4	2	2	1
Sri Lanka	5	1	8	6
Malaysia	6	8	3	3
Mexico	7	6	9	4
Brazil	8	10	7	2
Phillippines	9	4	4	4
Peru	10	9	1	9

Notes: In the first two columns rank 1 is given to the 'best' performer, and so on. In the last two columns, rank 1 is given to the country with the highest value of the variable, and so forth.

Sivard (1983): (a) percentage of school age population at school; (b) percentage of women among university students; (c) literacy rate; (d) physicians per head of population; (e) hospital beds per person; (f) infant mortality rate; (g) life expectancy at birth; (h) calorie and protein intake per head; (i) percentage of total population with access to safe water. The SEI therefore represents, in principle, an aggregation over entitlements to basic education, literacy, women's educational rights, health care, longevity, nutrition and basic sanitation. The best performer gets a rank of 1, and so forth. Column 2 shows the ranks according to the relative equalities of income distribution; thus Sri Lanka has the most egalitarian distribution in the sample while Brazil is the worst in this category. The ordering is based on data in Sen (1981) for any available year in the 1970s. The ranks for income distribution and SEI together provide a comprehensive overall picture of entitlements. Clearly, the lower the rank, the better the situation in terms of development. Column 3 gives the position for average military burden for 1975–80; the highest spender (Peru) is ranked 1, the next highest (South Korea) is ranked 2, and so on. The final column gives the growth rate of real per capita GDP (national income per head); again, the best achiever is ranked 1 while the worst has rank 10. Data for this—from World

Bank, *World Tables* (1983)—relate to the annual average between 1970–81.

A comparison of the four columns demonstrates the relationship between defence and entitlement to a better quality of life. For countries like Sri Lanka or Costa Rica the position is clear. Low military burden helps to improve entitlements in spite of the fact that growth is low. Argentina and Venezuela also have exceptionally high ranks for the socio-economic index showing their relatively eminent position in education, health and welfare. Military burden is relatively low. Thus a negative relationship between defence and development can be established. This is particularly significant since they have two of the lowest growth rates in the sample. Thus growth of per capita income is not necessarily contributing towards their high ranks in the field of welfare provision.

The position is reversed for countries such as Peru and Malaysia. The situation is most depressing for Peru with the highest defence burden and the lowest rank for entitlements as well as growth. Similarly, Malaysia's defence outlay (as a share of GDP) seems to be having a detrimental effect on its ability to improve the socio-economic index. Greater military burden seems to cause low entitlements. This is specially important since Malaysia has a high rate of growth (as well as the highest income per capita in the Asian subgroup) and we would expect some spin-off and feed-back for social welfare. The depressive effects of defence are therefore quite large.

There are a few 'outliers', particularly Brazil and South Korea. Defence expenditure as a proportion of GDP has always been low for Brazil. However, the country has been highly militarized during the period (in terms of coups, government control, vested interest of the ruling elite, internal repression, and so on). A low defence burden therefore causes growth to prosper; however, there is none of the trickle-down effect towards wider development in terms of egalitarian income distribution and improved quality of life. Military expenditure *per se* does not have a dampening effect on entitlements since it is relatively low in any case; however, militarization in a broader sense has its negative influence.

South Korea seems to be the only genuine exception to the general negative relationship. It seems that it is possible to have a higher military burden, greater growth and better entitlements as the South Korean example demonstrates. In our sample, this country has the highest growth rate, does well on the socio-economic index and has the second best performance in terms of income equality. But even here a cautionary word remains. South Korea has been helped tremendously by US military aid as well as by the 'spin-off' of the Vietnam war, leading to high procurement expenditure of the American forces. Thus the drain of resources from high MILEX was mitigated by aid, and growth reduction was lessened. It may not be easy for LDCs to 'do' a South Korea.

Defence, war and famines

Historically there has always been a potentially close connection between high defence expenditure financed by taxation in kind (usually food in medieval societies), the ravages of war and the incidence of famines. But the analysis of recent famines has not emphasized these interrelationships sufficiently. We propose to discuss some of these issues in the context of the three major famines discussed in Sen (1981)—the Great Bengal Famine, 1943, the Ethiopian famine, 1973–4, and that in Bangladesh, 1974.

The traditional explanation for the occurrence of a famine is the lack of available food (the food availability doctrine) due to, say, a drought. Oddly enough, most of the major famines actually started when food was still available; starvation was of course exacerbated by later loss in supply due to, say, crop failure, but the primary cause seemed to be that relative price changes so adversely affected the terms of trade of specific segments of the population, that it was not possible to acquire sufficient amounts of food required for subsistence. Occasionally, a very high general inflation masked dramatic price differentials leading to a loss in earnings of some people who consequently could not buy enough food to prevent starvation, or society did not recognize the entitlement to famine relief: the result was large-scale deprivation, famine and deaths due to starvation.

Sen (1985) asserts the relation between famines and loss of entitlements in the following way:

A person has to starve if his entitlement set does not include any commodity bundle with enough food. A person is reduced to starvation if some changes either in his endowment (e.g. alienation of land, or loss of labour power due to ill health), or in his exchange entitlement mapping (e.g., fall in wages, rise in food prices loss of employment, drop in the price of the good he produces and sells), makes it no longer possible for him to acquire any commodity bundle with enough food.

Famines can occur in a 'slump' caused, say, by a sudden loss in food output. Non-producers of food, particularly in the rural areas, may witness a loss of demand for their services; the resulting deterioration of their terms of trade, coupled with the rise in the price of food, and the absence of non-market transactions say from government famine relief, may force them into starvation. But even in a generally expansionary situation—a 'boom' such as described by Sen (1981)—the price of food may increase sufficiently to become scarce from the point of view of *effective* demand of sizeable segments of the population; even though food is available in aggregate, some will starve if their entitlement to subsistence is not recognized by society at large.

The Bengal famine of 1943 was precisely a boom famine induced by war-financed expansion of general industrial activity and a dramatic rise in the relative price of food. Large military expenditures increased the income of urban centres around military bases as well as that of the city of Calcutta; the price of rice (staple diet) went up relative to non-rice rural sector products such as wage income of agriculture labour or price of fish and so on. Famine began among the non-rice growers initially who bore the brunt of starvation. But rice prices relative to industrial products did not rise; so there was no incentive to grow more by farmers (rice growers); disease mortality was also very high; the consequent depopulation caused a subsequent fall in food output. The Bengal famine can be directly attributed to military causes, specifically high defence expenditure causing a distortion in the relative price structure leading to a loss in entitlement to sufficient food required to avoid starvation.

The Ethiopian famine of 1973–4 was concentrated in the Wallo, Tigrai and Hareghe (Ogaden) districts of the country (see details in Sen, 1981). Wallo had a crop failure in 1972–3; but it seems that the Tigrai province had a relatively normal output; yet the latter had a famine of quite severe intensity. In this case, at least, food availability doctrine is not appropriate. Again Sen (1981) suggests the failure to secure basic rights of entitlements. We believe that a major reason for this failure may have been related to internal insecurity and political problems. In 1974, there was a military coup in the country and Emperor Haile Selassie was deposed; one important reason given being the failure of the authorities to control the secessionist movement in Eritrea.

Interestingly enough Eritrea had a worse position in terms of food output but no famine in comparison with Tigrai. Again this is related to internal security and administration. The Eritrean Liberation Front (ELF) and the Eritrean Peoples Liberation Front (PLF) controlled large parts of the district, had a good food distribution system, recognized the entitlement of people to famine relief, and utilized their resources efficiently to build up a public feeding programme. The recent famine in Tigrai has also seen the Tigrain PLF mitigating the worst effects of the drought and the civil war; part of the reasons for the massive starvation deaths in that area is directly attributable to the military. Finally, the other major famine area was Hareghe, linked to the Somalian war in the Ogaden region. It is quite clear that the civil war in Ethiopia and domestic dissension are strongly implicated in accentuating the effects of the famine.

Bangladesh, around 1974, had somewhat similar features to Ethiopia though there were also major differences. The standard reasons given for the famine was the devastating monsoons and massive crop failure in July 1974. But, as Sen (1981) points out, famine started earlier, actually prior to crop failure. The price of food was rising rapidly from the beginning of the year and already the tell-tale signs, of the inability of large sections of the population to buy sufficient food to avoid starvation, were present. Data reported in *World Armies* (1983) claim that the price of rice rose by 400 per cent between 1971 and 1975. This was within a virulent inflationary regime where the GDP deflator increased by over 43 per cent between 1973 and 1975 and about 76 per cent between 1974 and 1975. The concomitant failure of entitlement to sufficient food, particularly by rural non-food producers, began the famine which was to become a major disaster after the adverse supply shocks.

The Bangladesh famine had no direct connection with the Pakistan civil war which had finished in 1971. Mujib-ur-Rahman became President in 1972. But internal dissension started almost immediately. There was a general expectation of a new civil war between two major factions of the recently constituted national army—the 'freedom fighters' who had fought the civil war and the 'repatriates' from the old Pakistan army. The memory of the recently concluded war was quite vivid; rational expectation on the basis of that information led people to hoard food; this gave rise to food price increases relative to other prices.

What conclusions can we derive from these rather disparate country studies? It is clear that high military expenditure in LDCs can cause an expansionary 'boom' famine and if society fails or is unable to recognize the rights of some people to get sufficient food then starvation will occur. This is particularly true during an external threat when governmental resources are scarce (financing the war effort) and rhetoric is abundant ('sacrifices are necessary'). Military expenditure, as in Bengal of the 1940s is a direct cause of entitlement losses. On the other hand, when food is genuinely scarce, say during a 'slump' famine, the military may help. If the military recognizes the right to famine relief they have the organization to deal with it. If food is available within the region or country the military may help to bring it to the destitute whose food availability has slumped. Lack of security, for example a civil war, may exacerbate the existing problems. Therefore appropriate defence expenditures, by increasing security, bringing peace, helping to organize relief camps, can help to avert the worst excesses of the slump famine. The final outcome depends on circumstances.

Conclusion

We can conclude briefly. The analysis shows that increase in defence burden, taking all direct and indirect effects together, may reduce entitlements significantly. There is no doubt that mitigating circumstances are present and it is even possible in some cases that defence spending may help the society to develop. But overall, a higher defence burden is associated with a lower quality of life and the failure of the country concerned to enjoy the fruits of development. Even if the military does not spend an excessive amount, an increase in militarization *per se*, as in the Brazilian case, may not be good for entitlement enhancement and development.

From an economic point of view this is not just a classic 'guns and butter' problem. It is quite easy to give country specific evidence to show that the military can increase entitlements, at least for significant groups of the population. It is imperative, at least initially, to take an aggregative cross-sectional view and find the relation between these two apparently disparate variables so important in the life of developing countries. The issues are complex and our framework is the first, to the best of our knowledge, to put it in some sort of structure.

Overall, military expenditure may be necessary for security, but it has to be carefully costed in terms of lost entitlements and capabilities.

Notes

Saadet Deger is grateful to the Economic and Social Research Council for financial support. We are grateful to seminar participants, particularly P. N. Mathur, Alfred Maizels, Robert Looney, Christian Schmidt and Ron Smith, for their comments. Thanks are also due to Amartya Sen for his encouragement.

5

Security and development in the Third World: some policy perspectives

W. SCOTT THOMPSON

Security, arms sales and development

The link between security and development has a curious history in government, at least in that of the United States, which is the perspective of this essay. The link itself in the past is most notable for its obscurity: but the few times it emerges are interesting. We search for it first through the media of history, secondly, the study of organizational charts, and lastly, the study of what are still current and unfolding events. Throughout this essay, the writer warns the reader that he has attempted to use his own peripheral role in these events as an organizational device.

Oddly, and historically, the link has been seen mostly in the context of developed countries. It is worth noting that the senior administrators of the Marshall Plan—an economic development scheme *par excellence*—were not innocent of military strategy and saw clearly the relationship between what they were doing and what their peers organizing NATO were undertaking, at least men such as senior administrator Richard Bissell, one of the plan's proconsuls, believed.[1] It was gospel that the runs on local currency would not stop, hot money would continue pouring into the United States, and virtuous economic development would not start, until Europeans felt confident of their future. By confidence the Europeans meant that someone was there to help them draw the line against further Soviet expansion on their continent. As late as 1976, no less than the Supreme allied Commander of NATO, Alexander Haig, could argue at a Defense Department Armed Forces Policy Council that expecting European economies to recover from their post-1973 recessions was useless until once again their confidence in their security was assured.[2] The subsequent attempt by one more junior Pentagon official—the present writer—to 'task' the analytic branch of the Office of the Secretary of Defense with an empirical test of the

Supreme Commander's hypothesis in the Third World, however, had a less exalted resonance in official corridors.

Another odd manifestation of the security-development nexus had to do with *American* development and other nations' security. Arms sales were always something of an embarrassment with no conspicuous bureaucratic home until the Kennedy administration became obsessed on the one hand with balance of payments difficulties and the desire to get itself a 'free lunch' in the foreign aid business on the other—from whence arose sales programmes of arms as a substitute for grant aid.

At least one remedy for the problem of arms sales was proposed by the Defense Department's International Security Affairs Bureau (its 'little State Department'), where a home was found for the new agency established to press arms sales, DSAA or Defense Security Assistance Agency. Conveniently, this was done at the same time that a logistics bureau was established to try to—in the euphemism of the day—'standardize' weapons systems in the alliance systems (that is, by selling American weapons everywhere) (Louscher 1977). The burden of DSAA was to convince others to 'buy American' and only gradually did the purported need for study to establish appropriateness of sales become established; only gradually did this become primarily a Third World affair.

There was always, however, considerable rhetoric about the presumably deleterious relationship between arms supplies and the development process in some circles (witness the outpouring of literature from the universities and from many policy-oriented organizations, so often showing what could be bought with a given amount of arms aid in the development field) without however delineating where the fungibility of this was (Ghosh 1984).

But it was as a result of the surge of weapons sales after the dramatic oil price increases between 1969 and 1973 that a serious counter-movement to the 'Sell American Arms' school of thought got underway in the bureaucracy. It had its start at the Arms Control and Disarmament Agency (ACDA), a self-contained agency housed in the State Department, which was annually in need of justification for its budget, and this was a time when Executive Branch custody of foreign policy was under serious Congressional branch challenge.

The counter-movement was not confined to ACDA. The 'bureaucratic gnomes', as Henry Kissinger liked to refer to them, existed throughout the government, indeed they were increasingly the dominant group, including some civilian personnel at the Defense

Department. The extent of their hold is suggested on internal evidence by a memorandum prepared in mid-1975 by a directorate of the Joint Chiefs of Staff, entitled 'A US Initiative for Limitations on Conventional Arms Transfers'. The report of course did not directly reinforce the new tendencies of the day, and somewhat presciently argued that 'most other supplier nations would welcome a self-imposed US restriction [on arms sales], since it would open new markets for their arms industries and enhance their ability to expand their foreign influence through arms transfers.' But implicitly accepting the momentum of the opposite position, it suggested that 'the concept of economically rewarding lesser developed countries for voluntarily curtailing conventional arms importations appears interesting. . . . it would afford the United States significant political "mileage." '3

All logic led to the drafting of an interdepartmental National Security Studies Memorandum (as they were then called) on conventional arms transfers, which is the way all business of the US government, other than that passing between cup and lip of the principals in (frequent) moments of inspiration, gets accomplished. As one of those who at one time 'had the action' on this Memorandum (which is to say had the power to initiate, or, more pertinently, stall, the process) the present writer notes that the dominant theme of the working group was for restraint in arms sales, *ceteris paribus*. Indeed it was a strongly held view in most cases.

Implementation, as it were, of the Memorandum never transpired during the Ford administration. Within the Pentagon, Kissinger's deputy secretary (now Governor), William Clements, kept his 'eagle eyes' open for those who thought that his Arab contacts 'whose natural state is to fight one amongst the other, shouldn't be able to buy the arms they need to defend themselves against the Commies.'4 The other deputy secretary of the day, Robert Ellsworth, put it more succinctly, 'Henry [Kissinger] uses arms sales as wampum.'4

There was a logic sequence put out at the Pentagon that bears closer scrutiny. One position paper, the argument of which is largely taken up and which can be quoted here at length without incurring a charge of plagiary, is as follows:

Foreign military sales are now on the cutting edge of US Foreign Policy, having become the primary instrument of foreign assistance to other countries.

[The] fact is that the Persian Gulf area had traditionally been under British protection, which changed when the British . . . withdrew 'east of Suez'—

just previous to the vast increase in oil prices. . . . These countries . . . knew that their wealth excited envy. . . . The new wealth gave . . . a new capability to acquire the sophisticated weaponry with which in due course they could protect themselves.

. . . most of these countries . . . have colonially-designed borders cutting across tribes and clans, adding to the instability. The governments seek to further their nationhood: to protect themselves against secession from within and inroads from without. This requires arms.

[The] fact is that the traditional form of international friendship—alliances—has evolved. Young nations do not want the formal ties of alliances yet need some of the functions that alliances traditionally served. Military sales is the new expression of cooperation . . . Considerable confidence must exist . . . and their international interests must be complementary. This is the new way of ensuring American access to critical areas of the globe without the explicit entanglement of alliances. . . .[5]

The logic was not confined to the Middle East. In a statement entitled 'Philosophy of Foreign Military Sales', drafted in DSAA, the Soviet moves in the Middle East were noted as precursors to similar moves in Africa, from which 'it would not be difficult to project the potential need for US military security assistance in sub-Saharan Africa in the future.'[6] Indeed.

The Carter administration took up office with a zealous commitment to change this policy. We can permit Zbigniew Brzezinski to summarize that particular *démarche*, as he does dismissing the whole issue in a few paragraphs of a large memoir. The administration, he writes,

attempted to generate an international consensus to slow down the sales of conventional armaments to the Third World. . . . America took the lead in emphasising restraint, with only a small increase in sales from $6.9 billion to $7.9 billion between 1977 and 1980, or 14 per cent over the four-year period. . . .

Unfortunately, the U.S. was unable to persuade its major allies, notably France, West Germany, the U.K., and Italy, to do the same. Sales from these four states . . . during the same period jumped from $6.9 billion in 1977 to $12.3 billion in 1980, a 78 per cent increase. This was an even larger increase than that of the USSR, which sold $9.6 billion in 1977 and $14.9 billion in 1980, for a 55 per cent increase during the period of the Carter Administration. [Brzezinski 1983]

This gives statistical muscle to the observation of a CIA analyst that arms sales are a function not of someone wishing to sell, but of people with money willing to buy, in circumstances where the Europeans are essentially forced by economic logic to sell all they can.[7]

Yet why, in the 1970s, a period of growing concern about arms sales, was there so little attention paid to the real cost of arms build-ups, why was nothing said or done about, at least, the trade-offs between security and development? The easy answer is that it is hard enough for economists specializing in development to get together in academe with political scientists studying arms transfers, where the obstacles to cooperation are surely problems of the mind; in the bureaucracy it is a matter of buildings, chains of command, frames of reference and, indeed, organizational charts.

No one anywhere in the US government has, or ever had, the responsibility to look at security and development together. At ACDA, which had a bureaucratic and policy tilt against arms sales and a responsibility to inform Congress of the need (or lack thereof) for every non-trivial arms sale, there is no such office. Dr. Janne Nolan, who worked in the front office in the agency's halcyon days under Jimmy Carter, tells of trying to stimulate such concerns: 'It wasn't possible to begin to get something off the ground'.[8] The Agency for International Development (AID) had no such office, only those of 'Policy Development and Program Review' and 'evaluation' under which such a title might have come. Instead we find co-ordinators for everything from environmental affairs to 'human resources', but nary a touch of security tarnish. And while the Assistant Secretary for International Security Affairs, Department of Defense, has a deputy assistant secretary who supervises DSAA and has a 'humanitarian assistance' office as well as one for international economic and energy affairs, there is none in which coordination is called for (or carried out) with AID or other development assistance organizations. One might have thought that in the State Department, on the other hand, there might be such an office: but there the bureau of politico-military affairs—even within its 'office of security assistance and sales'—advertises and contains no such work. Nor does the Policy Planning Council.[9] And if one looks at the armed forces, one is still less likely to find an admiral or general officer charged with security and development. Organizational charts once again say it all.

Reagan administration views

The Reagan administration came in with new priorities and none of the anxieties about military assistance of the Carter administration. There was a considerable pragmatism about rewarding friends and

punishing enemies worldwide at the expense of course of theory.
Indeed the bias was against abstraction. Yet in the end, it was in the
Reagan administration that, implicitly at least, it was seen that a link
between security and development was of the essence to the success
of its own, self-proclaimed hard-line, policies, if only *faute de
mieux*. We will see, in briefly examining later the cases of El
Salvador and the Philippines, how this transpired.

Reagan administration analysts, including some very good ones,
for example, Presidential Assistant, Geoffrey Kemp, an erstwhile
student of this subject, perceived the situtation in the following way
(Kemp 1979). As against what was happening as a result of the
political trends of and within the United States, there were the
external realities (the argument would go), to which US policy
occasionally related and sometimes even took into account (though in
the main it is tempting to conclude that US policy was far more
responsive to the dynamics of domestic politics). The spurt of arms
sales in the mid-1970s was of course a function of the new oil wealth. It
is less often noted that the new wealth created new temptations for
those nearby, for which the traditional recourse has been to arm
oneself more heavily. Only on the American campus of the late
twentieth century did this tendency prove to be a cause for comment.

Academic trends of course give rise to counter-trends, and we
have seen in the case of arms spending studies no exception:
examples include the work of Benoit, and in a related but clearly
more sophisticated form, Neuman and Harkavy, who have all shown
inter alia the spin-offs, as it were, of Third World arms expenditures
ranging from the feeder roads built in India for the army but which
expanded farmers' markets, to the technological proficiency introduced into Saudi Arabia by way of military modernization, however
expensively (Harkavy 1979).

What has been substantially ignored—except in policy circles
where the acceptance of the thesis had a self-serving motive—is the
possibility that arms expenditures were what they were said to be or
what they traditionally represented. With respect to the former, the
newly rich Third World states averred to be frightened of external
threats. The academic persuasion has been to see this as the
psychiatrist sees his patients' call for explanations—'what are you
really saying and why are you saying it?' Robert Rothstein, in a
significant paper, for example, attributes arms increases to 'per
capita income growth rates, the "contagion effect", competition
among arms sellers, internal inter-service rivalries, the behaviour of

post-coup governments, and the revival of Cold War conflicts and attitudes.'[10] Only the first half of the last stated reason deals with the possibility of external realities.

The fact is that, fortuitously, the oil wealth came at the same time as the (perceived) enhanced Soviet involvement and, indeed, interventionary behaviour in the Third World; it coincided with the collapse of South Vietnam—which King Faisal sought to avert through Saudi subventions, so close a connection did he see (Snepp 1977). Perhaps it is now easy to see how some of us overreacted to the new Soviet power projection capabilities;[11] but at the time there was more than a modest element of prophecy in fearing a trend that led by the end of the decade to a massive Soviet invasion of a neutral country.[12] In other words those who wanted to see threats were perhaps not simply imagining them, even if, in the end, these threats turned out to be more self-contained than it was at first thought. (If nothing else, trends beget counter trends.)

Then there is the question of what arms increases traditionally represented—namely the attributes of statehood, and the development, alas, of the characteristics of state systems, which is to say traditional conflicts over everything from resources, treatment of nationals, and boundary areas. The point that seems to evade notice is that the first generation, or even half generation, of the 'new states', prior to the great increase in arms expenditures, represented a false dawn—and a soft data base from which to project the later trends. The international system was, far more than we choose to remember, an American protectorate (admittedly one acting often most effectively through surrogates) with a well cordoned Communist enclave. The new states (and the old ones like Iran) started off with high ideals of new patterns of inter-state relations—Kwame Nkrumah's Institute of Truth comes to mind (Thompson 1969) —that were especially attractive to states without arsenals and with the 'glue' of independence that was not to come unstuck for some years. Indeed, glue is briefly intoxicating, as was independence, and that too bought time for the new states.

In time new states became 'not-new' states, and had interests including preservation of even the most artificial boundaries (Jackson and Rosberg 1982: 1). Arsenals got incrementally bigger, until leaders got used to honour guards and then began looking covetously at neighbours in some cases. The more traditional the pattern became, the more the sermons were a descant to the reality: it is no accident, it seems, that the most pious state of Asia and Africa respectively was the first in its continent to sponsor a veritable invasion of a neighbour (India in Bangladesh, Tanzania in Uganda). The attractiveness of the cause in each case hardly alters the point. Armies had become useful.

Armed force, in short, became the new-old midwife of international politics. Nations disappeared[13] through force of arms, and nations were tested in war and in some cases even found their spirit through their battles, as had historically been thought to be the case, prior to the advent of the new received academic wisdom.

A new view of Africa, for example, is seen in an article by Sanford Ungar (1985), a writer who, more than any other, might be expected to be less sympathetic with the trend. Headlining his piece that Africa was 'starving with arms aplenty', he found the following underpinnings of the trend a necessary part of the explanation:

Most African countries inherited illogical and unstable borders. . . . Several face the constant worry that their most prosperous regions may try to secede.

In addition to the official total of two million refugees in Africa, millions are displaced within their own countries, and this contributes to instability.

. . . where few symbols of economic development and national achievement exist, the military domain may be the only available source of pride.

Impoverished countries sometimes buy advanced weapons for the same reasons that the poor in the United States buy Cadillacs: they are expensive to maintain and they may soon fall apart . . . but they make the owners feel good in the meantime.

These are parts of a paradigm of the world the changing of which would not come easily.

Thus perhaps it can be seen how it became a commonplace of Reagan administration officials that theory, ideals, whatever notwithstanding, if African states might be seen in that light by a liberal, how much more easily it would be to justify large sales to important states in the Third World with real money to spend, with real threats to their security, and a desire to do serious business with Washington. And as we had learned in the Carter administration, not to do so affected only our sales, not their purchases. Even a poor state like Pakistan, which obviously had learned over the years to play the American system to its advantage, could more easily sell its case when Soviet war planes overflew border areas routinely as the US, China, Saudi Arabia and others intervened in Afghanistan through Peshawar and elsewhere along the Pakistani border. The fact that new supplies gave Pakistan new capabilities against India, partly remedying the sharp change in India's favour in the balance of power that occurred in the 1970s, was not really interesting to the new Washington realists.

And yet, and yet: it could hardly be gainsaid that something was different, if only because the new academic wisdom was at least in part picked up by Third World elites (or, rather, counter-elites) as a critique of their own governments, and because rising expectations of political standards were generalized through the world system by television, education and radio.

Emergent trends

The hopeful case (even the adjective betrays a bias) rests on trends and the new discovery of old realities. Just as the greatest academic alarm at arms purchases came from sharp increases from un-realistically low bases, a slowing down inevitably came as a number of problems intervened: for one thing oil wealth did not accumulate forever (and oil-financed weapons purchases could be cancelled, as the Ayatollah Khomeni showed). The old problem of absorptive capability had new variants: as the Soviet ambassador not unfairly replied to a mocking Ambassador Jeane Kirkpatrick at the UN in June 1972, 'not 27 Soviet MIGs knocked out of the sky [by the Israeli air force] . . . but 27 Syrian pilots. . . . '[14] And too many of the rest of the pilots failed to re-enlist—a serious problem in all burgeoning Third World services.[15] Anyway, the regimes (as with Syria) had a political problem with their training.

But that is not enough of a trend on which to end hopefully, as was promised. For I promised that the first clear focus on the nexus of security and development was in the Reagan administration. To some, this may seem ironic with respect to so conservative a regime, one with the views described above. Consideration of this propo-sition ought, however, to be made along with the sound historic dictum that liberals always implement conservative programmes, and vice versa; the nineteenth century (viz. Bismarck's social programme) is a testament to the proposition, and much twentieth century history as well. The occasions for such may be multifarious, but the reason always has to do with the way historical contra-dictions must be resolved and contradictory political support bases sustained.

In the early 1980s, any president would have to deal with budget deficits and declining congressional support for overseas activities; the proposition that the funding of a major counter-insurgency effort abroad (so much more costly than an insurgency, Reagan activists would remind us in early 1986) could find sufficient constituency was from the first not serious.

Yet it was equally serious that the Reagan administration would not permit a communist victory in El Salvador. Whether the high rhetoric of the administration's early pronouncements, in particular those of General Haig, or the president's more general expressions, beneath it lay a commitment. Conveniently, the insurgents, in early 1981, believing an impotent lame duck president also to be supine and hoping to push him over in the very dark twilight of his administration, had led Jimmy Carter as his last foreign policy undertaking to start military assistance to San Salvador on the eve of the Reagan inaugural. Yet even in the early 'honeymoon' the Reagan administration could not find support for more than an eight-figure military assistance programme in El Salvador.

But what does $50,000,000 buy in the 1980s? Three-and-a-half helicopter gunships—for running the war American-style? But we had seen what that had cost in Vietnam. Or two helicopters and a half a combat plane? How was that going to help save El Salvador? As this writer prepared an article on this subject in early 1981 (Thompson 1981: 78) he found the new administration already asking these troubling questions.

Another line of development that reinforced these questions was the incipient programme to encourage democracy in the world, which of course would have implications for national policy on the question of development and security. What happened is that the March 1982 parliamentary elections in El Salvador astonished the US administration: the turnout was at least double their own best predictions. The administration believed the elections to be largely free—and 'put' a certifiable right-winger in power of whom even arch-conservative Senator Jesse Helms could not disapprove. Perhaps there was something in that old democratic idea after all, despite Col. D'Aubuisson's brief emergence at the helm. It did at least provide proof of some slippage in the Kirkpatrick thesis that authoritarian regimes should be supported while totalitarian regimes condemned.

At that time the president had a commitment to address the British parliament but the subject of this important address had not been agreed upon. 'Project Truth' had been around since mid-1981, but had languished in the programmes bureau of the United States Information Agency as merely a reactive policy tool, and now the president decided to give it some new flesh—in what was to emerge as 'Project Democracy.' For how did you square the circle of insurgency-defeating, 'Commie-bashing', and leaving the air 'signed with your honour when you could not enlarge the budget'? The structure for dealing with insurgency came from the Department of State, the anti-Communist rhetoric and policy from the White House, making it palatable to foreign audiences from the US Information Agency.

The way to win was to stand for democracy, but that meant both security and development. This was fine when the adversaries were the communist insurgents in El Salvador—Ferdinand Marcos was not yet tottering. You could even caution the Soviets, as Reagan did in the June 1982 speech to parliament, promising that nuclear weapons were no protection against a people's infection with the desire for democracy.[16]

Saying this was easy, but implications in policy flowed. To be sure, 'Project Democracy' as a structure proved fragile and a shadow of its envisaged self; and the president did not wait long to go back to the antipodes of his earlier style of *proclamata*. But meantime things were happening in El Salvador; aid was still pegged in eight figures, but the insurgents had at least been slowed down. It came to be seen in 1983–4, however, that the *sine qua non* of continued progress was political reform—and an end to right-wing terror. That meant getting d'Aubuisson out and getting Duarte in—as president, in the 1984 elections. I believe that future records will show that the US Government determined to support him in all plausibly deniable ways and in some other ones too; and that the sophisticated electorate, knowing its dependence on US aid for economic recovery and an end to the insurgency, understood American desires which largely coincided with its own.

Model provinces, where land reform and administrative reform had gone hand in hand with the development of people's militia, were touted as the answer; and indeed it looked that way, once Duarte was elected president in 1984, giving more flesh to Reagan's democratic idea.

Other reinforcements came along. The Kissinger Commission report, though not published until early 1984, held hearings throughout this period, and everything it said and did reinforced the lessons already acquired; the chairman was not known to proceed in a vacuum or without inspiration. Thus it enunciated 'three principles' for American success in Central America: democratic self-determination, economic and social development benefiting all, and 'cooperation in meeting threats to the security of the region.'[17]

It almost seemed the new conventional wisdom. Brent Scowcroft, speaking for the Atlantic Council which had undertaken a report as well, told the Congress that the 'United States should pursue its broadly defined security interests through regional development. Solid support for socioeconomic development must be a major component of long-term U.S. security policy in the Caribbean Basin.'[18] And the 'conclusions and policy recommendations' of the study were sub-titled 'Security Through Development'. True, the reports were riddled with inconsistencies (which for example Richard Feinberg of the ODC provided tellingly for the Congress).[19] But the burden had shifted. The argument for military assistance was compellingly and inextricably involved with the case for development.

A CIA analyst recently said, *per contra*, that 'Security and Development are mutually exclusive' for all the bureaucratic reasons that were outlined earlier. The argument here is that such is no longer so. The final nail in the old coffin of separateness was driven in by none other than Ferdinand Marcos.

The US administration had forced the issue of Marcos's legitimacy in November 1985 precisely because the security of the Philippines (and hence of American bases) was at risk through the failure of Marcos's development strategy. The insurgency was gaining very rapidly indeed, as the national income declined and 'crony money' went to Hong Kong and New York. Marcos had to go, lest the US lose its bases, it was that simple. There had been no development, other than of first family purses, and the result was simply catastrophic. Ambassador Kirkpatrick's thesis that authoritarian governments were no danger to the US and could evolve democratically was laid to rest by Marcos's flight. Marcos's authoritarian bona fides were nowhere in question, but his capability to evolve was. The lesson was that you had to link development and security to lick communists fighting progressive allies, and you had to do the same with authoritarian allies. But in both cases, the nature of the regime had to bend to the link-up of the two: in El Salvador that led to Duarte's election, and in the Philippines to Marcos's departure. The lesson may have been learned other than through the instruction of some who 'knew it all along', it may have been learned because there was nowhere else to go and nothing else to do given congressional and other constraints—but it was no less learned.

Indeed, on the very eve of our London deliberations President Reagan removed another large foundation stone out from the structure Jeane Kirkpatrick and others have built, and added a similarly large chunk to a new theory of democratic development in security. In calling for Congress to transfer $100 million for Contra funding purposes, Reagan promised to resist despots of right and left, building democracy within regional frameworks of security. 'We use our influence to encourage democratic change, in careful ways that respect other countries' traditions and political realities as well as the security threats that many of them face from external or internal forces of totalitarianism.'[20] One need only see 'development' as a subset of democratic development—as I do—to realize that American theory as practised by government has come a long way.

Notes

1. Personal discussions.
2. Armed Forces Policy Council, 23 September, 1975, author's files.
3. 'A US Initiative for Limitations on Conventional Arms Transfers', prepared by Deputy Directorate for International Negotiations, J-5, OJCS, June 1975, author's files.
4. Author's files, FMS Working Group meetings, 1975–6.
5. Draft article, unpublished, written by the author, 1976.
6. 'DOD Philosophy on Foreign Military Sales', undated, c. 1976, author's files.
7. Interview, S. Rose, 1986.
8. Personal communication, 1986.
9. Information from current telephone directories, US Government.
10. See Chapter 8 of this book.
11. See W. S. Thompson (1978) for a possible example.
12. On the other hand, see the prediction made by the present writer in the records of the California Arms Control Symposium, July 1979, that 'there would be 100,000 Soviet troops in Kabul by Christmas.'
13. See The Economist, 'When Nations Die', 26 October 1985.
14. Personal files, during author's stint as delegate, SSOD II, New York, 1982.
15. A point I owe to S. Rose.
16. For text of the speech, see New York Times, 9 June 1982.
17. See the 'National Bipartisan Report on Central America', US Congress, Senate, Committee on Foreign Relations, 1984.
18. Ibid., p. 137.
19. US Congress, Senate, Committee on Foreign Relations, 1984, p. 196.
20. New York Times, 14 March, 1986.

6

The creation of an international disarmament fund for development

JACQUES FONTANEL AND RON SMITH

The International Conference on Disarmament for Development, sponsored by the United Nations and held in Paris in July 1986, did not excite much media or public interest in either Britain or France. The Conference resulted from an initiative by the French president, which follows a long diplomatic tradition originating in the proposals advanced by Edgar Faure and Valery Giscard d'Estaing. In his speech of 28 September 1983, François Mitterrand set the following agenda:

1. to measure the military burden and to overcome the differences on data and estimates to obtain a standard accepted by all;
2. to estimate the economic effects, domestic and international, of the growth of military expenditure;
3. to measure the relation between the evolution of military expenditure and the main factors contributing to international economic disorder;
4. to examine the possibility of meeting social goals (health, technical training, agricultural development in the Third World) using the resources freed by an organized progressive reduction in military expenditure in the major countries.

In order to achieve the fourth objective it is also necessary to ensure a favourable economic effect from the reductions in Military Expenditure and to determine how the process of conversion should be organized.

The French president asked for a Conference to be called on the link between Disarmament and Development and the creation of an International Disarmament Fund for Development (Fonds International de Desarmement pour le Developpement: FIDD).

In her response to the Commission on Disarmament France has insisted on the responsibilities of the great powers for the arms race and the necessity to establish a right of compensation for those states that directly suffer as a result of international tensions: the 'disaster victims' of the international system. For them development aid needs to be provided through a comprehensive assistance programme, which takes account of the military dimension to the problem. With respect to resources, the objective to be attained is a Fund equivalent to 1 to 2 per cent of world military expenditure, that is between $9 and $18 billion. This is a considerable sum given that the UN Programme for Development has a budget under $1 billion.

The link between armaments and development can be maintained by the nuclear powers making a contribution proportional to their nuclear weapons. These funds should add to (and not substitute for) traditional development aid. Funds would be directed firstly to the least developed countries and particularly to those affected by conflicts.

The UN Institute for Disarmament Research (UNIDIR) has prepared, at the request of the UN General Assembly, a report on the creation of a FIDD, which emphasizes the destructive effects of the arms race on world security and the negative impact of military expenditure on national economies. It puts forward four essential principles.

— All proposals for such a Fund must rest on the willingness of the great powers to disarm.
— It is necessary to define a form for the Fund which will promote longer term progress towards international security through disarmament and development.
— The Fund should serve as an institutional link between disarmament and development; a link which has not been systematically developed in any international institution, past or present.
— The Fund would require co-ordinated action among states. Each country will need to perceive participation in the Fund as being in its own interest.

From an institutional point of view, UNIDIR presented two solutions: either the creation of a new organization, or the use of an existing organization for the management of the funds which would maintain a distinct identity within the organization.

The proposal to create such a fund has political and economic aspects. This chapter will examine the economic and organizational aspects in terms of how the resources available to the Fund might be acquired, and the contribution such a Fund might make to disarmament and development.

Clearly there are a range of criticisms that can be made of the approach itself. It can be argued:

— that although there are linkages between military spending war and economic performance, disarmament and development are distinct objectives that may best be achieved by separate processes;
— that large international bureaucracies, such as the proposed Fund, are often ineffective and perhaps even counter-productive ways of meeting desirable objectives;
— that certain kinds of aid to poor countries may hinder rather than help the development process.

Rather than discuss these arguments, this chapter takes the proposal, to create a Disarmament Fund for Development, on its own terms and examines the economic details involved.

Resources

In order to finance the Fund it is necessary to determine who the contributors should be; how their level of contribution should be determined, in particular the role of level of development and of level of armament in the definition of contribution rates; and how the basis of national contribution should be verified. Three principal methods of collection have been proposed—disarmament dividend, voluntary contributions and a tax on arms. Each of these methods will be examined in turn, then some specific proposals discussed.

Methods

Disarmament dividend. This method envisages the sums freed following measures of disarmament being invested in the essential needs of the population. This approach is favoured by the experts who produced the United Nations report on Disarmament for Development. They argue for the movement of resources from the military towards other types of expenditure; whether internal, for education and health for instance, or external, in the form of development aid. However there are many problems.

If disarmament is identified with arms control agreements between the major powers, it has to be recognized that these tend to release very few resources. If the Fund were linked to such measures, the agreements would need to include an estimate of the sums that would be eventually freed and available for distribution as development aid, further complicating the negotiation. It would be preferable to link the Fund to reductions in military expenditure, but this implies the acceptance of a common precise definition of military expenditures. Trying to obtain such a definition is another UN enterprise.

A procedure of verifying the process of disarmament is required. Verification would be helped by the technical and political acceptance of the matrix of military expenditures and the method of international comparison recommended by the UN expert group on the measurement of military expenditures. Verification of military expenditures raises fundamental problems about secrecy and trust between states. There is also the problem that subscriptions based on the resources freed by disarmament are likely to provide only a transitory revenue for the Fund, rather than sustained resources.

The use of the disarmament dividend to aid development does not necessarily require the creation of a Fund to organize it and disarmament itself raises domestic political problems of conversion. This is particularly the case for countries with a large arms industry or whose balance of payments and employment depend heavily on arms exports.

Voluntary contributions. Voluntary contributions leave each state to determine their own contribution, on the model of a number of specialized funds and agencies of the UN. This is the easiest procedure to implement and already provides significant resources for a number of UN programmes; but it has enough disadvantages to mean that it is not regarded as a sufficient source of funds. The resources would be limited, there would only be a symbolic link between disarmament and development, and a system so flexible to exclude all reference to and constraint on the arms race would lose credibility. It is necessary to establish a closer link between disarmament and development than is provided by voluntary contributions.

Voluntary contributions would face particular difficulties during a world economic crisis. The developed countries threatened by inflation and unemployment are unlikely to be generous to LDCs in the absence of an obligation owed to the international community.

An arms tax. A tax on armaments where the tax base is determined on the basis of an agreed measure of military effort, has the advantage of furnishing the Fund with a continuing flow of resources while penalizing the states who are heavily armed, by obliging them to transfer extra resources to the poorer countries. It also provides an incentive against higher military expenditure by increasing its cost.

However, it raises considerable difficulties. The problem of comparison and definition of military expenditures arises again. The difficulties of international comparison would make it impractical to link this tax to the absolute level of military expenditures. However, measures based on percentages, which can be compared across countries, such as the share of military expenditure in GDP or public expenditure, discriminate in favour of the richer countries who are better able to support their defence burden. Another alternative is to tax the arms trade, but this discriminates against the countries who have to import their arms, particularly the poor countries.

This proposal also has the implication that the amount of aid available to the Less Developed Countries will increase when the arms race accelerates, which creates a paradox, and an incentive to the recipients of the aid to encourage the acquisition of arms by donors. In addition, it is probably not politically feasible for the tax rate to be set sufficiently high to provide an incentive against arming. The advantages of the tax are the incentives it provides against arming, the verification which it implies for military expenditures and the resources it provides for the poorest countries. The disadvantage is that it could only be implemented in a climate of trust, which does not currently prevail.

Specific proposals

The objective is to chose a method of collecting resources which will be acceptable to the countries involved and which links Disarmament and Development. Hugo Sada and Alain Pipart (UNIDIR, 1984) suggest a combination of different types of contribution for different types of state. They regard the preferable method, the automatic payment of an agreed percentage of the military budgets of the heavily armed states, as facing a number of great difficulties in application. However, it seems to them that a guaranteed minimum obligatory element is needed to link disarmament and development. They consider that the five large nuclear powers have a particular responsibility in matters of international security, and that they should engage to contribute to the Fund a sum based on the number of nuclear weapons. This has the advantage of providing a precise measure of the armaments of each state and all that is required is to fix the rate per weapon to determine the sum each state is liable to pay. Other forms of voluntary contribution are envisaged for other developed states based on the percentage of GNP, or government budget, devoted to military expenditure.

This system has two dangers. First, it puts the five nuclear powers in the same category though their level of development is different, and it is not evident that they all should be accorded the same status. Second, although the calculation of the number of nuclear weapons is easier than military expenditures, it does not permit a correct appreciation of the force of each state and it gives perhaps too much weight to stocks as against investment. It treats the weapons of 1975, which remain in the inventory, as being of the same value as the weapons newly installed in 1986.

This method emphasizes armaments but forgets development. The developed countries which benefit directly, by treaty, or indirectly by the nuclear umbrella of the superpowers are not taxed, with the consequence that China, a poor country, has to finance the Fund while a rich country, like Japan does not.

Marek Thee argues that the disarmament dividend must constitute the fundamental formula for the activities of the fund. To avoid dispute he proposes to adopt the contribution principle based on the general order of magnitude of military expenditures. A system of taxes will be put in place to avoid making tolerable the arms race on the basis of a formal or informal agreement among the interested countries. In addition voluntary contributions will be encouraged. For its creation the FIDD needs to receive an initial subscription of 0.5 to 1 per cent of world military expenditures. The five nuclear powers would make a contribution of 60 to 65 per cent of the budget (24 to 25 per cent by the US and USSR, 4 to 5 per cent for the other three). The rest will be furnished by UN members in proportion to their declared levels of military expenditure. Thus all states will be contributors, with a higher rate of tax for the nuclear powers.

This proposition has a number of difficulties. The problems of orders of magnitude must not be underestimated. The estimates of military expenditure are very different depending on the sources used. If the tax on arms is presented as desirable, the terms of its applications are not explained. It could be based on military expenditures or represent a tax on the construction (and eventually the possession) of each missile. One could also imagine different tax rates for different types of equipment. It seems better to take account of a measure using a harmonized definition of military expenditure. Again is difficult to imagine this Fund functioning without considerable trust between the states.

Evaluating the propositions

The objective of the exercise is to mobilize and use resources in order to provide incentives for disarmament, symbolize the link between disarmament and development, and create some institutional momentum. From the point of view of resources the fundamental questions are then: who pays, on what basis, in what form and how much?

With respect to who pays: there is no doubt that the richest, most heavily armed states should be the principal contributors. But how is this group to be defined: the superpowers, the large powers, the nuclear powers, the richest states, the most heavily armed, the permanent members of the Security Council, all states? The problem is complicated because there are both poor heavily armed states and rich lightly armed states, and there is no obvious way to take account of the specific features of each case. In particular, the security needs of states differ and there is no objective basis for deciding whether a particular state is 'over-armed' relative to its needs.

It is very difficult to establish a just criterion that can both reduce the arms race and help the developing countries. It would be an anomaly if developed countries protected by a superpower did not have to pay, while a poor country like China would be a principal contributor. The criterion of being a nuclear power does not put sufficient weight on the link between disarmament and development.

There are many principles which seem applicable:

1. The countries which furnish the resources should be the countries judged as having high incomes according to the UN definition.
2. The developing countries may participate in providing resources, but are not bound by the international agreement.
3. The developed countries which do not benefit by a treaty or military protection have a lower obligation unless their military expenditures are relatively high, for example over 3 per cent of GNP.
4. All the other developed countries should participate in the creation and financing of the Fund.

5. The international regional organizations can contribute voluntarily to express unity of action among the countries which they represent and to develop the image of cooperation necessary between states. The purely economic international organizations might be excluded, but it is reasonable to expect a contribution from those with a military function such as NATO and the Warsaw Pact. The participation of the alliances would have the advantage of making concrete the link between disarmament and development and having a certain symbolic value.
6. The institutions of the UN and the principal organisations for development and regional integration should be involved in the operation of the Fund.

With respect to the basis of contribution: the agreement could be expressed in terms of the physical numbers of weapons, nuclear or conventional, as is usual in arms control negotiations. The agreement could refer either to stocks of weapons, with perhaps some allowance for age and quality of the weapons, or it could refer to the construction of weapons or to net additions to the stock of weapons. An assessment based on military expenditures raises more difficulties than one based on physical counts, because of all the problems of definition, measurement and comparison. Verification will raise difficulties whatever the scheme.

The resources available to the Fund are likely to be provided in many different forms. The obvious form is the donation of money by the contributing states. However, in a number of cases, the currencies contributed will be non-convertible and could only be used for purchases from the state that provided them. These states will thus receive contracts as a counterpart of their aid. In certain cases, particularly for conversion purposes, the gift of goods and materials could form part of the contribution, including perhaps military products freed by disarmament, which could be put to civilian uses. In addition, if the Fund made development loans as well as grants, the repayments and interest payments would, in the longer term, provide an additional source of finance.

The final question is how much finance the Fund will have. To be effective, the Fund needs to have substantial resources, and the rate of contribution has to be assessed accordingly. Total military expenditures are so large that quite small percentage contribution rates yield considerable revenues. The Soviet Union has proposed a 10 per cent reduction in the military budgets of the permanent members of the Security Council, and the transfer of 10 per cent of this sum to the developing countries. Currently, this represents about $6 billion. The Sada–Pippart proposition involves about $1 billion; the Thee proposition, involves the contribution of between half and one per cent of total military expenditures, which represents between $4 billion and $8 billion of aid. In practice, given the economic situation facing the contributors, it is unlikely that such sums could be realised.

Contribution

A Disarmament for Development Fund would redistribute the resources liberated by a reduction in military expenditure in such a way as to contribute to development. The precondition for the effectiveness of the Fund, is a real measure of disarmament or at least a reduction in the speed of the arms race, which would reduce the insecurity of the system. The economic position of the developing countries is very serious. The international financial system is threatened by the large outstanding debts, and international monetary instability threatens the weaker countries. Economic insecurity itself increases international instability and encourages rivalry thus fuelling arms races.

The role of the Fund would be to use development aid to reinforce the process of disarmament for development and to reduce this economic insecurity. In order to see how this might be done, it is necessary to define the beneficiaries of the fund, the criteria used for distribution, and the form of the contribution the Fund could make to the international system.

The Less Developed Countries would not be the only beneficiaries of the Fund. The developed countries would also benefit through the reduction of the arms race, and the release of resources for other purposes. There is no doubt that after the initial difficulties associated with the conversion of military industry, the developed countries would gain from the reduction in defence expenditures. The dividends from disarmament would benefit the system as a whole. The initial contributions from the developed countries should make allowances for the costs involved in reducing production in the arms industries.

In disbursing aid the Fund may take account of various considerations. Since it is necessary to maintain a link between the activities of the Fund and disarmament, it should be a principle that countries involved in war or who are excessively armed do not have access to the aid, while the poor countries who make a real effort to disarm should have privileged access to the Fund. It should also attach a high priority to projects which aid the conversion of arms industries to peaceful uses. Disbursement of the aid could be made dependent on recipients providing information on their levels of military expenditure.

In general, aid from the Fund will be complementary to other international development aid, and the grants and loans will be distributed on similar terms. However, the Fund should also have a specific role in providing a link between disarmament and development.

Alain Pippart and Hugo Sada suggest five specific types of action that the Fund may support. These include financing peace-keeping operations; supporting the creation of nuclear-free or conflict-free regional zones; providing investments, such as transport and communications, which encourage cooperation in potential war-zones; help to the victims of war and insecurity; and the encouragement of regional disarmament measures. These proposals involve a very narrow conception of the link to disarmament. Care would need to be taken to ensure that the Fund was not placed in a very delicate position, by making military–political interventions in situations which may have East–West dimensions or in which there is no willingness to compromise by the participants.

Another possibility is to use the labour and capital embodied in military forces for economic purposes. For instance, a state may offer or lend some military specialists to provide infrastructure in poor countries, such as construction of bridges and development of airports. It may provide military personnel and equipment as part of disaster aid. This already happens to a certain extent and raises other difficulties associated with possible militarization of the development process and the use of troops provided under humanitarian cover for other purposes.

It seems necessary to broaden the scope of the Fund beyond such narrow military dimensions and extend its actions to three fundamental problems of development: conversion of military industries to civil application; expansion of civilian Research and Development in the Third World; and the improvement of agricultural production. Thus the fund would confront the major issues in development, the diversion of resources to arms, the lack of technology and the prevalence of hunger. The aid to R&D would also counteract the belief in some Less Developed Countries that the promotion of military industry is a way to obtain technological spin-offs. In general, the most effective way of providing the aid would be through loans at low interest rates, which would provide some incentives for productive investment in conversion, technological development and agricultural production.

Although there are many problems associated with the distribution of the resources of the Fund, which would need to be resolved; the Fund does have the possibility of making a major contribution, both symbolic and effective, to the promotion of the processes of both disarmament and development. Given the potential of the Fund, it seems worthwhile conducting a serious analysis of how it could be constituted and organized in order to judge whether the project is feasible and desirable, and the extent of its contribution to the international system.

Note

We are grateful for support from the CNRS & ESRC for a project on the Defence Efforts in Britain and France. The chapter has also benefited from comments made at the Colloquium on Defence, Security and Development.

PART III
Determinants of Defence Expenditures

7

The causes of military expenditure in developing countries

ALFRED MAIZELS AND MACHIKO K. NISSANKE

Introduction

The past decade has seen a rapid expansion of defence expenditure in many developing countries. It is highly probable that this trend may be detrimental to their domestic development since military spending can act as an unproductive consumption expenditure without having the sort of Keynesian multipliers that increase output and growth in developed economies. However, little empirical analysis has yet been attempted to answer the question as to why, if military expenditure does, in fact, retard growth, do developing countries increase such expenditure? The present Chapter attempts a quantitative assessment of some of the more important factors which influence the level of military expenditure in developing countries by means of cross-country multiple regression analysis. We choose a recent period, the average of the years 1978–80, to investigate empirically the determinants of defence spending.

The next section sets out the major issues in the field and suggests how they can be systematically organized and analysed. The third section gives the empirical results which build upon the theoretical discussion. The final section concludes briefly.

The causes of defence spending in developing countries

A number of recent quantitative studies have analysed the impact of military expenditure on the economic growth of developing countries (Benoit 1973; Benoit 1978; Ball 1983; Deger and Sen 1983; Deger and Smith 1983; Frederikson and Looney 1983; Faini, Arnez and Taylor 1984; and Deger 1986). For a critical review of the literature, see Maizels and Nissanke (1986). Almost without exception, they have taken such expenditure as exogenously given. This may run counter to a traditional neo-classical approach which views the role of the state as maximizing national welfare and balancing, at the margin, the welfare benefits of additional security derived from defence spending with its opportunity cost in terms of foregone civilian consumption.

However, neo-classical theory is difficult to apply to most developing countries; its central tenet, of a politically neutral state weighing the security needs of the nation against welfare losses arising out of reduced consumption to pay for defence, may not have much significance for most less developed economies. Rather, state security in these countries will generally involve the need for safeguarding the legitimacy of the ruling elite as well as the suppression of domestic opposition groups. In addition, of course, there will be the need for protection against possible external aggression. Defence spending, therefore, should be related to the need for military force to keep the ruling elite in power as well as to deter possible threats from aggressors. This will be particularly true for military governments—and these now seems to be in the majority (Sivard 1983)—but also for civilian governments which will try to use their control over the military for similar purposes.

Strategic conflicts between neighbours in the Third World must be one of the major reasons for the rise in defence spending. Conflict and tension between Arab countries and Israel, Iraq and Iran, India and Pakistan, Greece and Turkey, as well as the relatively high defence burden (military spending as a proportion of national product) in these countries, clearly demonstrate the importance of regional belligerence in explaining military expenditure.

In addition to these two factors, that is, internal conflict and regional tensions (or wars), a third element may also have become significant in recent years as an influence on the military expenditure of developing countries, namely their degree of involvement in either of the global power blocs. To the extent that a developing country adheres to a global political–strategic alliance, provides facilities for foreign military bases, and depends on a superpower or its allies for its military equipment and personnel training, it may also come under pressure to expand its own military establishment, partly to enhance the potential of a foreign military base, and partly as an instrument in support of power bloc regional policy.

The foregoing discussion suggests a useful, and pedagogical, classification framework to analyse the proximate causes of defence spending. The basic distinctions are those between domestic (national), regional and global determinants. The various military influences under these three categories are mentioned above. In addition, it is important to emphasize the political factors as well as the economic linkages. The matrix of nine elements now incorporates military, political and economic causes distinguished at the national, regional and international levels. Table 7.1 sets out the details of the schema. We now examine them in some detail.

Consider first the determinants of defence spending that emanate from military activity. The vested interests of the military establishment will push it towards higher security-related expenditures. This consideration is closely related to the power of the military, even in a country with a civilian government; the more powerful the military in relation to the civil authority, the greater the chance that the military can increase its share of the government budget and the national product. Secondly, internal repression of opposition groups may require more military resources than if such groups were left free. More important, such repression may lead to civil wars. There is little doubt that over the postwar period civil wars in developing countries have been far more destructive of life and property than

Table 7.1 Potential causes of defence spending in developing countries; a schematic presentation

	Domestic	Regional	International
I. Military influence	1. Vested interest of military establishment 2. Internal repression 3. Civil war	4. Regional war 5. Regional tension	6. Foreign military aid
II. Political factors	7. Nature of State and government	8. Regional alliance	9. Member of global power bloc
III. Economic linkages	10. Economic development 11. Growth 12. Government budget 13. Military-industrial complex	14. Regional economic co-operation	15. Available foreign exchange 16. Role of foreign capital 17. Influence of aid donor

have inter-state wars. Over the period 1945 to 1976, for example, Kende (1980) has recorded 102 separate civil wars (of which 73 were anti-regime), with an average duration of three-and-a-half years, while in this period there were 18 inter-state wars between developing countries, with an average duration of seven months.

At the regional level, tension, conflict and wars between neighbouring countries are potentially important in bolstering defence spending. It should be noted however, that many of these inter-state wars have been closely related to civil wars in progress in one or other of the combatant nations. It is even possible for a foreign country actively to encourage and help strategically the continuation of civil conflict. Examples (countries with civil wars listed first) have been Ethiopia–Somalia, Uganda–Tanzania, Lebanon–Israel/Syria, Cambodia–Vietnam, Cyprus–Turkey and Pakistan (Bangladesh)–India. At the global level, military activity is fostered by foreign military aid. Whether this increases or decreases the domestic defence burden is a debatable point. Aid may take off the pressure from security and threat concerns of the recipient government and help it to reduce its budget on defence. On the other hand, if aid is related to precommitment towards additional domestic spending on complementary inputs of military activity, then the defence burden may rise.

Turning now to the political factors (elements 7 to 9 in Table 7.1), these are more general in nature and difficult to quantify. The nature of the state, military or civilian government, can be exected to have some influence on defence spending in predictable fashion. Membership of regional alliances can be conceivably important though in practice most LDCs are not involved in such alliances. The importance of being a part of global power rivalry has already been mentioned.

The economic linkages of military spending may be extremely crucial, particularly in setting an upper constraint to defence related activities. The level of economic development is of course very important. Structural change, arising out of the attempt to develop, may accentuate social conflict and force governments to spend more on defence. A rise in per capita incomes may mean that societies' concern for 'security', a non- inferior good, will increase, thus calling for higher military outlay. Real income growth is expected to impose a binding constraint on spending on defence, as will the size of the state budget since military spending in developing countries is always publicly funded. Though the influence of the military–

industrial complex has been emphasized in the literature, this does not seem to be important for LDCs since arms production is still in its infancy, in general, though there are a few major exceptions.

The economic linkage at the regional level usually relates to regional economic cooperation such as that among ASEAN countries. Though this has an implicit military dimension (perceived threat from China and Vietnam for ASEAN), in practice policy coordination between defence and economic factors have not proceeded far. Much more important are the economic factors at the international level and their interrelationship with military spending: specifically, economic factors include the availability of foreign exchange; the potential influence of foreign capital, in the form of transnational corporations, on the socio-economic structure of host countries; and the potential influence of major aid donor governments on the domestic and foreign policies, including military strategies, of these countries.

The relevance of foreign exchange, which derives from the need of all developing countries to purchase military equipment, particularly sophisticated equipment, from developed countries, was especially notable when oil-exporting countries in the Middle East began programmes of rapid military expansion following the sharp rise in oil prices in 1973 and again in 1978–9. By contrast, developing countries with chronic balance of payments deficits can modernize or expand their military hardware only by restricting imports for civilian purposes, or by becoming client-states of a global power bloc.

It is difficult to prejudge a priori the influence, if any, of transnational corporations on military expenditure. To the extent that their operations lead to national disintegration, as some dependency theorists maintain, the resultant increase in social divisiveness and conflict could be expected to lead to greater internal repression of disadvantaged groups and, to that extent, to higher levels of military expenditure. On the other hand, transnationals are likely to concentrate their investments, *ceteris paribus*, in countries with low levels of political instability so that, to that extent, there is likely to be a negative relationship between the magnitude of foreign direct investment and the level of military expenditure.

It is equally difficult to prejudge the probable influence, if any, of a major aid donor government on the level of military expenditure of a developing country. In this case, much would depend on whether, as is often the case, the major aid donor was also the chief member of a global power bloc, in which case the presumption would be that heavy dependence on that country for both aid and arms would tend to be associated with a higher level of military expenditure than if both aid and arms were obtained from a variety of sources. If, however, the dominant supplier of arms belonged to an opposing global power bloc from the dominant supplier of aid, the host government could come under conflicting pressures; this would not be a stable situation, and would presumably not last for very long.

The empirical results

The three levels of distinctions, the national, regional and inter-national levels, as well as the division between military, political and economic factors, are emphasized in the following empirical analysis. Cross-sectional regressions for a large sample of seventy-two developing countries, utilizing data of annual averages for the years 1978 to 1980, are used to identify the significant determinants of defence spending. The dependent variables are the military burden (ratio of defence expenditure to GDP) and the military share (as a ratio of central government expenditure). Separate regressions were also run for Africa, Asia, and Latin America; these are reported elsewhere (Maizels and Nissanke 1986).

The variables, chosen to exemplify the features noted earlier in Table 7.1, need to be specified. We look first at the national and regional levels. The close interconnection between the nature of the government, domestic repression and the vested interest of the military prompted us to use a single variable to represent all these concepts together. A scored dummy variable is used: countries with civilian governments are given a zero score; countries under military rule are scored 1, 2, or 3 according to whether the use of violence against the public is rated as 'none', 'some' or 'frequent'. In similar fashion, since wars of various kinds are closely related with each other, a dummy variable for inter-state and/or civil wars (between 1973 and 1980) is utilized to distinguish countries participating in a conflagration. Economic development is represented by (log of) GDP per capita in US dollars. This is a simplification, but is adequate for the purpose at hand. As discussed earlier, GDP growth (average for 1973–80) and the ratio of central government expenditure to national product are also included as explanatory variables.

At the international level, the political, strategic and military influences are closely related. These are represented by a single variable, arms suppliers concentration, which adequately represents implicit adherence to a global power bloc as well as foreign military aid. The concentration is measured by a 5 point score for the proportion of arms transfers coming from the principal supplier country; a higher score implies greater involvement with super-powers and more defence-related foreign aid.

The three economic factors, at the international level, require close scrutiny. Foreign exchange is crucial to sustain a modern defence sector and developing countries may find this to be a binding constraint. Its effect is represented by the growth of foreign exchange availabilities (exports of goods and services, aid and the net inflow of long term capital) deflated by the import price index, used in log-transform, over the period 1972–3 (average) to 1979–80 (average).

The potential influence of foreign direct investment in a host developing country was measured in several complementary ways. First, estimates were made of the proportion of the total stock of fixed assets (excluding the government sector and housing) which was under foreign control. As indicated earlier, different views of the role of foreign penetration of the economies of developing countries would lead to opposing expectations of the relationship between the degree of foreign penetration and the size of the military establish-ment, and hence of the military burden. Second, the relative change in the stock of foreign capital assets, from 1973 to 1980, was measured to ascertain whether there was any significant association between changes in foreign ownership and changes in the host country's military effort. Third, the degree to which the foreign capital stock is concentrated in the hands of the controlling developed country was represented by a 5 point score, depending on the proportion of subsidiary and affiliated enterprises of trans-national corporations of the principal developed country involved. This concentration variable is relevant to testing the hypothesis that countries in which foreign capital investment comes mainly from a single dominant investing country are more susceptible to that country's influence on its development policies, including its military policies, than are countries having a diversified foreign investment structure.

Various regressions, with alternative combinations of the in-dependent variables, were estimated by Ordinary Least Squares; the results are essentially similar. We report two empirical equations in Table 7.2, one each for military burden and share. The equations are

Table 7.2 Regression results for defence expenditure

| | Military spending as a ratio of: | |
| | GDP | Central govt. budget |
	(1)	(2)
1. Military factors:		
i. Inter-State or civil war	2.43**	7.68**
	(2.89)	(3.40)
ii. Military government/use of	0.65**	1.33**
violence	(2.63)	(2.16)
2. Domestic economic factors:		
i. GDP %	n.s.	n.s.
ii. GDP growth rate	n.s.	n.s.
iii. Central government spending	0.21**	n.s.
as ratio of GDP	(7.1)	
3. Global political/strategic alliance	0.63**	2.45**
	(2.82)	(4.12)
4. External economic linkages		
i. Growth of foreign exchange	2.79**	4.73*
	(4.06)	(2.44)
ii. foreign direct investment		
a) ratio to total capital stock	−1.15**	−2.59**
	(−3.59)	(2.93)
b) foreign investor	n.s.	−1.38
concentration		(−1.46)
R^2	0.651	0.517
n	72	72

** denotes significance at 1% level, * significance at 5% level, and n.s. means non significance.

well specified with all the different levels (national, regional, global) and factors (military, political, economic) making significant contributions to the overall explanation. The explanatory power of the equations is also high, given the wide heterogeneity of developing countries and the size of the sample.

It is clear that military activity has a high and significantly positive effect on defence spending (both as a proportion of GDP and total government budgets). A country at war may be expected to have a higher military burden of the order of almost 2 per cent. It will also need to spend about 8 per cent more on the military (as a proportion of government spending) relative to other developing countries. Military governments, as well as those with greater use of violence, also tend to spend more on defence (given GDP or State budget) and the coefficient is highly significant.

Turning now to the domestic economic linkages, neither GDP (per capita) nor growth rate seems to exert significant effects on defence. However, as equation (1) shows, central government expenditure has a strong positive influence on military spending. The 'income effect' is of the order of 20 per cent; thus a $1.00 increase in total government spending will raise the defence allocation by 20 cents, a not insubstantial amount.

Moving now to the international factors, we find that the variable used to represent adherence to a global political–strategic alliance, that is, the degree of concentration of foreign arms suppliers, was found to be highly significant. Countries depending wholly or mainly on only one external supplier of military equipment have, on average, a proportion of military expenditure to GDP which is some 2 per cent higher than countries with widely diversified sources of supply. The corresponding difference for the proportion of the military component of the central government budget is 6–7.5 per cent. These differences strongly suggest that adherence to a global power bloc is indeed likely—as discussed earlier—to lead to pressures on governments to expand their military programmes.

Finally, consider the external economic linkages. Availability of foreign exchange has a highly significant role in expanding defence outlay. It is clear that modern armies are import-intensive and this may create difficulties for civilian imports at times of foreign exchange shortage. Foreign direct investment, representing the penetration of foreign capital, is negatively related to defence. It seems that transnationals prefer to invest in countries with low military expenditure, possibly corresponding to low levels of political instability.

Concluding remarks

The study is a comprehensive attempt to investigate theoretically and empirically the major determinants of defence expenditures in developing countries. The results suggest that military budgets are a product of complex interrelationships; national, regional and international linkages are important; so also are the economic as well as strategic–political factors, in addition to the purely military ones. Differences in relative size of defence burdens are not solely a reflection of differences in wars or tensions between neighbouring developing countries. The reasons for defence expenditures are more complicated. More generally, domestic factors, particularly the need perceived by ruling elites to repress internal opposition groups and the ability of governments to raise resources, as well as external factors, including relations with the global power blocs and the availability of foreign exchange to buy armaments abroad, are also major determinants of defence spending.

The topic is important, particularly in the light of research that shows the negative effects of defence on development and growth. These related issues need more analysis—specially for individual countries, utilizing time series data. An analysis of the relative dynamics of defence and civilian shares in government budgets would be particularly useful in the current climate of financial stringency and would have wider implications for our understanding of the causes and effects of defence spending in developing countries—a subject of considerable importance in development theory.

Data sources

Inter-State war or civil war: Sivard (1983); International Institute for Strategic Studies, *Strategic Survey* (various issues); Hartman and Mitchell (1984).

Military government/use of violence: Sivard (1983).

GDP growth rate (1973–80): United Nations, *Handbook of World Development Statistics* (1982).

GDP per capita: World Bank, *World Tables* (1983).

Military expenditures and GNP: ACDA, *World Military Expenditures and Arms Transfers* (1985), 'constant 1982 dollars' series.

Central government expenditure: World Bank, *World Tables* (1983).

Foreign exchange availability: UNCTAD, *Handbook of International Trade and Development Statistics*, 1983 Supplement (1983).

Foreign direct investment:

(i) *Ratio to total capital stock*: authors' estimates of capital stock, based on extrapolation of cross-country regression for OECD countries of current replacement value of capital stock (excluding housing and government

sector) on energy consumption. Value of foreign private direct investment (book values) from OECD, *Development Co-operation* (various
issues), adjusted to current valuation. Log-transformed.

(ii) *Change in foreign capital stock*: OECD, *Development Co-operation*
(various issues). Log-transformed.

(iii) *Foreign investor concentration*: United Nations, *Transnational
Corporations in World Development: A Third Survey* (1983). Scale
value assigned as follows, depending on percentage of principal
investing country in total number of subsidiaries/affiliates of transnational corporations: $0 =$ up to 20 per cent; $1 = 21$–40 per cent; $2 = 41$–60
per cent; $3 = 61$–80 per cent; $4 = 81$–100 per cent.

Aid/GDP ratio: OECD, *Development Co-operation* (various issues). Ratio in
1978–80 (average) as percentage of ratio in 1972–3 (average). Log-
transformed.

Arms supplier concentration: ACDA, *World Military Expenditures and
Arms Transfers* (various issues). Scale values as for foreign investment
concentration.

Note

The authors are grateful to the Leverhulme Trust for financing this research
which forms part of a wider study of the economic relationships between
developing and developed countries.

8

National security, domestic resource constraints and elite choices in the Third World

ROBERT L. ROTHSTEIN

Introduction

A central question in any discussion of Third World military expenditures is why the ruling elites, faced with so many competing demands for the use of very scarce resources, nevertheless spend substantial and in some cases growing amounts on defence and security.

No single answer to this question has gained general acceptance. A wide variety of hypotheses have been advanced to account for some arms spending decisions in some periods. These, together with case studies of national defence decision-making in developing countries, have provided valuable insights but have been less useful in establishing a general conceptual framework to explain the security choices of ruling elites in the Third World.[1]

The assembled evidence appears to show that there are many Third World security problems; that there is often a complex inter-action of internal security threats and external power factors; and that weakness, instability and severe resource constraints tend to focus the attention of elites on questions of regime survival and on the pursuit of short-term relief. In many countries, core values and basic interests are threatened by a range of economic and environ-mental pressures; it is evident that the relevant concept of national security is far broader than encompassed by the classical concen-tration on external enemies, defence composition and military expenditures. At the same time, there is increasing differentiation within the Third World.

A satisfactory conceptual framework to account for Third World security choices requires a differentiated analytical approach, consistent with the variety of factors and circumstances revealed by the empirical evidence. The first step is essentially pre-theoretical. Neither grand theorizing nor another round of case studies will suffice. What is needed is a mapping exercise, an attempt to categorize and differentiate developing countries on the basis of a few key variables so that like can be compared with like. This is the purpose of the present chapter. Section two, below, contains such a mapping exercise. Section three assesses some of the ways it may contribute to devising a conceptual framework which can facilitate the quest for genuinely explanatory hypotheses.

Threat perception, resource constraints, and legitimacy

The difficulties of conceptualizing the security decisions of the developing countries should be apparent. On the one hand, there is no such thing as 'the' security problem in the Third World: differentiation within the Third World itself is growing (from different growth rates, levels of development, resource endowments, political orientations, and so on) and there are unique factors in each case that make grand generalizations inherently suspect. On the other hand, there may be enough similarities to suggest that certain common patterns do exist that at least provide a useful *starting* point for analysis. Threat perception by the ruling elites is likely to be significant in nearly all cases but the threats vary greatly in origin and intensity and perceptions are also likely to be affected in varying degrees by elite judgements about the effectiveness and legitimacy of their own regimes. We shall assume that the interaction of these variables provides a framework for most Third World security decisions and that the framework is sufficiently general to be relevant despite the many differences among Third World states. To provide a brief background and context, some general comments on these variables seem necessary. The comments are obviously meant only illustratively.

We shall assume that the main priority of Third World ruling elites is regime survival.[2] This commonplace is worth emphasizing because the resources that the elites can dispose to assure survival are strikingly limited. Consequently the need to use available resources to insure short-run survival is very strong. These elites are also usually preoccupied with questions of order and stability, which implies essentially the durability of the regime and the relative absence of violence.[3] The key question is whether these goals can be achieved by effective decision-making and voluntary citizen compliance with governmental policies or whether repression and other unfortunate policies seem necessary.

Another factor that seems common in most developing countries is the centrality of the state. While the state takes many forms in the Third World in almost all cases it has great power and autonomy because of its central role in providing security and instituting and managing the process of economic and social development.[4] The functions that the state performs in poor, weak and badly-integrated countries—state–nations rather than nation–states—are particularly crucial. The state must meet the growing demand for certain public goods (security, infrastructure, education, and so on) and for certain kinds of large-scale organization and central guidance. It must also choose an internal development strategy and an orientation toward the international economic system. Moreover, in most cases some share of available benefits must be used to reward followers and protect existing gains, functions that become increasingly important as demands escalate, effectiveness declines and instability threatens. Competition for the control of the state, the major source of power and wealth, is crucial, but also likely to seem dangerous to the winners. It is not surprising that genuine democracies are scarce (competition and participation being dangerous), that nearly 90 per cent of the developing countries are authoritarian, and roughly 40 per cent are under direct military rule. In these circumstances, security decisions are very likely to become a euphemism for using what power the state has against potential or actual internal dissidents. Sharing (limited) power is less attractive or more risky than amassing power to retain control—although amassing enough power to do much more is difficult.[5]

Domestic failures and rising international economic turbulence over the past decade have generated great pressures on the ruling elites and the state apparatus. This can be conceptualized in terms of a substantial resource gap.[6] Maintaining an equilibrium between rising demands and available resources no longer seems possible. Efforts to increase the 'supply' of resources or to decrease the 'demand' from citizens are imperative, but extraordinarily difficult. The governing elites usually do not have the resources to increase growth rates, and greater efficiency in the use of existing resources is either unlikely or insufficient to meet the level of demand. Transforming the economy in response to new patterns of comparative advantage is difficult and risky and foreign resource transfers, which might facilitate a transition, are unlikely to fill the gap. Decreasing demand pressure by persuading citizens to accept even greater austerity will probably increase internal dissidence, and altering priorities and seeking non-economic goals is likely to be possible only in a few cases—as, for example, in Iran under Khomeini. With no spare resources to buy off the discontented and with commitment to the idea of the state itself frequently very weak, it is not surprising that many of the elites have chosen to increase military spending since it seems the only means of maintaining some degree of stability and avoiding a military coup.[7] In any case, how effective the ruling elite is in dealing with the resource gap will have an important impact on security decisions.

The absence of resources sharply narrows the range of elite choices and makes repression and higher military spending more likely, but it also has an impact on the legitimacy of the state. Legitimacy relates to whether citizens are loyal and willingly support state policies—whether they accept the authority of the state and believe existing institutions are in some sense appropriate.[8] Illegitimate governments must use most of the resources they dispose to stay in power and to secure compliance; conversely, legitimate governments can expend relatively more of available resources on public goods. The degree of perceived legitimacy by the ruling elite is thus likely to affect how threats are perceived and how resources are employed in dealing with threats. Legitimacy is of course not associated with a single form of government: democratic regimes with some form of constitutional representation are generally legitimate, but established monarchies, theocracies, and perhaps even some Marxist regimes can also achieve some degree of legitimacy.

Governmental effectiveness is related to legitimacy in the sense that loyalty and support are not likely to survive the state's decreasing ability to fulfil the needs of its citizens. Effectiveness alone, however, does not determine the degree of legitimacy. Effectiveness is largely an instrumental value but legitimacy is largely normative and perhaps ultimately emotional. In contrast to democratic regimes, which rely on some degree of consent by the governed, the mostly authoritarian regimes of the Third World must rely more heavily on effectiveness as the primary form of legitimation—except for quasi-theocratic regimes such as Saudi Arabia and Iran. Note that neither legitimacy nor effectiveness are either/or notions but rather fall along a shifting continuum. In addition, in most regimes, although to different degrees, the most critical component of judgements about legitimacy and effectiveness is compliance and support by politically active elites.[9]

In many developing countries the relationship between effectiveness and legitimacy has seemed to follow one general pattern. As the governing elites seek to protect their own interests and as they seek to reward friends and potentially dangerous enemies with a large share of a 'shrinking pie', the state itself no longer seems to represent the national interest but rather seems to be the spoil of spoils for special interests—a robber state. The state thus loses legitimacy, decreases effectiveness, hastens the politicization of ethnic conflict, increases instability, and may even generate the belief in external enemies that an attack is necessary or justified (as with Tanzania against Uganda). Security policy can be reduced to an effort to keep the lid down on a boiling pot, rather than an effort to diminish the grievances that increase incentives to revolt. The resources that are available to the ruling elites are likely to appear insufficient to develop but perhaps sufficient to repress (more or less) successfully.[10] Simultaneously whatever symbolic resources the state possesses are also devalued.

A state that confronts declining effectiveness and legitimacy is obviously unlikely to attract external aid and investment, unless it appears crucial because of ideological or geopolitical considerations. Also, since the state itself remains indispensable for both national and parochial reasons (especially the latter as resources decrease and the state controls access to whatever is available), regional cooperation is likely to look less attractive than maintaining control of the state apparatus, in part because regional gains are generally modest in the short-run and in part because internal decisions on arms spending may exacerbate external tensions. The fact that there may be large opportunity costs implicit in increased military expenditures is also not likely to be very persuasive to governing elites, unless the costs are much more salient than they seem likely to be, or unless external donors react more negatively than seems likely. The 'opportunity costs' of not spending on the military may seem much higher in terms of elite survivability.

Metaphorically, the point of the argument made thus far is that the 'poverty trap' must also be understood as a 'security trap'—and vice versa. It must also be emphasized, of course, that this interpretation of the importance of effectiveness and legitimacy, as one component of security decisions, is a sketch with many variations. Both variables are difficult to estimate and require some degree of subjective judgement by analysts.[11] Moreover, rapid shifts in effectiveness, and perhaps somewhat slower shifts in legitimacy, may also be likely in some cases. For most developing countries, the capacity to respond to citizen needs and demands is limited and very vulnerable to sudden shifts in resources, regimes and ideologies. We can only hope to make relatively accurate judgements about strengths and weaknesses at any particular period.

Judgements about internal decisions must be joined to judgements about more traditional security issues: threat perception, reflecting the varied threats these countries confront, and threat intensity, which can be divided (crudely) into high or low intensity. If we make the same sort of distinctions for effectiveness (high or low) and legitimacy (high, medium, low), the result is the matrix depicted in Figure 8.1. Placement of the countries in the different cells is based on judgements by a number of expert groups, supplemented by discussions with a few individual experts and, in a few cases where consensus could not be reached, by decisions of the author.[12] The 'mixed' threat cell was most controversial, meaning, in this context, an internal conflict that has spilled across borders either in the sense of sanctuaries for internal dissidents or some support by external ethnic or ideological allies—but not a full-scale international war combined with internal conflict. As such the mixed threat presumably implies less need for massive military spending than a major external conflict but more than for a relatively contained internal conflict. Finally, one very important point needs to be kept in mind: the judgements about country placements were made in May and June of 1984. Thus they do not reflect current conditions.

The use of four variables in the matrix is not meant to imply that other factors are irrelevant. Personal, unique, or idiosyncratic factors are likely to be present in each case.[13] By their nature, it is not possible to include such variables in the matrix. Thus the matrix seeks to reflect summary judgements about the interaction of four crucial variables, variables that seem likely to affect in some fashion nearly all Third World security decisions. Rather than simply listing all the internal and external factors that might affect security decisions—an endless list—we have made some critical decisions about the relative importance of one set of four variables in a particular context. Deviant cases and mistaken expert judgements will always be present and will always undermine more elegant conceptualizations. Still, while the matrix is at best a starting point for analysis, one hopes that it is more realistic than resting content with a few general statements about threat perception. Note that the

		High Legitimacy: Government Effectiveness High	High Legitimacy: Government Effectiveness Low	Medium Legitimacy: Government Effectiveness High	Medium Legitimacy: Government Effectiveness Low	Low Legitimacy: Government Effectiveness High	Low Legitimacy: Government Effectiveness Low
EXTERNAL	Intensity: Low		Costa Rica	Taiwan			
EXTERNAL	Intensity: High	Israel, Saudi Arabia	Cuba	South Korea		Iraq	Somalia
MIXED THREATS	Threat Intensity: Low				Kenya, Ecuador, Tunisia		
MIXED THREATS	Threat Intensity: High		India, Zimbabwe	Libya, Kuwait	Morocco, Iran, Jordan, Peru, Nicaragua, Thailand		Pakistan, Syria, Oman, Bangladesh, Lebanon, Angola, Mauritania, Ethiopia, Mozambique, Chad, Sudan, Guyana, El Salvador, Honduras
INTERNAL THREATS	Threat Intensity: Low	Ivory Coast, Venezuela	Jamaica, Barbados, Colombia, Tanzania	Singapore, Malaysia, Trinidad & Tobago	Algeria, Mexico, Senegal, Brazil, Gabon, Panama, Benin, Nepal, Malawi, Egypt		Haiti, Sierra Leone, Togo, Burundi, Paraguay, Rwanda, Indonesia, Congo
INTERNAL THREATS	Threat Intensity: High		Argentina	Cameroon	Zambia, Dominican Republic, Sri Lanka		Philippines, Uganda, Chile, Guinea, Liberia, Bolivia, Cape Verde, Uruguay, Guatemala, Burma, C.A.R., Madagascar, U.Volta, Mali, Niger, Nigeria, Zaire, Ghana, U.A.E.

Figure 8.1 Country classification by legitimacy and threats

Figure merely provides a classification scheme, which is not 'right' or 'wrong', but rather more or less useful and suggestive.

One variable that might have been used to supplement the other variables in the matrix is regime-type, especially the distinction between civilian and military regimes. However, this distinction no longer seems as useful or important as it once did. The general consensus among most analysts now seems to be that the military have some influence in all regimes, thus suggesting a continuum (not an either/or dichotomy), and that military regimes tend to act much the same as civilian regimes in economic and social matters— an unsurprising outcome since both kinds of regimes face the same internal and external constraints.[14] There is also very little evidence that military regimes act more aggressively than civilian regimes, automatically spend more on arms, or interpret threat situations in a unique manner.[15] Thus in terms of an explanation of patterns in Third World security decision-making, a simple distinction between civilian and military rule is probably not very useful.[16]

In placing countries in different cells in the matrix one might hope to rely on something more objective than the judgements of experts. Various quantitative measures, for example, might be used to supplement subjective judgements, although I have not attempted to develop such measures here. However, a large element of subjectivity will probably always be present, if only because elite and government statements about security threats are not very reliable. All ruling elites tend to insist that they are spending on the military to deal with threats to the nation, not themselves, all or many use or even develop external threats to divert attention from domestic failures or to gain access to foreign arms, and most ruling elites deny the existence of an internal threat for as long as possible because such threats obviously have a large impact on foreign investment and tourism. In any case, no elite wants to be accused of repressing its own citizens—although this has been a burden many have deemed it necessary to bear. In any case, given the unreliability of public statements about threat perception, there seems to be no alternative but to rely on expert judgement to sift through fact and fantasy.

Given the fact that conditions prevailing in the spring of 1984 determined country placements, a proper statistical test of the accuracy of expert judgements will require 1984 and 1985 data on military expenditures. Such data is not yet available. In any event, there will be difficulty in using straightforward statistical tests because, for the elites who make the actual decisions, the two sets of variables are mixed together in a single judgement. Some notion of effectiveness and legitimacy is thus already incorporated in threat perceptions. In effect, the separation of the variables in the Figure reflects expert judgements about relative weights, not practical judgements about specific decisions. However, to get a very crude indication of whether this approach *might* at least be potentially useful, simple unweighted averages for military expenditures in 1983 were calculated. Percentages of central government expenditures rather than percentages of gross national product were used on the assumption that the former were a more accurate indication of elite concerns and priorities. The results are shown in Figure 8.2.

Note that the statistics reflecting combined averages seem to indicate that this approach is useful and that country placements are relatively accurate. If we look at the west to east axis, in each case high legitimacy countries spend less on average than medium legitimacy countries and the latter spend less than low legitimacy countries. If we look at the north to south axis, countries facing a strong external threat in each case spend more than countries facing a mixed threat and the latter spend more than countries facing primarily an internal threat. Comparisons between individual boxes are difficult because too many boxes either have few or no entries, but they also are interesting. In most cases where comparison was possible countries facing high-intensity threats spent more than countries facing low-intensity threats (except in two intersections: external-medium and internal-medium) and countries of high legitimacy spent less than countries of low legitimacy (except in two intersections: internal-medium and external-low). Most of the anomalies represent boxes with only a single entrant, which is obviously insufficient to suggest either the presence or absence of a pattern.[17]

It should not be necessary to emphasize how tentative, preliminary, and provisional these results are. The available data are not very reliable, it is too distant in time from the period of expert evaluations, and the latter can be notoriously erratic. In addition, perhaps the use of additional variables (for example, duration of threat, longevity of regime) would yield even better results. Finally, it is worth once again reemphasizing that certain factors that might be crucial in individual cases (personality, history, culture, and so on) have not been included; the framework provided here suggests where to begin, not where to end.

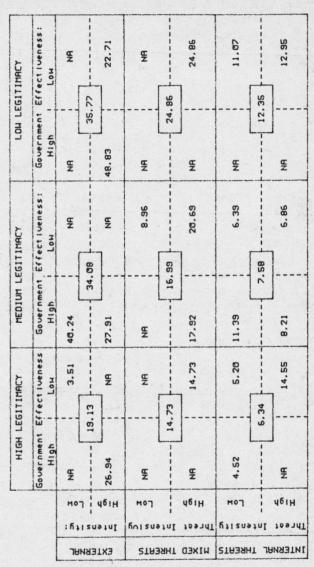

Figure 8.2 Ratios of military to central government expenditures 1983. Unweighted mean of the Military Expenditure/ Central Government Expenditure ratios for countries assigned to each cell in Figure 8.1. Numbers in the boxes at the intersection of dotted-lines are means of the ratios for countries assigned to the four adjacent cells. NA indicates no country is assigned to that cell in Figure 8.1 except Cuba where data are missing. *Source*: ACDA, *World Military Expenditures and Arms Transfers* (1985).

Is there any practical or conceptual significance in this mapping exercise? Do the states in the same cell follow similar policies, and do states in different cells follow different policies? One might ask these questions, for example, about arms procurement policies, the type of force employed, and even the decision-making process itself. These comparisons await further research but we can at least suggest some general insights that emerge from this approach to Third World security decisions.

Connecting some missing links

The Figures emphasize that there is no such thing as 'the' security problem for developing countries: the type of threat and its intensity make a difference. This judgement also implies something about which countries should be compared with which countries: who is spending 'too much' or 'too little' on arms depends on the order and intensity of the threat. The Figures also make the more arguable point that internal conditions—how effective the government is in either meeting or containing citizen demands and to what degree it can count on voluntary citizen compliance with its policies—make some difference in security decisions.[18] This may not be true in all security decisions, especially against an intense external threat, but it seems true in most other cases. This point is bound to be arguable since threat perception is the more salient and immediate factor in the calculations of insecure elites, it is always useful to such elites to attribute their problems to external enemies, and the effectiveness–legitimacy variables are more diffuse and difficult to measure and evaluate. This does not mean, however, that these latter variables are irrelevant. What we seem to have is a shifting and complex pattern of interactions, not the dominance or irrelevance of any particular variable or set of variables. Perhaps another way of making the point is to suggest that the effectiveness–legitimacy variables may set the broad constraints within which threats develop and elites make choices about how to deal with them.

This argument represents a challenge to what is generally called 'structural Realism'. This doctrine asserts, inter alia, that structural conditions (primarily the distribution of power) largely determine outcomes in the international system, irrespective of the nature of the actors within that system.[19] The argument here maintains quite the opposite, that the nature of the actors within the system interacts with power factors—and other things—to produce a complex and varied pattern of responses to apparently similar external pressures. The dispute between structural Realists and their critics can probably never be definitively resolved, since some of the issues at stake involve subjective judgements and values, but it is clear that the argument presented here should provide some support for the critics of structural Realism.

Resource constraints are also suggestive about why it has been so difficult to detect differences in economic and social performance between military and civilian regimes. The type of regime is less important than the pressures created by escalating internal problems and an increasingly unstable and hostile international environment. All regimes, whether radical or conservative, successful or inept, are in increasing need of external resources and thus required, willingly or not, to adjust policies to the dominant international ideologies.

A recent study by Hicks and Kubisch (1984) is interesting in this regard. They analysed thirty-two countries that decreased government expenditures in real terms one or more times from 1972–80 in order to see which economic sectors were reduced more than proportionately and which were protected more than proportionately (relative to the cut in total expenditures).[20] Their results show that the defence sector was well protected but so also were social welfare expenditures; by contrast, the production sector and the infrastructure sector bore the main brunt of the cuts. As the authors suggest, presumably the (relative) protection of the social sector reflects the strong short-run bias of besieged governments. Cuts in social welfare spending have direct and immediate political costs (especially in rising unemployment), whereas cuts in production and infrastructure affect primarily long-term growth prospects (Hicks and Kubisch 1984: 38). In addition, I have separated the military from the civilian regimes and made some rough comparative calculations. The military regimes followed the same general pattern as the civilian regimes, but were well above the mean for the whole sample in production and infrastructure cuts, very slightly above the mean for social welfare cuts, and considerably below the mean (30 per cent) for cuts in defence expenditures. Perhaps this implies that one of the key differences between military and civilian regimes is that the former are able and willing to take more extreme actions against citizens and for their own interests, actions that civilian governments would also like to take but lack sufficient control to do so.[21]

There may be one rather surprising exception to the argument that regime-type is not a very powerful explanatory variable. Note that in Figure 8.1 there is a strong over-representation of relatively democratic regimes in columns 1 and 2. Despite the possession of very limited natural resources and very difficult internal conditions in some of these countries (for example, Jamaica, Tanzania), most have been surprisingly stable. In addition, most spend very little on arms. For example, the Caribbean states, Costa Rica, and Colombia spend under 1 per cent of their GNPs on arms and even a rich oil exporter like Venezuela, which spends a little over 1 per cent, has not emulated some of the other 'oil rich' states. Perhaps this implies that the legitimacy provided by democratic institutions provides a better defence against the failure to meet rising citizen demands than does repression and increased military spending. Implicitly there may be a trade-off in which citizens are willing to accept some degree of shared economic deprivation in exchange for political institutions that provide a degree of genuine political participation and competition.[22]

I do not mean to carry this inference too far because the democracies themselves differ in many ways and there is no formula for gradual conversion to democracy. In effect, the difficult economic and political conditions now prevailing may mean that the existing democracies are a special case in the Third World, not a harbinger of the future. Whether the recent turn to democracy in several Latin American countries is a refutation of this pessimistic judgement or a case of 'premature' democracy, due primarily to the ineptitude of the previous military regimes, is unclear. The latter will be more probable unless the new democracies receive much greater external support than now seems probable. Also, of course, the democracies are far from trouble-free and some have only a precarious degree of stability. Some degree of effective performance is also necessary if legitimacy is to survive, as one can see from the popular coup against democracy in Nigeria and the erratic steps toward and away from democracy in countries like Peru, Argentina and Uruguay. The fact that none of the democracies (except perhaps the special case of Israel) has had the degree of economic success of the Asian 'gang of four' (Hong Kong, South Korea, Taiwan and Singapore) and that this has seemed to provide some justification for authoritarianism (the 'military as modernizers' school, now largely defunct, or the 'technocrats with tanks' school favoured by some analysts) probably implies that the special cases are likely to remain special.[23]

Nevertheless, the placement of the democracies in Figure 8.1 does provide some very tenuous support for the connection between democracy and (relative) stability. It may be obvious but still worth noting that low levels of defence spending provide more resources for development and that the propensity for coups may be restrained by the limited role of the military and the absence of large military resources. This is not to deny that interventions by weak military forces have occurred. Still, the decision to intervene may seem riskier and less a 'natural' response to economic deficiencies in democratic countries. Unfortunately how to move from unstable authoritarian regimes to stable democratic regimes is far from clear.

Many Third World elites have been very conscious of the linkages between security and development. In some cases, especially in Latin America, the military has tended to see development largely as a tool of security and to emphasize a development strategy of rapid industrialization, private enterprise, and an open-economy, export orientation. This has frequently also been joined to hostility against political institutions—order before development—a bias against agriculture, and a gamble on the continuation of an open trading system. This combination of policies, which has worked reasonably well for some of the newly industrializing countries, now seems much more dangerous in an unstable and potentially hostile international system. Whether the correct response to these conditions is, as the United States and various international institutions insist, an even greater commitment to a liberal trading system, joined to an emphasis on more efficient uses of domestic resources, is unclear.

Several points follow. Whatever the development strategy adopted, more and more developing countries are becoming increasingly dependent on a much less generous international system. In addition, since domestic development programmes are doing badly in much of the Third World, rising insecurities among ruling elites will continue to ensure that a large share of available funds will be spent on the military. There is not much point in telling such elites that opportunity costs of defence spending are high. If the elites lack the resources to meet citizen demands, using available resources to facilitate short-run survival is not irrational or surprising. Finally, the linkage between domestic security and development choices and the provision of greater international resources is bound to become more salient; additional resources from abroad will not guarantee more spending on development and less on security, but the absence of such resources ensures that security will continue to get the highest priority.

The probability that additional external resources will be provided is not great.[24] However, if the developed countries believe that patterns of Third World military expenditures are dangerous, either because they injure long-term development prospects or because they generate unstable local arms races (even if the initial impetus is internal), then it is a mistake to act as if the international development debate is largely tangential to the security issue. In effect, Third World security, barring a few cases of direct external aggression, cannot be dealt with on its own terms. Analysing security as a discrete issue in isolation from other internal and external issues does not suffice.

It is of course true that, if more external aid were to be provided, some of it would be misused by corrupt or incompetent ruling elites. Moreover, increased material resources create the possibility of more effective response to citizen needs but they do not guarantee that the possibility will be grasped. Still, while there will be exceptions and anomalies, in a great many cases the provision of more resources is the most plausible means of improving the local climate of insecurity. It does not guarantee success but it is not clear that any feasible alternative is more likely to succeed.[25] One seeks here not only to increase the availability of non-military alternatives but also to affect the perception that security can come only from the barrel of a gun.

Conclusions

Concentrating on narrowly defined problems of threat perception or illustrating the opportunity costs of military spending are necessary but not sufficient if we want to understand Third World security problems. Security problems are also linked not only to internal conditions (effectiveness and legitimacy) but also to the nature of the international environment. These complex and shifting relationships have largely been ignored in the security literature, in part perhaps because of disciplinary boundaries and skills and in part perhaps because there are exceptions either because of the presence of genuine external threats or the dominance of irrational and brutal leaders such as Idi Amin or the 'Emperor' Bokassa. Nevertheless, the continued decline of domestic development prospects and the likelihood that the world economy will grow more slowly in the rest of this decade suggest that the security and development debates will be increasingly linked.

The approach suggested here is unproven and untested. Even if generally correct, it does not simplify the analytical problem, although it may complicate it usefully. Nor will this approach provide policymakers with unequivocal answers to their problems or with a sharp reduction in uncertainties. The implications of the argument in this paper are primarily long-run in focus and even then do not guarantee desirable outcomes such as a reduction in military spending, increased stability, or improved development prospects. The most that can be said is that this approach is interesting enough to justify further work and that it may ultimately permit us to begin classifying security problems more accurately and to begin asking questions that are more conceptually and practically productive.

Notes

1. For a critical review of prominent explanations of Third World security decisions, see Rothstein (1987).
2. Other priorities include increased autonomy and an increase in national incomes, but elite survival takes precedence over both. For a discussion, see Rothstein (1977: 194 ff).
3. Stability is a controversial and ambiguous term with a variety of meanings for both practitioners and analysts. For an interesting discussion, see Hurwitz (1973: 449–63). The ambiguities are not surprising, given that the developing countries are in the midst of great change and given that the origins and causes of instability vary greatly. In the abstract, one assumes that a fully adequate concept of stability must incorporate a capacity to adapt, effective decision-making, and a reasonable degree of legitimacy. But given the focus on immediate survival, the values chosen seem to reflect what the ruling elites mean by stability.
4. For more extended comment on the state, see Rothstein (1984: 553–76). The growing role of the state also means that 'now disaster is attributed, like the rise in oil prices or the high cost of living, to the misrule of governments. . . . ' (Austin 1984: 207).
5. There are some exceptions to these generalizations, especially in regard to the strong governments of the East Asian 'success stories'. These governments have amassed sufficient power to be able to go beyond merely hanging on, but it is not clear how well they will continue to perform if their gamble on an export strategy becomes even riskier and if the new classes created by economic success also begin to demand a greater share of power.
6. The implications of the resource gap for policy-making are discussed more fully in Rothstein (1977: 186–99).

7. If not actually increasing military expenditures, the choice may be to cut it less than other sectors of the economy. There is empirical evidence for this tendency, which will be discussed below.

8. I follow here Lipset's definition of legitimacy as the capacity of a system to engender and maintain the belief that existing political institutions are appropriate (Lipset 1960: 77). An external component should probably be added to the idea of legitimacy these days, in part because of normative pressures and in part because developing countries, desperate for support, are increasingly compelled to pay something more than lip service to external demands by potential donors. But I shall not pursue this issue here.

9. I do not mean to suggest that using legitimacy as a standard is easy or trouble-free. There are many problems in defining the term, in assessing how much legitimacy a regime actually has, in dealing with its manipulation by ruling elites, and in recognizing that some apparently legitimate regimes (Iran, Libya) may violate international norms or behave reprehensibly. However, alternative standards are just as ambiguous, if not more so, and legitimacy is a useful value or standard to assess all regimes.

10. If it is necessary to rely on imported weapons, their relative increase in cost in comparison with available exports probably makes development prospects worse. Whether there is sufficient 'compensation' for this loss in terms of greater military efficiency against internal and external enemies is a question that can be answered only in detail. The same probably holds true for the question whether increased dependence on foreign military and/or economic aid also decreases legitimacy.

11. Note that effectiveness is not equivalent to possessing or not possessing natural resources. We are concerned here with estimating the government's success in meeting at least the minimal (felt) needs of its citizens. Thus even success in extracting revenues is not sufficient; also necessary is some judgement about whether the government uses the revenues efficiently and for the benefit of all. In short, countries with no or few natural resources but with a skilled population and a relatively efficient government can be ranked higher than countries rich in natural resources but with corrupt and incompetent governments (say, Zaire). The same sort of combined judgement is also necessary for rankings on legitimacy: one is assessing the shifting intersection between popular support, government performance and perceptions of likely movements in particular directions.

12. The judgements were made by several regional groups within the Washington chapter of the Society for International Development. I would also like to thank Professor Brian Weinstein of Howard University and two State Department officials who prefer to remain anonymous.

13. Some of these factors are incorporated in the expert judgements but some also are presumably ignored or misperceived.

14. Helpful on these matters is Jackman (1976: 1078–97). Also valuable is Bienen (1980: 168–90).

15. One ought also to note that military regimes themselves vary greatly. Some are very nationalistic, seeking a strong state, a strong army, and close ties to the international economy. Others are obsessed with security, stability, and anti-communism. In short, there is a spectrum of military regimes running from the most radical to the most reactionary.

16. Military regimes may not differ greatly from civilian regimes on socio-economic matters, but they do tend to differ politically in their hostility to democratic institutions and the 'messy' style of democratic politics. There may also be a military bias toward rapid industrialization and central government control of decision-making. Thus, there are real differences between the two kinds of regimes, but these differences are less salient on the issues under discussion here.

17. I have varied the Table in a number of different ways (for one example, by differentiating Internal, low intensity; Internal, high intensity plus Mixed, low intensity; and Mixed, high intensity plus all External; and High Legitimacy plus Medium, High Effectiveness; Medium Legitimacy, low effectiveness plus all Low) but the results have been the same. Thus, I have not included that material here.

18. This argument conflicts with some radical arguments which maintain that military spending is largely fueled by 'supply' pressures from the developed countries. The radical argument overlooks the fact that there are some genuine external threats and that internal factors can be as or more important than external factors. For some radical arguments, see Eide and Thee (1980).

19. The most prominent recent statement of this argument is in Waltz (1979).

20. Hicks and Kubisch (1984: 37–9). Their sample is smaller than one might expect because very high rates of inflation have kept nominal expenditures rising.

21. Perhaps this also suggests that there is, after all, something to the distinction between civilian and military regimes on socio-economic issues. However, the evidence is too sparse to come to any clear judgement.

22. For further comment, see Rothstein, *Peaceful Transitions from Authoritarianism*, A Report prepared for the Office of the Historian, Department of State, June 1985.

23. It is worth emphasizing that many authoritarian governments performed as badly as the democratic governments in terms of economic growth. Moreover, the successful authoritarian governments, as in East Asia, may have created social and economic pressures for some movement toward

democracy. And if these governments begin to perform below citizen expectations, as has begun to happen in some cases, they too may have to rely on the trade-off of increased political rights for (somewhat) diminished economic performance.

24. Except perhaps for the heavily indebted countries and a few others perceived as important on ideological or strategic grounds. Note the difficulty that the African states have had recently in extracting firm commitments for greater resource transfers—despite massive needs and despite promised domestic policy shifts.

25. Much of this aid will have to go to central governments that have not been very efficient or equitable. Unfortunately, strengthening the central government may be a necessary preface to achieving other ends, since there is not likely to be much movement away from repression until or unless the ruling elites feel that their own security is not immediately threatened. The acute moral and practical dilemmas that this raises should be clear, although most developed country governments, while paying lip service to political democracy, have not had much difficulty in supporting existing regimes that seem to offer short-term stability and predictability. Still, some developing countries have at least begun to move away from tight state control of the economy, partly because of inefficiency and partly because of external pressures—but how far this will go and whether it will generate a movement toward political democracy is unclear.

PART IV
Arms Transfers to the Third World

9

Current trends in arms transfers

MICHAEL BRZOSKA

The aim of this chapter is to outline some of the changes in the structure of the arms trade with the countries in the Third World in the last decade or so and to present some thoughts about future developments. The approach is a structural one—it emphasizes changes in the framework and the structure of the arms market within which political decisions and events in both supplier and recipient countries influence volume and composition of arms transfers to the Third World.

The arms boom of the early 1970s

The arms trade had, according to available statistics, a period of unprecedented growth in the 1970s (see Figure 9.1). This period began before the 1970s, but was fuelled by various factors increasing in importance in the early 1970s. One of these factors was the rise in the price of oil (and also some other raw materials); another was the changed attitude of the superpowers towards arms transfer policy. The Nixon administration in the United States had formulated a policy of arms transfers to friendly regionally dominant states in the place of more direct forms of military involvement (Sorley 1983). The Soviet government began to view arms transfers as a source of revenues in addition to political advantages.

The arms boom of the early 1970s was also supported by a procurement cycle. A number of countries had received large numbers of weapons in the 1940s and 1950s, when surplus weapons from World War II, or shortly thereafter, were transferred. The demand for replacement of these weapons became stronger in the 1970s. There also were—as always—some new technological developments receiving much attention, such as guided electronics in traditional weapon systems.

The expansive phase of the early 1970s was still marked by the elements of a hierarchical system—despite its use as an instrument by Western suppliers to recycle money paid for oil and other raw

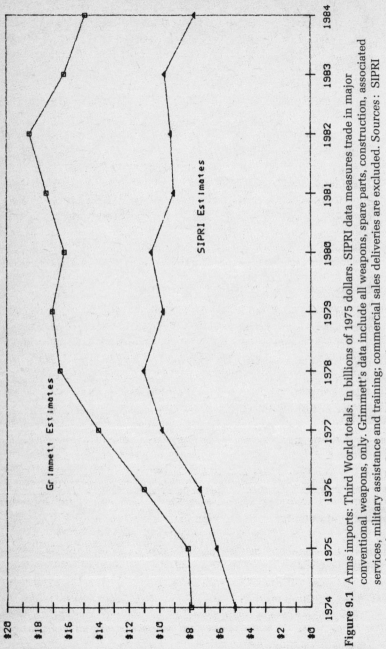

Figure 9.1 Arms imports: Third World totals. In billions of 1975 dollars. SIPRI data measures trade in major conventional weapons, only. Grimmett's data include all weapons, spare parts, construction, associated services, military assistance and training; commercial sales deliveries are excluded. *Sources*: SIPRI Yearbook (1985); R. F. Grimmet (1982; 1985).

materials and by Eastern suppliers to gain hard currency. The French government especially, and following it the West German and Italian governments, looked at arms transfers primarily in a commercial way. But the market shares of these producers were small and both the two superpowers and most recipients attached much political weight to arms transfer decisions. The world was rather tidily, if dangerously, divided up into zones of influence and dependence. In the transfer of weapons both the efforts by Third World governments to break up the world hierarchy and by the industrialized states to strengthen it fused in the early 1970s. The struggle for a new world economic order, led by OPEC, gave many Third World countries the means to buy weapons as a symbol of greater political importance. It was at the same time in the political interest of the great powers to transfer weapons and in the economic interests of all producers to sell weapons.

In the early 1970s the postwar structure of the arms market reached its highest stage. This structure was dominated by the United States and the Soviet Union as suppliers with mainly political aims in their arms transfer policies. The United Kingdom, France and other suppliers acted similarly, though on a smaller scale. Their allies in the Third World were the main recipients. As the 1970s moved ahead, some of the elements that have come to characterize the current, different structure of the arms market— such as increased production in the Third World, increased competition among producers and a less hierarchical structure—became clearly visible.

The interim stage of the late 1970s and early 1980s

Arms imports continued to increase in the late 1970s into the early 1980s, although less spectacularly than in the early 1970s. Much of this continuation of the former trend can probably be attributed to the dynamics of political processes. There are, for example, the dynamics of local or regional arms races that accelerated in the first half of the 1970s, such as between Iraq–Iran, India–Pakistan or Argentina–Chile. Also to be considered are the lead times of arms orders, and these increased with the boom in the first half of the 1970s. Additionally, there is also something like 'vogues' in international relations, and in the 1970s it was much in vogue in many regions of the Third World to arm. Then there was, in a number of cases, the vicious circle of militarization.

Militarization can best be described as an interactive process of increasing influence of the military sector on the various levels of society (Skjelsbaek 1983; Brzoska 1984). It makes good sense to distinguish analytically among (1) a military level proper, which measures the increase in the means to perform military actions such as fighting wars, both internally and externally; (2) an economic level, capturing increased costs of the military sector; (3) an ideological and cultural level, on which an increased importance of military values or values connected with the military, such as nation, honour and order, can be seen; and (4) a political level, on which an increased political influence of the military is felt.

Militarization is fuelled by economic crises and by the weakness of civilian political institutions. In the 1970s such processes of militarization were recorded in a number of countries. In fact, only states with stable political structures (such as India and the Arabian monarchies) seemed to escape the trend towards militarization which accompanied the worsened economic situation of the late 1970s.

Modern weapons systems also have a central position in the process of militarization: they symbolize the—usually outstanding— technological competence of the military; have an effect on the need to modernize at least part of a country's industrial sector; and affect the need to train a share of the country's workforce in modern technology. Their contribution to the military level proper is contradictory, as witnessed by the Iranian example. But the short- comings of modern weapons as direct means of securing political rule are overcome by their value as indirect means. In addition, they can be complemented with military efforts more directly oriented towards regime stabilization, such as counter-insurgency weapons and training of special forces.

Some West European countries were, however, in the late 1970s, in danger of becoming victims of a quite different vicious circle, based on the economic effects of arms exports. Economic problems, especially in the labour market, made it difficult for governments to keep political control over arms transfer policies. It could be shown again and again that the denial of an export licence would result in short-term economic disadvantages, such as the loss of employment, foreign exchange, and contributions to nationally-financed weapons projects. With these arguments, the arms industries were allowed to increase their capacities further. The pressure to export grew. The financial rewards of arms exports in the first half of the 1970s attracted more and more producers into the armaments sector, both in the traditional West European producer countries, such as France, the United Kingdom, the Federal Republic of Germany, Italy, Belgium, Sweden and the Netherlands, and in other countries, such as Spain, Austria and Greece.

While the political demand for weapons remained high, the means to acquire them diminished. There was no new international economic order; instead, raw material prices, with the exception of oil, fell. Many Third World governments realized that the increase in earnings for some among them had decreased the earnings of others and a world-wide economic crisis began to be felt. Borrowing became widespread, not only, but also, for weapons (Tullberg 1985; Brzoska 1983). Government budgets and foreign exchange balances were overstretched in order to keep up with the promises of the 1970s. Arms imports contributed to the destruction of the dream of a new and just economic world order. They cost foreign exchange and diminished the long-term chances to increase the economic independence of Third World countries.[1] They became a source for the further expansion of budgets and foreign indebtedness. In the late 1970s the Third World was more directly in the grip of multinational institutions and banks than ever before. The symbols of greater political freedom of manoeuvre—modern weapons systems—had a high price.

The Carter administration in the United States was first to see the consequences of these trends and to act in a systematic way. It was made easy for the administration as US arms exports had increased so rapidly in the early 1970s. Some clients, such as the government of the Shah of Iran, also gave some indications of where things could go.

One element recognized in the Carter administration was that the costs of grandiose arms import programmes crippled economic development. This required efforts to limit arms transfer to the Third World and to stop the dynamics of arms races in the Third World—in the interests of both recipients and the United States. Another factor was that unlimited arms transfers threatened to weaken the political positions of the superpowers in the Third World. This reasoning was also in line with efforts to limit arms transfers.

Little is known about the Soviet attitude towards arms transfer control at the time (Krause 1985; Kozyrev 1985). But the Soviet willingness to discuss arms transfer limitations with the United States, despite lamentations from many of its Third World allies, indicated that the ideas discussed in the United States might not have been without counterpart in the Soviet Union.

The Carter administration—in addition to the problem of defining its aims—underestimated the political interests of many Third World governments in their arms import programmes and the commercial interests of arms producers, both in the United States and in West European countries.

The Carter administration soon began to retreat in view of the difficulties. The talks with the Soviets were stopped, arms were given to those demanding them, and at the same time plans were drawn up to change from arms transfers back to a policy of greater reliance on the direct use of force (building up the Rapid Deployment Forces). There are indications that the Soviet Union also adapted its Third World arms transfer policy, giving priority to more direct forms of military involvement (for example, in Ethiopia and Afghanistan) and decreasing the importance of arms exports for its trade balance with the Third World.

Some features of the mid-1980s

In the mid-1980s the arms market is marked by low growth rates, stagnation, and even decline. The sources for this situation have to be sought in the Third World and in the relations between the industrialized and Third World countries. The suppliers are not the source of limitation in the arms market; quite the contrary, they have increased their efforts to sell weapons.

The arms market in the early 1980s is characterized by the decreased demand among many of the long-time recipients of arms and the increased supply from both long-time and newly established arms suppliers. It has, in large measure, become a buyers' market. Recipients can choose among many offers. More often then not, the financial and technological arrangements for a weapons sale are more decisive than the quality of the weapons system. A case in point is the Indian procurement of new howitzers. In this case, producers from Austria, France, the United Kingdom, the Soviet Union, the United States, Italy and Sweden all demonstrated their products and negotiated financial terms.

Third World arms production

One factor leading to change in the volume and structure of the arms trade is the growing production of armaments in a number of countries in the Third World (see Figure 9.2). Third World arms production has grown substantially since the mid-1960s, the result of both increases in production capacities in countries with established arms industries and the initiation of production in more countries.

Third World arms production is concentrated in a few countries. Even in the countries with large arms production capacities, self-sufficiency is far away (see Figure 9.3). Dependence on inflows of technology and components remains strong in all countries where the production of state-of-the-art technology is attempted. Even with respect to major conventional weapons, large arms production capacities do not guarantee a high level of self-sufficiency.

Third World arms production has influenced the arms market in several ways. First, while it has not eliminated dependence on the main suppliers of weapons, technology and components, it has changed it from direct political dependence to an economic form of dependence. States are less vulnerable in times of crisis, since they are better able to maintain and repair the weapons in their arsenals and to produce ammunition and at least some of the necessary spare parts.[2] The Iranian resupply in its current war with Iraq provides an example of this phenomenon. While the Iranian arms production programme of the 1970s was over-ambitious and did not result in much production of modern weapon systems, experience in repair of some of the systems and familiarity with general weapons technology was gained. This was then used both to maintain and repair the weapon systems bought in the 1970s as well as weapon systems bought from a large variety of sources in the 1980s.

Second, the increasing demand for arms production technology—both to substitute for direct import of weapon systems and to complement the import of weapon systems—has benefited some exporters more than others. The Soviet Union and the United States have been more reluctant than West European producers to part with arms production technology.[3] For the West European governments it was less important that political leverage decreases with the delivery of arms production technology. They were also less afraid that technology could become available, via some Third World country, to hostile military establishments. Their main concerns were commercial—that the transfer of production technology bred future competitors. In the 1970s and early 1980s it has been the 'newcomers' among the West European producing states who are especially eager to export arms production technology—for example,

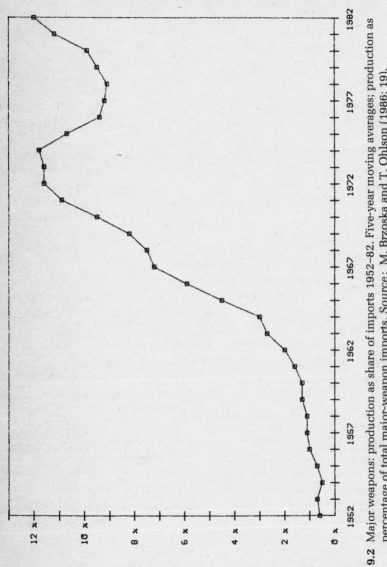

Figure 9.2 Major weapons: production as share of imports 1952–82. Five-year moving averages; production as percentage of total major-weapon imports. *Source*: M. Brzoska and T. Ohlson (1986: 19).

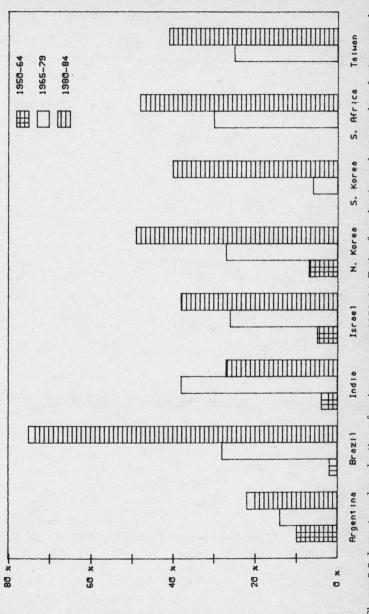

Figure 9.3 Imports and production of major weapons 1950–84. Ratio of production values to values for imports plus production of major weapons. Source: M. Brzoska and T. Ohlson (1986: 28).

Italy, West Germany and Austria. Only in the mid-1980s, for example, did the French arms industry engage in more active promotion of arms production technology.

Third, some developing country arms producers have turned into arms exporters. Governments in the Third World—such as those of Brazil, South Korea, Singapore or Egypt—are even less concerned about political control over arms exports than West European exporting states. Although the share of Third World arms exports in the total imports of major conventional weapons in the Third World has remained comparatively small—around 3 per cent in the period 1981–5 (SIPRI Yearbook 1986)—this has further eroded the position of those exporting states which try to achieve political goals through their arms exports.

Economic crisis

Among the reasons usually given for the recent stagnation in the arms market, the economic crisis in almost all Third World countries is the most prominent (Ingrassia 1985; ACDA 1985). This explanation is plausible, since less growth in GNP and government income decreases the financial basis for military expenditures and procurement outlays. It also derives empirical support from inspection of the trends in arms imports and economic indicators in the 1970s and 1980s. But arms transfers have not moved simply in parallel to economic aggregates in the last decade. There was faster growth of arms transfers in the 1970s—and there is a sharper decline in the early 1980s.

The relation of changes in the level of Third World imports of major conventional weapons to changes in economic growth can be seen in Table 9.1. Both in the early 1970s and in the late 1970s, many more Third World countries experienced increases in the level of GNP/GDP than decreases. At the same time, levels of imports of major conventional weapons increased in most countries, though not in all countries. In the early 1980s, GNP/GDPs were still increasing in the majority of Third World countries, although in fewer countries than in the 1970s. At the same time, the level of imports of major conventional weapons declined in a majority of Third World countries.

A similar difference between the 1970s and early 1980s can also be found in a comparison of the levels of major weapons imports with changes in the growth of GNP/GDP. Already in the late 1970s,

Table 9.1 Clusters of countries: imports of major conventional weapons vs Gross National Product (number of countries from Third World group)

	Change in level of imports of major conventional weapons	
	Increase	Decrease
Change in level of GNP/GDP		
1971–5/1966–70		
Increase	33	13
Decrease	2	2
1976–80/1971–5		
Increase	46	10
Decrease	3	3
1980–4/1976–80		
Increase	16	32
Decrease	6	10
Change in growth of GNP/GDP		
1976–80/1971–5		
Increase	17	6
Decrease	25	2
1980–4/1976–80		
Increase	7	6
Decrease	13	36

Notes

1. 1980–4 levels and growth rates of GNP/GDP computed from preliminary data and estimated from averages where data are missing.

2. All changes computed on basis of five-year averages.

Sources: SIPRI Data Bank; GNP/GDP based on IMF estimates.

growth rates of GNP/GDP were falling in more than one-half of the Third World countries. At the same time, the level of imports of conventional weapons increased in the large majority of countries. In the early 1980s, GNP/GDP growth rates declined in most countries. At this time, the level of imports of conventional weapons also fell in more than two-thirds of the Third World countries.

The effects of worsened economic conditions were evidently combined with a cyclical movement in arms procurement in the Third World. Several factors contributed to this cyclical pattern.

First, there was the build-up of arsenals of major weapons in the 1970s. In the early 1980s, this trend is changed. While arms imports have stagnated since the turn of the decade, military expenditures continued to grow at least until 1983 (SIPRI Yearbook 1986). Figure 9.2 also indicates that the trade in major weapons began to stagnate before the trade in other weapons, spare parts and services. In addition, there was the problem of indebtedness which called for reductions in budget expenditures even in cases where GNP/GDP continued to increase.

Table 9.2 Shares of economic regions in world economic and military sectors, 1983 (in per cent of world total)

Economic regions	Population	GNP	Total imports	Major weapons imports	MILEX
Low-income economies (per capita GNP less than $440)	50.4	5.0	3.1	9.9	7.5
Lower middle-income economies (per capita GNP $440 to $1640)	14.4	4.1	6.1	19.6	2.3
Upper middle-income economies (per capita GNP more than $1640)	10.8	8.5	13.2	26.7	3.1
High-income oil exporters	0.4	1.8	3.8	10.8	5.0
Industrial market economies	15.7	66.8	65.0	25.4	52.4
East European non-market economies	8.3	13.7	8.8	7.5	24.7

Notes: Column 4 computed on basis of imports of major weapons 1981–5.
Sources: World Bank, World Development Report 1985; SIPRI Data Bank.

Table 9.2 shows that the relation between economic aggregates and arms imports is quite different for groups of countries with different levels of economic activity. In the low income group, imports of major conventional weapons are comparatively small— not much larger than the share in world military expenditures. Military expenditures are mostly used to pay the wages of soldiers and officers. (Compared with economic aggregates, both arms imports and military expenditures are relatively large for this group of countries; compared to population, they are small.) For the two middle-income groups, there is a different set of relations. Here, the shares in world-wide major weapons imports are much higher than the shares in military expenditures (and much higher than the share of these groups in world population, GNP, or total imports). The group of high-income oil exporters are heavy military spenders and arms importers—but they use their military expenditures even more for the build-up of infrastructure than for the import of major weapons. For the industrial market economies, which are the largest military spenders in the world, the share of world-wide arms imports is much less than the share of military expenditures. These countries as a group are more than self-sufficient in arms production.

From these data, a kind of substitution cycle for arms imports can be deduced. As national income grows, for countries at the lowest level of per capita income, expenditures on weapons substitute for expenditures on personnel—and the weapons have to be imported. As national income grows, for countries at higher levels of per capita income, domestic production of weapons substitute for imports. This, of course, is only a general trend, modified by factors such as size of the armed forces, depth and type of industrialization, and political decisions. Also, there is no uniformity in the growth of national income; recent years have shown significant differences among countries are more likely, even in periods of a growing world economy. Some countries advance, while others stay behind.

The size of the arms market and its composition are influenced by these various movements, since it is the middle-income groups of Third World countries which are the most prolific arms importers. Should there be a lower rate of growth among the middle-income countries, this would reduce the probability of an increase in arms imports even if the economic situation improved for the Third World as a whole.

Increased competition

In the early 1970s it made sense for all producers to increase their arms exports without much restriction. While it tended to become partially counter-productive for the superpowers at an early stage, for the Western European and the Third World suppliers expansion of arms exports was economically attractive. The attraction even increased with the emergence of economic problems in many producing countries.[4] There was less domestic demand which could substitute for arms exports. The share of arms exports in arms production has increased in the most important West European arms exporting countries—in some, such as Italy or France, earlier than in others, such as the United Kingdom and the Federal Republic of Germany (SIPRI Yearbook 1986).

Increasing supply and decreasing growth of demand resulted in tougher competition. This expresses itself in a number of ways. For example, offsets have become a regular feature of arms transfers (Neuman 1985). In the 1980s, not only the quality and the price of the weapons system are important in negotiating an arms import order, but in many cases the financing conditions are decisive. Buyers can often negotiate very favourable financial conditions. The Brazilian government in 1984 was able, in an extreme case, to negotiate a credit of $200 million for the import of helicopters valued at $100 million. The rest of the credit could be spent on other imports from France.

Another salient feature is the greater marketing efforts of arms producers. There are the traditional outlets of information such as advertisements in the trade press, arms fairs and presentations to governments and procurement agencies. These have increased substantially in the 1980s, with a number of new trade journals and new exhibitions (mostly now staged in Third World countries, close to the customers). There are also the 'non-traditional' practices of the arms market—such as paying high commissions and using intermediaries familiar with the specific interests of a customer. It is difficult to document with hard facts, but it appears that both the involvement of private arms dealers and the payment of commissions have increased in the 1980s.[5]

Hierarchical changes

The shares of the United States and the Soviet Union in arms imports of the Third World have declined in the past decade (SIPRI

Yearbook 1985; Grimmett 1982). Their insistence on using arms transfers as an instrument of domination has brought them into disfavour in the eyes of many potential recipients. In general, there is a less hierarchical structure of the arms market (see Table 9.3).

The number of cases has decreased where only one of the biggest exporters is predominant in the arms imports of a Third World country. This phenomenon is most visible in the case of the United States, and least visible in the case of the Soviet Union. The Soviet Union has a number of clients which, due to lack of finance or political choice, do not consider alternatives to supplies from the socialist countries. The United States and the Western European countries also have such clients, but for most recipient governments there is a choice among suppliers. In a number of cases—such as Nigeria, Kuwait and India—this choice even includes the socialist countries. For Third World countries which can pay for their

Table 9.3 Shares of dominant exporters in imports of major conventional weapons by Third World countries (in number of countries from Third World group)

	USA	USSR	France	UK	Number of Third World countries
More than 90%					
1966–70	9	7	6	2	88
1971–5	9	8	3	4	97
1976–80	3	9	1	3	107
1981–5	3	9	5	2	110
More than 66%					
1966–70	20	17	13	5	88
1971–5	25	14	12	7	97
1976–80	16	20	9	5	107
1981–5	16	18	8	5	110
More than 50%					
1966–70	22	17	13	11	88
1971–5	29	16	15	7	97
1976–80	18	22	13	7	107
1981–5	18	21	15	7	110

Source: SIPRI Data Bank.

weapons, the hierarchical structure of the arms markets has largely broken down.

Arms exports have lost much of their political leverages. They are still a tool of diplomacy—for the United States, the Soviet Union and also other states—but in a different way. They are more indications of reversed leverage, and of the attempts by the sellers to receive the favours of the buyers. An example of this is the willingness of the United States government to supply F-16A aircraft to Thailand, Singapore and possibly Indonesia. For a growing part of the market, however, political considerations are secondary. It is the economic gains that are most interesting. It is seen as a beneficial side effect of arms exports that they stimulate political relations, but few supplier-governments attempt to use them for purposes of political leverage.

There are many elements of the present situation which resemble the pre-World War II period, when there was little government control and economic considerations ruled the arms market.

Possible future developments

The present decline in arms transfers is largely explained by short-term economic conditions and cyclical procurement factors on the side of the recipients. It can therefore be argued that the volume of arms transfers will increase again, if and as economic conditions improve and weapons grow increasingly outdated. Also, weapons are used in conflicts and the number of conflicts has not decreased in the 1980s (Gantzel 1986). But there are also some other structural influences on arms transfers—such as Third World arms production, internal political development in Third World countries and vogues in international relations—which may preclude a return to an arms market with high growth rates.

On the other hand, there is no reason to assume a reduction in the supply of weapons for export. National security policies of the main suppliers emphasize the necessity of maintaining a broad arms production capability to satisfy domestic needs, even where excess capacities and other structural problems have become difficult to reconcile with the profitable management of the industry. The pressure will continue to compensate for the increasing complexity of weapons systems and decreasing numbers of produced items by expanding exports. Arms production which is underwritten by national security needs domestically can be exported at non-commercial terms—although it may be encouraged to earn as much as it can abroad in order to help finance ever-increasing R&D costs. It is mercantilistic logic which is at work here.

In the arms market, this is accompanied by commercialization. Arms deals are accomplished through offsets and financial arrangements. Exporters may be required to sacrifice political goals if they want to get orders. Exporters with some political goals are persuaded to drop them. On the whole, arms transfers lose their outstanding political usefulness for suppliers.

The arms market is becoming less hierarchical; it is more a multipolar than an oligopolistic structure. There are still many customers who, because of lack of finance, have little choice in selecting their suppliers; they must try to receive weapons as military aid. But even at that end of the market, things are changing. Exporters, especially from Third World countries, specialize in upgrading, modernizing and the production of low-priced weapons systems.

One factor constantly working against further erosion of the position of the main suppliers, with their advanced arms industries, is technological progress in arms production. This is heavily concentrated in the countries with the largest R&D programmes. If countries try to import the most modern weapons that are on the market, this favours some exporters over others. There is a tendency for exporters in the middle range of technology—between the cheap-and-simple end and the high-technology end, such as Italy and Austria—to experience difficulties in finding customers.

These developments tend to put greater responsibility for arms transfers control into the hands of the Third World countries, where it is seen to be in their economic and political interests to limit armaments. The capacity of the superpowers to impose control over arms transfers is correspondingly reduced; even if the superpowers might be prepared to limit their own arms transfers, other suppliers will step in. Third World arms control also has the advantage of not being imposed but being achieved by the parties concerned. The less hierarchical structure of the arms market means that the chances of the Third World to sort out its security problems and come up with some limitations are improved. Third World arms production can be encompassed in a limitations regime, if transfer control is expanded to armaments control aimed at force levels.

One obligation of the exporting countries must be to reduce the pressure emanating from their arms industries so that Third World limitation regimes are not threatened by the commercial activities in some exporting companies. They can also help via the improvement of the world economic situation and the strengthening of Third World democratic institutions, thereby reducing the dangers of militarization processes. In addition, it would facilitate Third World arms limitations if the superpowers could agree on means to constrain their conflicts in the Third World and reduce their efforts to recruit allies and build up intervention forces. The current trend towards more intervention capabilities and threats towards the Third World undermines all efforts to enhance Third World security from within the Third World.[6]

There is currently not much to be seen in terms of Third World attempts at arms limitations. There are some hopeful signs in Latin America and South Asia, but not more. A prediction of Third World agreements for limiting armaments would currently be most unsound if judged by visible actions. But the logic of it is compelling and might influence politics.

When the Non-Proliferation Treaty was signed in 1970, the prediction that there would be no further Third World states admitting possession of nuclear weapons was very risky. Still, in that case, the political logic of trying to limit nonconventional weapons in the Third World has so far succeeded. In the conventional field, things are more complicated, since more actors and different interests are involved—and the interests of superpowers, other suppliers and Third World governments are mixed in a different way. Still, the underlying logic, that it would be better to use resources for development purposes rather than for weapons, which cannot provide permanent security, remains the same.

Notes

1. For an early statement about the incompatability between a continuation of arms transfer patterns and a New International Economic Order, see Lock (1981).
2. Still, in the mid-term, even more advanced armaments producers remain vulnerable in the supply of spare parts and ammunition. See Harkavy (1984) and Subrahmanyam (1986).
3. See the statistics in Brzoska and Ohlson (1986); for a detailed discussion of United States policy on transfer of technology in this field, see Klare (1983).
4. An econometric investigation showed differences between exporting countries: for the United Kingdom, the United States and the Federal Republic of Germany, military expenditures and arms exports were

negatively correlated; but the opposite was true for France and Italy. See Smith, Humm and Fontanel (1985).

5. A revealing case was made by the military government that took power in Nigeria on New Year's Eve, 1983. One of their charges against the Shagari government was that extensive use of bribes from arms import deals had been used for the election campaign. In the Iraq–Iran war, private dealers play an important role as intermediaries for both sides. An account of some deals originating in Belgium is found in Ralet (1982).

6. This is eloquently argued in Subrahmanyam (1986).

10

Arms trade and the Third World: Spain's growing participation

ARCADI OLIVERES

Introduction

The inclusion of this chapter's title in an international volume on defence, security and development can be taken as a sign of the interest which the Spanish presence in the world armaments market has awakened in recent years, as was first made evident in the appearance of Evamaria Loose-Weintraub's article (SIPRI Yearbook 1984) dedicated entirely to the production and exportation of arms within the framework of Spain's new defence policy.

This presence in the world market certainly is new, as also are the studies on the subject which are beginning to appear. In fact, the secrecy on such matters that prevailed under Franco's rule, as well as the reduced size of the sector, made it difficult during that period to conduct the kind of economic analysis which was made in other areas of industrial production.

It may come as a surprise that we speak of the 'reduced size' of the armaments sector during a period when the country was ruled by a pre-eminently military government. This apparent paradox can be understood, however, by considering the fact that the military objectives of the time were basically aimed at controlling the Spanish people and that this control could be carried out effectively using light arms, with no requirement for large-scale investment.

Thus, the present appears to be the right time to encourage, in Spain and to some extent in the other Latin countries, the kinds of arms-industry studies which, until now, have focused primarily on English-speaking countries.

Growth of the Spanish armaments industry since 1982

The growth of the Spanish armaments industry and trade is a post-Franco phenomenon which began to take off in 1982. The year 1982 is important in this account for several reasons. Spain officially joined NATO on 30 May, the Spanish Parliament having passed the 'Armed Forces Sustenance and Investment Budget Act' five days earlier; these two elements defined Spain's medium-term armaments policy. The victory of the Partido Socialista Obrero Espanol (Spanish Worker's Socialist Party) in the legislative elections of 28 October of the same year, and the ensuing implementation of its Economic Programme, established the context of industrial policy.

We can identify three factors which converged to enlarge the demand for armaments in Spain: the goal of modernizing the defence apparatus to bring it into line with that of NATO; the capacity to mobilize considerable financial facilities; and the determination to stimulate growth of certain industrial sectors which could replace those undergoing reorganization. The higher demand for armaments could logically be expected to spark new production or, by default, importation.

Discussion of the firms that would be responsible for this new production, and thus become the focus of its growth, must refer primarily to enterprises related to the national industrial development agency, the Instituto Nacional de Industria (INI). Since its creation in 1941, the INI Defence Division has been structured around three firms: Empresa Nacional Santa Barbara, Empresa Nacional Bazan, and Construcciones Aeronauticas. These three firms are dedicated to military production and cater to the Army, the Navy and the Air Force, respectively.

Other firms also associated with INI but dedicated to more specific lines of production should be identified. CETME, engaged in light arms production until a few years ago, now serves as a Research and Development company for the military industry. ENASA participates in the production of armoured vehicles. ENOSA produces military applications of optics. INISEL is responsible for electronic warfare *matériel*. DEFEX coordinates and organizes the exports of the listed firms and other private companies.

In recent years this sector of industry has grown rapidly, as is shown by the data appearing in Table 10.1 for sales, exports, investment, and research expenditures in the period 1976–86. Over this span of years, production of the sector has risen from 1.3 per cent to 1.6 per cent of the Spanish industrial gross domestic product.

This growth has, however, been accompanied by other characteristics which should be noted. First, employment in the sector has remained practically unchanged—in the 26,000 to 28,000 range—throughout the period. Second, the sector is importantly dependent

Table 10.1 INI Defence division performance indicators, 1976–85
(in millions of pesetas and number of workers)

	Earnings				Research	Workforce
				Investment	Expen.	(number of
	Gross	Net	Exports	Expen.	(a)	workers)
1976	28,777	489	7,124	2,143	773	26,054
1977	32,183	755	10,757	1,730	285	26,054
1978	36,708	2,662	10,757	1,146	409	25,607
1979	36,198	3,702	13,575	4,457	432	25,471
1980	64,002	3,159	17,641	3,765	261	26,049
1981	73,730	2,381	36,594	3,815	1,114	27,400
1982	109,859	1,000	53,903	6,449	1,749	28,341
1983	132,349	6,528	72,878	7,185	1,749	27,923
1984	144,229	16,623	89,182	6,253	1,903	27,478
1985	122,809	19,633	44,959	6,312	2,300	27,295

Notes: the data included here (except for research expenditures) refer to the three most important firms of the INI Defence Division—*Santa Barbara*, *Bazan* and *Construcciones Aeronauticas* (CASA)—for which continuous information is available. Although information on the armaments sector is incomplete, these three firms account for some 65 per cent of the total for the sector—or, at least, that part of the sector which is known.

(a) Total research expenditures for public and private firms. Projections of research expenditures are 7,419 million pesetas in 1986 and 30,000 million pesetas in 1990.

Sources: Mir (1986), 'El complejo militar-industrial espanol', *Mientras Tanto* (for 1976–81 data); *Fomento de la Produccion*, *Campeones de la exportacion* and 'Las 2000 majores empresas espanolas' (for 1982–5 data); Mir (1986a), 'L'estructura i politica militar-industrial espanyola des de finals dels 70' (for research expenditures data).

on evolving technology, particularly that of such subsectors as aeronautics and electronics, which have received priority treatment. Third, the overall economic performance of the sector has been marked by consistently negative net earnings, which are made up by public subsidy—clearly demonstrating that the criteria at work are more political than economic. Fourth, and in contradiction to the persisting negative net earnings, there has been a continuous and significant investment effort in the sector. Finally, it should be added that there is not sufficient information yet available to evaluate the performance of the group of private firms in this sector;

their significance is probably greater than that usually attributed to them.

Spanish arms exports

The most important result of the recent expansion of the Spanish armaments industry has undoubtedly been the growth of its exports. The prospect of export growth has also been used as one of the most common political justifications for enlargement of the sector.

Economies of scale normally require a level of production greater than domestic absorbtion; foreign markets are needed for this sector to be profitable. This is clearly the case in Spain where arms exports are intended to compensate in part for the considerable volume of foreign exchange being spent on the importation of weapons systems, as part of the defence modernization plan.

In organizational terms, Spanish arms exports are carried out by three firms in which INI participates directly or indirectly: DEFEX, CIREX and ALKANTARA.

DEFEX is the focal point for arms export activity. Its shareholders are the most important firms of the sector, both public (Santa Barbara, Bazan, Construcciones Aeronauticas, INISEL) and private (Plasticas Oramil, Esperanza y Cia, Explosivas Alaveses, Instalaza, Placencia de las Armas). Together with its subsidiary CIREX, DEFEX is responsible for the promotion, sale and financing of arms exports and it maintains offices in Madrid and Washington for these purposes.

As a complement to DEFEX, of which it is a subsidiary, ALKANTARA Iberian Exports Ltd. is primarily dedicated to the Middle East market—which is very important for Spain—and maintains representatives in Nicosia, Riyad and London for that reason.

At the same time, as an indirect means of promoting exports, Construcciones Aeronauticas maintains subsidiaries in Indonesia (Airtech Industries, which builds parts of fuselages) and in the United States (CASA USA, Inc., which acts as a business agent).

An overview of the 1976–84 period confirms the relative importance of growth in exports. Over this period, for the three main firms of this sector (Santa Barbara, Bazan and CASA), the current value of total sales increased by about 50 per cent, but exports more than doubled. The composition of arms exports during the years 1976–85 consisted of the following products:

Naval shipbuilding	47%
Aeronautical production	15%
Explosives and munitions	15%
Vehicles	15%
Electronic *matériel*	6%
Other products	2%
Total arms exports	100%

It is difficult to quantify the value of these arms exports by destination because the statistical information available from the State Customs Office is unreliable. These transactions are often recorded without specifying the contents of the material being expedited, or camouflaging the material with such vague descriptions as 'miscellaneous' or 'machine parts'. The process used to expedite arms shipments abroad sometimes seems designed to hide a guilty conscience underlying the transaction. The shipments are customarily made in vessels flying a flag of convenience (such as Liberia, Gibraltar, or Panama) and depart on the weekend in order to pass unobserved.

None the less, the available information about these shipments is sufficient to demonstrate that the bulk of Spanish arms sales abroad are made to countries of the Middle East and Latin America. It can also be shown that, during the period 1981–5, the value of Spanish arms sales to the Third World comprised between 3 per cent and 5 per cent of the total value of such sales—placing Spain between twelfth and fourteenth place in the world ranking of arms merchants.

These magnitudes are confirmed by information on international arms contracts assembled by the International Institute of Strategic Studies (IISS) and published in the volumes of *Military Balance* for the years 1983–4 to 1985–6. The IISS reports that, of the 427 most important contracts registered in those three years, 17 correspond to transactions in which Spain was the supplier-nation and 12 to transactions in which Spain was the buyer-nation. The sum of these Spanish contracts constitutes 6.8 per cent of the world total–a proportion far higher than Spain's share of world population or production.

The fact that there was a significant number of transactions in which Spain was the buyer highlights another important aspect of the Spanish arms trade. Spain is a substantial importer of arms supplied by developed countries. It should be noted that, as a result of her 1983 contracts with McDonnell Douglas to purchase seventy-two F–18 Hornet jets, Spain became the United States' major arms customer in that year.

Financing arms exports and use of foreign development aid

It should be acknowledged that success in penetrating the present-day international arms markets is not attributable solely to better product design, quality, or price. It generally requires other conditions—which can be of greater importance than quality or price factors—such as compensatory business arrangements, counter-trade agreements, provision of financing facilities, or political events.

In the case of Spanish arms exports, there are important differences between sales made to developed countries (a small part of the total) and sales to developing countries. Some shipments made to industrialized countries are the result of concessions granted to Spain as compensation for her purchases previously made in those countries. These arrangements account for the majority of Spain's arms-export contracts with France and the United States.

With respect to Spanish arms exports to developing countries, the attractive element almost always consists of the financing aspects of the transactions. There are two exceptional cases: Spain's relationship with Indonesia and Chile is based on the installation of subsidiaries or sub-contractors of Spanish firms in those countries.

Aside from these two cases, the provision of payments facilities and concession of easy credit are significant features of the Spanish arms sales transactions. An example is provided by the sale of arms to Egypt, which represents the largest transaction of this kind carried out by Spain up to the present time. The contract which effected this sale was signed in August, 1982, and included the supply by Spain of 600 BMR-600 armoured vehicles, 1,200 coaches, 10,650 off-the-road lorries—and a later supplement of 2 frigates and 2,000 Land-Rovers—at a total value of 170 billion pesetas. Egypt's inability to finance this astronomical sum resulted in Spain's offer to cover as much as 85 per cent of the purchase total value in the form of 'easy' credit facilities provided by the Banco Exterior de Espana (Spanish Overseas Bank), while the remaining 15 per cent was financed by *fondos de ayuda al desarrollo* (foreign-aid development credits: FAD).

It is this use of development-aid financing which seems to underlie a large number of Spanish arms exports transactions—

although the information is incomplete and hypotheses about this practice remain subject to confirmation. None the less, it is known that nine of the nineteen countries which have received Spanish aid through FAD credits are at the same time important customers for Spanish armaments; these customers are Angola, Gabon, Equatorial Guinea, Morocco, Mauritania, Mexico, Peru, Sudan and Turkey. It should be acknowledged that this is the normal practice of many arms-exporting countries, but it does demonstrate Spain's willingness to participate energetically in an international market in which political and economic interests override ethical considerations.

Legal regulations and intermediaries

Unlike many European countries, where a tradition of arms exportation has led to the creation of regulatory legislation, in Spain supervisory policy is almost non-existent: the basic norm is to sell without asking any questions. The attitude underlying promotion of arms sales, attributable to the firms involved as well as the government, was illustrated by an item which appeared in *La Vanguardia* on 4 April 1986, which stated, 'The possibilities of exporting to Latin American and Third World countries seem to be quite real. It might be better for these countries not to buy armoured tanks, but if they have to buy them then they might as well be made in Spain.'

In theory, there are some institutions devoted to arms traffic control. First, there is the Comission Interministerial reuladora del comercio de armas y explosivas (Inter-Ministerial Arms and Explosives Trade Regulatory Commission), created in 1978. The Commission reports to the Secretary of State for Defence who, in turn, refers instances of arms shipments abroad to the Government; authorization for the shipment must be granted in accordance with the final destination certificate which endorses the merchandise. The legal loopholes derive from the fact that this authorization is only necessary in the case of 'war *matériel*' as defined by an especially obsolete regulation from 1944—and only applies to shipments destined for 'zones of conflict' whose specification is particularly ambiguous. The reality is that there is no effective follow-up to confirm the destination of the merchandise; even more important, there is a notable lack of oversight by any parliamentary supervisory commission.

This legal laxity in the matter of international arms sales frequently enables Spain to play the role of intermediary in the export transactions of third party countries for which certain destinations are prohibited. Thus, for example, Spain was recently cited together with Italy and Paraguay in the trial of the Düsseldorf firm Rheinmetall, accused of having exported arms to Argentina during the military dictatorship, to South Africa and to Saudi Arabia—all with the help of the countries listed. According to information furnished during the trial, Spain's participation consisted of re-expediting a shipment of anti-aircraft guns by providing a change of vessel.

There are political and diplomatic connotations of this attitude respecting international arms trade. One example was provided in a recent session of the United Nations Human Rights Commission convened for the purpose of condemning the Indonesian government for genocidal actions carried out in East Timor. The Spanish delegation abstained from voting on the resolution of condemnation—for fear, it would seem, of possible consequences on business relations between the firm CASA and its Indonesian subsidiary NURTANIO.

Final comments

The description of the defence industry sector in this chapter permits us to characterize the Spanish position as that of a country with an armaments industry in an intermediate stage of development, but with a clearly expansionist aim which requires the search for markets among Third World countries.

This intermediate stage of development is further demonstrated by the fact that, while arms sales are normally channelled toward the domestic market or Less Developed Countries, Spain's more sophisticated arms acquisitions depend on importation—especially from the United States and France. We may observe that Spain has a level of technological development which combines domestic patents with foreign licences, although the use of the latter is limited by the Co-ordinating Committee for Eastern Trade (COCOM) agreements.

The expansionist tendency is perhaps the clearest feature of the current industrial and commercial panorama. The armaments sector and others closely related to it have emerged as a result of 'reindustrialization.' In the list of seven sectors which the Finance Ministry Planning Office has designated for future priority development, five (electronics, data processing, defence itself, aeronautics and new development areas) are clearly involved directly or indirectly in armaments production.

It is useful to identify the reasons for the selection of these sectors, and legitimate to ask whether or not they constitute the best option. We conclude this chapter by considering these questions.

Both the Defence Minister, Narcis Serra, and his Secretary of State, Eduardo Serra, have justified expansion of the armaments industry and trade by reference to three hypothetical benefits: employment, technology and the balance of trade. In brief, it is their reasoning that, at a time when it is difficult to identify promising sectors for industrial development, the armaments sector offers the possibilities of sales in foreign markets and meeting a public need. They expect that expansion of this sector will (1) create jobs, directly and indirectly; (2) require the generation and acquisition of technologies whose applications will later spill over into civilian activities; and (3) bring about substantial earnings of foreign currencies through the placement of a significant amount of this production in foreign markets. Advocacy of this schema is accompanied by the spectre of unemployment and the mirage of 'modernization' as the panacea which will bring about the reorganization of the country's industry.

The questions of employment creation and technological innovations attributable to military industries have been studied for some time in many countries of the world; the empirical evidence from these studies corroborates the conclusion that military production is less effective than civilian production in both creation of jobs and technological innovation. At the same time, the expansion of the world arms trade does not seem to offer favourable economic prospects to the Less Developed Countries, as demonstrated by various reports on this subject drawn up by the United Nations. Nor are the present circumstances very favourable for the arms-exporting countries: France, for instance, is experiencing difficulty in placing its military products abroad. We may also observe that, regardless of the export trade, development of the armaments industry requires enlarged domestic consumption of military *matériel* paid for by the State, generating substantial costs for the public budget.

Taken together, these factors would seem to indicate that, from a strictly economic point of view, the prospects for the development of the Spanish armaments industry are not as promising as the authorities have tried to indicate—and public opinion has come to believe.

If, in addition, we consider the ethical aspects—which can by no means be left out of account—we could come to the conclusion that, in the case of Spain, the path taken since 1982 is not the best one to justify speaking of the country's active participation in a policy of peace and world development. Our only hope is that there may still be time to change.

11

Arms transfer control: the feasibility and the obstacles

HERBERT WULF

Not surprisingly international initiatives to limit or reduce the volume of arms trade or to prohibit the transfer of the most sophisticated weapons have more or less failed. Neither agreements between exporting countries or among importers, nor UN resolutions, have led to desirable results.

Despite official declarations from governments in the West, East and South underlining the necessity of controlling the arms trade, growth rates of exports of the weapons industry outranked growth rates of almost all other kinds of trade during the last decade.[1] When proposals that link or associate disarmament and development are made by government, it is usually the armaments of the perceived adversary which are criticized and the need of a policy change in other countries which is meant.

Policy makers in NATO countries draw attention to the dynamics of armaments in Warsaw Treaty countries and vice versa. Governments in Third World countries criticize the huge overkill capacity in the North while at the same time Third World countries are themselves criticized for using their limited resources for military ends.

The Palme commission (see Palme 1982) concluded that it is rather unrealistic to expect disarmament to take place if one waits for government initiatives. This is a remarkable, extraordinary and pessimistic assessment from an elite that is at present, or was in the past, part of the centre of political decision making. What is the history of arms transfers? What initiatives for arms transfer restraint have been taken in the past and what has been the result of these initiatives?

Pattern of arms transfers to the Third World

The historical pattern of arms exports into Third World countries has been one of constant increase in both the volume (until the end of the 1970s) and the complexity of weapon systems. To understand the feasibility and the obstacles of arms transfer control it is essential to look at the motives for arms transfers.

The use of military force is not a new phenomenon in that part of the world which is today called developing or Third World. Distinct phases of militarization and an intensified flow of arms in the post-World War II period can be identified. (The use of violence in these regions, of course, did not begin with the period of colonization.)

The process of decolonization, partly a result of weak post-World War II positions of the colonial masters, was not at all peaceful. In several cases armed conflict forced European countries to give up their colonies (for example, Indonesia, Algeria, Vietnam, Angola, Mozambique). In other countries European and Japanese positions were given up and replaced by US influence. The manifest US superiority in practically every field after World War II has been of great influence for the evolution of military doctrines in the Third World. Military aid programmes, installation of military bases, specialized training centres for foreign military officers and export of US arms (usually second hand World War II equipment) on credit or grant basis led to an inflow of weapons into the Third World.[2] The recipients—in many cases—were the military forces that had previously served as colonial armies, with the function of controlling internal unrest and fighting the anti-colonial struggle.

Since the end of the 1940s and early 1950s arms have increasingly been supplied by the United States to Third World countries with reference to the Cold War between East and West. Countries bordering the Soviet Union and its socialist allies in Europe and Asia were generously supported and supplied with weapons free of cost or at reduced prices to guard against what was perceived as Soviet expansion or to even roll back communism. A system of several military alliances was founded or bilateral military treaties concluded and a string of military installations established.

The Soviet Union and its allies entered the international scene as a major but restrictive weapons supplier only after 1955. After the death of Stalin the Soviet government more actively tried to establish friendly relations with Third World governments outside the socialist group of countries. The leaders of the nonalignment movement, particularly Nehru of India, Peron of Argentina, Soukarno of Indonesia, and Nasser of Egypt were considered as possible collaborators, even though they were not anti-capitalist, but anti-imperialist. Soviet economic and especially military aid programmes were particularly aimed at the Middle East and were accepted in several countries. Until 1970 only twenty-nine developing countries had received weapons from the USSR while the United States had exported military equipment to almost all countries of the Third World. A decade later more than forty developing countries imported military equipment from the Soviet Union (SIPRI 1971: 10–11; SIPRI 1973: 299; ACDA 1985: Table III).

West European arms suppliers (France, Britain) that had lost ground to US companies tried—almost exclusively for economic reasons and to a lesser extent for political ends—to recapture a share of the market in their former colonies. At a later stage (especially since the early 1970s) West German producers competed by offering the export of arms production technology, licences and transfer of know-how for indigenous Third World weapons productions.

During the 1960s a crisis in development and development theory was apparent and led finally to an intensification of armaments in the Third World. Military expenditures increased, more resources went into the importation of weapons and *coup d'états* ocurred in many countries for the explicitly stated reason of replacing incapable politicians and taking charge of development policy. Only then did development sociologists begin to study, on a reasonably systematic scale, the role of military. A theory of 'modernization', was formulated and research was concentrated on the military elites as an agent of social change (Albrecht, Ernst, Lock and Wulf 1974: 177–80). The military was identified as a key group that was able to promote development due to its technological competence, managerial skill, organization and social cohesion. At the same time this analysis offered the legitimacy necessary to intensify military aid and arms supplies to undemocratic governments and military regimes (Wolpin 1973; Wolpin 1981).

A policy change was adopted in the United States during the Nixon administration. In 1969 as a result of the Vietnam experience the Nixon doctrine was formulated, emphasizing the self-reliance of Third World armed forces in their fight against outside aggression and de-emphasizing US involvement by stressing the need of burden-sharing. As a result of the Nixon doctrine the Military Assistance Program was substantially reduced and the major portion of arms exports were carried out under strictly commercial terms.

During the early period of *détente* the political situation in the Third World was astoundingly stable. The Nixon administration expected continued stability that would limit Soviet chances to expand its sphere of influence. This faith in stability, on which *détente* was built, was not well founded. A second wave of revolutions (after a first wave in the 1950s and early 1960s in the process of decolonization), starting in Ethiopia in 1974, swept a number of Third World countries, especially the former Portuguese colonies (Halliday 1983). United States–Soviet competition in the Third World was enhanced and the hope of US governments to preserve the status quo was wiped away.

Since 1973, when oil prices increased dramatically several Third World countries have had almost unlimited hard currency funds at their disposal. A substantial part of these funds has been used for arms imports. Growth rates of arms imports, never experienced before in the period since World War II, led to increased armament, especially in the crisis-prone Middle East, and at the same time resulted in recycling the oil income into the traditional financial centres in the West.

This trend has been reversed since the end of the 1970s. Arms imports of Third World countries have been stagnating or have decreased in some years, neither because suppliers were reluctant to export nor because importing countries had changed priorities from armaments and underdevelopment to disarmament and development. Two reasons have to be mentioned. First, many developing countries are increasingly developing—with assistance from the West—their own arms production industries, particularly in Brazil, Israel, India, and Argentina, but also on a somewhat limited basis in Taiwan, South Korea, Singapore, South Africa, and so on.[3] Second, and probably more important, several of the major importers are highly indebted—as has been mentioned above—while oil exporting countries have had to substantially lower oil prices and have thus been obliged to cut imports, including in many cases imports of arms.

Past experiences and future initiative of arms transfer control

If governments cannot be expected to promote disarmament, as was stated in the Palme commission's report introduction, who can? What is to be done? What kind of initiatives have been taken to control the flow of arms into the Third World and what were the effects?

Direct measures on the international level

International agreements between supplier-countries The best known initiatives to control conventional arms transfers on the international level has undoubtedly been the so-called 'conventional arms transfer talks' (CAT)[4] suggested by Jimmy Carter, former President of the United States. During his election campaign in 1976 restraint of the extraordinary growth of arms trading with the Third World was one of Carter's campaign issues. After his inauguration President Carter took the initiative to negotiate with the Soviet Union. Carter specified in a policy directive that arms sales would be an exceptional foreign policy instrument, to be used only in instances where transfers would contribute to the national security of the United States. The United States unilateral restraint was implemented before the CAT negotiations started in so far as a dollar volume ceiling was placed on new commitments. However, it soon became apparent that this policy was not strictly applied since certain countries and commercial sales were excluded from these restrictions. Carter stressed, that he expected his unilateral approach to be positively received by the Soviet Union. He hoped to reach an agreement that would lead to an exporters' cartel.

Examples of different kinds of such export cartels still exist. One of the more or less functioning cartels is the so-called coordinating council of the majority of NATO countries plus Japan (COCOM) for the control of military related technology transfers to the Warsaw Pact Treaty countries (Krause 1981: 196–7). The decisive differences between the COCOM model and a conventional arms export cartel are, of course, that in COCOM only Western countries are members and that COCOM attempts to deny certain technologies to a group of countries that is perceived as a common enemy. A conventional arms export cartel would consist of countries with very different and often even conflicting interests.

The London Suppliers Club, an informal group of major nuclear technology producing countries, is another parallel example. The task of this club is to prohibit the proliferation of military-relevant nuclear technology. The success of the London Suppliers Club is not extremely convincing since many developing countries, with the help of industrialized countries, have been able to develop the technological potential to produce nuclear arms at present or in the near future.[5]

Export cartels could be implemented on different levels. One possible concept is a global approach, which would establish an agreement between the major arms exporting countries like the United States and the Soviet Union (together totalling approximately 70 per cent of the global arms trade) as well as France, Great Britain, the Federal Republic of Germany and Italy (together totalling an additional 20 per cent of global arms transfers). An agreement between these countries could restrain or reduce the volume of arms export. An alternative to this quantitative approach could be qualitative reductions of certain arms technologies. The difficulties experienced in trying to find global solutions are most pertinently illustrated by the CAT negotiations. One of the problems of the global agreement is that it neglects to consider the need for regional restraint. There exist a number of regional arms races, for example in the Horn of Africa, the Near East and on the Indian sub-continent. The intensity as well as the duration of wars fought in these regions has been influenced decisively by arms supplies. The 1965 war between India and Pakistan for example had to be terminated within a relatively brief period when the United States and Great Britain, the major suppliers of arms at that time, agreed upon an effective embargo against the two adversaries. Another example is the French embargo against Israel in 1967 at the time of the Six Day War. One example of a regional agreement—almost forgotten in the meantime—was a US/USSR/UK/ French agreement to withhold arms deliveries to the Middle-East that held from 1947–55.[6] Both the experience of several Arab–Israeli wars and the CAT negotiations between the United States and the Soviet Union in 1978 prove how difficult it is to agree on steps to regulate the arms transfer on a regional basis. After differences of opinion within the US adminstration on a regional versus a technical approach had been decided in favour of regional regulations, the Carter administration suggested the establishment of working groups on regions and proposed Latin America and Sub-Saharan Africa, given the relatively low levels of arms transfers by either side to these areas. The Soviet delegation was, however, more interested in legal principles regulating global arms transfers, particularly in defining criteria for potential recipients. The suggested guidelines were intended to permit arms transfers to those countries that needed arms for self-defence but not to those countries that used arms in wars of aggression. A compromise including legal, technical, and regional criteria as well as guidelines was ultimately negotiated. After Latin America and Sub-Saharan Africa had been discussed the Soviets proposed consideration of China and the Persian–Arabian Gulf. At that time United States–Chinese relations were somewhat normalized while the US Gulf region policy was being delicately influenced by the instability of the regime of the Shah in Iran. The US National Security Council suggested stopping the negotiations in order not to endanger US foreign policy in these regions. Despite the fact that the Soviet government had accepted the US proposal to expressly discuss geographic regions the US delegation was not entitled to take up the Soviet suggestion. Instead the US delegation was instructed to discuss only Latin America and Sub-Saharan Africa.

Blechman, Nolan and Platt (1982: 148) conclude that CAT failed primarily

because the talks were conducted against a backdrop of deteriorating U.S.–Soviet relations, a volatile Middle East and an increasingly difficult political situation for the Carter administration at home. Bureaucratic confusion, personal rivalries, and tactical errors complicated these problems. Most important, in 1978 Carter made two contradictory decisions: first, that CAT should be a political rather than a technical negotiation; second, that the international political relations upon which it would impinge were too sensitive to discuss with the Soviet Union.

Import agreements Instead of approaching conventional arms transfer limitations on the supply side, it is possible to develop demand-side models for arms import restraint. Again, the point of departure could be the negative economic impact and political destabilization resulting from regional arms races. Agreements on import restrictions could, for example, be modelled on the agreement of Tlatelolco; this agreement prohibits nuclear arms in Latin America. Participating countries could either agree on a quantitative ceiling or on the prohibition of specific weapons systems. An obstacle to the implementation of such an agreement is, of course, the existence of conflicts and the perception of neighbouring countries as enemies. A precondition for the success of an agreement would be the acceptance of the principle of solving conflicts peacefully. Growing economic pressures led in 1974 to such an initiative by eight American countries. These eight countries declared in Ayacucho (Peru) their intent to negotiate regional limitations of arms transfers. Despite a repetition of this declaration by the eight and an additional twenty Latin American and Caribbean states in 1978, arms imports to Latin America have grown substantially during the last few years.[7]

UN agreements and embargoes On several occasions limitations of arms transfers have been proposed and arms embargoes have been agreed upon within the United Nations Organization. General agreements, however, failed as a result of widely differing opinions about appropriate criteria and standards. Various Soviet initiatives, aimed at establishing eligibility criteria for potential recipients (such as liberation movements) or for the prohibition of arms transfers (to aggressors) were not accepted. It was no surprise that the initiatives failed as a result of differing opinions on definitions of 'aggression' or 'limited self-defence'. The final declaration of the First Special UN Session on Disarmament in 1978 in which member states promised unanimously to start negotiations between the main suppliers and recipients of arms to limit conventional arms transfer, never went beyond this stage of declaration. A possible model for such an agreement could be the Non-Proliferation treaty. In contrast to the above discussed control agreements it is neither an export nor an import cartel but an agreement that has been ratified by nuclear as well as non-nuclear countries, that is, both potential suppliers as well as recipients have agreed upon the goal of the non-proliferation of nuclear arms.

Several controversial arms embargoes exist within the United Nations[8] but the UN member states have never succeeded in unanimously imposing an effective arms embargo; the success of those embargoes which have been imposed has been rather limited. The arms embargo against South Africa, for example, is openly ignored by several countries and circumvented by other countries which supply military-related technology.[9]

National control measures

Instead of trying to reach international agreements, the possibility of unilateral national measures can be taken into consideration. The advantage of such a stratgy is, of course, the chance for both independent decision making and for the initiation of a programme of action. The disadvantage of unilateral national restrictions or prohibitions is that the total volume of arms transfers might not be reduced due to the fact that other suppliers might compensate for the decreasing supplies. 'If we don't deliver, others will', is one major argument of the arms transfer protagonists. The supply of weapons by some forty countries (SIPRI Yearbook 1984) to Iran and Iraq during the war in that region seems to be a case in point, that is to say, arms will be supplied whenever there is demand.

Several arguments in favour of unilateral national measures can be raised. First, there are positive examples from the past. During the war in Vietnam the United States decided not to interrupt the flow of military supplies to North Vietnam, while the Soviet Union chose not to supply certain weapons to North Vietnam that might have threatened US Navy vessels operating in the Gulf of Tonkin. Another example where unilateral restraint by one superpower was reciprocated by the other is in the case of the delivery of military equipment to both Koreas. The United States and the Soviet Union demonstrated mutual restraint during the 1970s. The Soviet Union did not supply mobile air defence systems, while the United States resisted supplying the most modern models of US fighter aircraft. This situation did not change until 1981 when US F-16 fighter aircraft were supplied to South Korea; since then Soviet restraint has also subsided (Blechman, Nolan and Platt 1982: 140).

Second, the use of arms supplies as a foreign policy tool has not been so successful as is sometimes claimed. Manipulation of client regimes by means of supplying or withholding arms has in numerous cases been a failure.[10] Restraining the arms flow by unilateral national measures does not necessarily offer a leading edge in military competition in the Third World to those countries that are not willing to carry out a restrictive arms export policy. Politics with arms is not a zero sum game in which losses to one side are a gain to the other. It is not the case that revolutionary governments will, in all circumstances, align themselves with the Soviet Union and disrupt relations with the West.

The emergence of communism in a Third World country cannot automatically be equated by the Soviet Union as a significant addition to its own power or sphere of influence. Soviet influence in developing countries is not at all very high. The economic and political model is neither well accepted nor is it admired or imitated. In most cases it is the only alternative to the dependence/dominance relation to capitalist countries. From an American point of view revolution in Third World countries cannot automatically be considered as an establishment of hostile military bases. Nationalist regimes do not want to be the pawns of either of the two camps or their major powers (Barnet 1984).

Third, a policy of unilateral national measures is more than a mere symbolic act done for internal opportunistic reasons. The reversal of the arms transfer dynamic into arms transfer control can be initiated by national restrictions. Even so if practically all arms exporting countries, with the exception of the United States and the Soviet Union, could reduce global arms transfers by only a few percentage points, this could be a basis for a credible international initiative.

Indirect control measures

Reduction of military expenditures International agreements to reduce military expenditures, especially in the two main military blocks of NATO and WTO have been proposed many times. Such measures could possibly have an indirect effect on the arms imports of Third World countries especially if the programmes of armed forces and weapons procurement that are specially intended for Third World intervention could be restricted. In the period 1963 to 1965 the United States and the Soviet Union successfully practised the making of secretly agreed upon cuts in their military budgets. These reductions were finally reversed due to the American engagement in the Vietnam war (Leitenberg 1981).

Use of military expenditure reductions in development assistance Far reaching suggestions to redeploy resources that are presently used by the military for development purposes have been proposed many times within the United Nations (Thee 1981: 53–8). Already in 1950 a General Assembly resolution stressed the necessity of the member states reducing their military expenditures to a minimum and of using these resources for development and prosperity by particularly taking into consideration the needs of the under-developed world. In 1974 a report by a group of experts of the United Nations suggested reductions of military expenditures of the permanent members of the security council by 10 per cent. Why did such proposals fail? NATO countries insisted that such a suggestion could be implemented only if one knew what each country was spending on its armed forces and if the same elements were included for all countries. The Soviet Union and its allies, as always, refused to supply detailed statistics on their military expenditures, even though the Soviet government herself had suggested such cuts already in the 1960s and again in 1973. Several initiatives of that sort have been proposed and in 1978 the French government suggested an international disarmament fund for development.[11]

Tax on armaments The report of the Brandt Commission (Independent Commission on International Development Issues 1980) proposed a tax on arms transfers that could benefit development aid.

Within the United Nations it was proposed to institute a tax on armaments based on the military budgets of states. This tax would amount to 5 per cent of military budgets and be paid to the United Nations to be used exclusively for development assistance. There was, however, no agreement on this proposal. One of the counter arguments was that the positive aim of development should not be related to armaments, because one of the results of such a tax would be that the higher the military expenditures the higher would be the development fund and vice versa. More significant, however, were objections of the major military powers that were not in favour of such a proposal since they would have to carry the main burden of such a tax.

Increased development assistance for countries with low military expenditures   More convincing could be a concept that uses the level of military expenditures as a criterion for development assistance in recipient countries. Initiatives within developing countries for regional arms restraint could thus be assisted by development aid to try to reduce social and economic conflict.

IMF conditionality and debt moratoriums   Arms are exported only when these exports are financed. This might be an effective leverage for arms control. SIPRI has registered stagnating imports of major weapons to Third World countries due to the decreasing income of oil exporting countries as well as due to the high debts of several developing countries (SIPRI Yearbook 1984). Among the group of major arms importing countries of the past that are heavily indebted are countries like Argentina, Brazil, Peru, Chile, Ecuador, Turkey, Venezuela, Zaire, and Zambia; problem cases are also Israel, South Korea, the Philippines and Indonesia. Several debt moratoriums have been necessary in the past and can be expected in the future as well.

It is hardly possible to guess to what extent debt in developing countries has been caused by arms imports (Brzoska 1983: 271–7). It has been proposed to the International Monetary Fund that a policy of conditionality related to imports of arms be adopted instead of imposing the usual conditionality and austerity measures that result in the long-term destruction of social and economic life in the Third World (freezing of wages, cutting of public food programmes, subsidizing of food prices, and so on).[12]

Prohibition of arms advertisements Needless to say, a demand for arms exists in developing countries. This demand is stimulated additionally by intensive advertisement and the sales campaigns of the producing companies of industrialized countries, partly in cooperation with specialized government agencies. An express prohibition of arms advertisements in newspapers and magazines and of arms exhibitions would be one means of controlling one of the driving forces of the arms dynamic in developing countries.[13]

Conversion to civil production Arms are also exported since this is a profitable business and helps to keep production capacities utilized. Excess production capacities, especially in Western European countries, and stagnating demand for certain weapons categories are causes for increased export activities. Conversion to civil production is one means of reducing economic pressures upon arms export companies.[14] It is at the same time possible to introduce unilateral national measures.

Obstacles

Numerous reasons have to be mentioned why prospects and perspectives for controlling and reducing the arms trade are rather bleak. Some of the major reasons are listed in the following pages.

(1) One difficulty is the lack of data to verify international agreements. Arms control agreements can effectively be verified only if generally accepted standards and criteria exist. Arms control and disarmament agreements have often been rejected due to verification problems. As far as arms transfers are concerned only two institutions, the United States Arms Control and Disarmament Agency (ACDA) that bases its publication on CIA information, and the Stockholm International Peace Research Institute (SIPRI) that uses public sources, publish global statistics on arms transfers. Yet their estimates of the volume and characteristics of arms transfers are disputed due to methodological problems. Proposals to establish a UN arms trade register along the line of the example of the pre-war League of Nations register have been suggested, but have not been approved. Correctly, several governments in developing countries have drawn attention to the fact that an arms trade register would only record the arms trade but would not register the bulk of arms produced that are bought by the armed forces in the producing

countries. The same argument can, of course, be used against all arms control proposals.

(2) Besides this more or less technical and organizational problem, other more fundamental obstacles must be mentioned. We are experiencing at present a fundamental international crisis, a crisis of the nation–state system. This system has amply demonstrated both its incapacity to guarantee the survival of mankind and its ability to create increased tensions. The dangers of a nuclear war are mounting; conventional wars can be seen daily. The crisis of the legitimacy of the existing world order (or should we call it world anarchy) leads many world leaders to resort to power politics and violence as a mean of settling conflicts. Military expenditures and arms procurement are not only devoted to nuclear weapons or programmes of major arms but to some extent to the creation of intervention forces, euphemistically called 'rapid deployment forces'. As long as no strict non-intervention policy is adopted by the major Powers and their allies, Third World governments are likely to resort to armament and arms imports as a means for defence against outside aggression.

(3) The above policy is not without precedence: historic patterns show that the armament and the use of force have been constituent elements in capitalist development. Repression and the use of arms are foundation stones of European history and also a factor in creating underdevelopment. The transfer of resources from the colonies to Europe was characterized by robbery and plunder and the destruction of societies. It is a bloody history. The methods have changed today: straightforward gunboat diplomacy and the use of military force have to some extent been replaced by more subtle methods of coercion.

(4) Besides several factors which 'push' for increased arms trade in supplier countries, there are 'pull' factors in importing countries as well. In recipient countries, agreements to reduce arms transfers are considered as a possible threat to their sovereignty. Supplier cartels are looked upon as neo-colonial or patriarchal notions and are therefore rejected. As long as the two major military blocs keep the arms race going, thereby affecting also security in Third World countries, efforts to regulate arms exports are based on a weak moral position. The problem of armaments and arms transfers is first of all a problem of the two big military alliances of NATO and the Warsaw Treaty Organization. The major part of the military potential of the World is concentrated in these two alliances: all of the nuclear

weapons (except for Chinese nuclear forces), at least 70 per cent of military expenditures, at least 90 per cent of arms production facilities, and about 80–90 per cent of arms exports. Unless the military system in the two major military blocs is changed, Third World criticism of the militarization in the North and its huge over-kill capacities should be taken seriously. Starting with apparently rational purposes—to advance capitalism, to protect socialism, to deter attack or to prevent war—the major powers have accumulated vast stockpiles of weapons which serve none of these ends. These stockpiles are neither a defence nor a security system since they increasingly create insecurity and instability. But this does not mean that there is no need and scope for developing countries to try to resolve their own conflicts peacefully or reduce their own arms procurement.

(5) Arms are used today in the World to solve conflicts of internal nature as well as with neighbouring states. Arms are used to crush rebellions, to break strikes, to implement counter-insurgency strategies, to deter aggression from outside, or to fight for territories or resources. The ideology of national security has proved to be an effective instrument that is carefully managed by the elites in the Third World to maintain, not to change, the existing economic order and political system. The cost of militarization has been borne most heavily by the poorest.

(6) An exploitative international division of labour exists that gives rise to conflict. A North–South dominance/dependence relationship increases tensions and it is not unrealistic to expect that some of these tensions will lead to war as they have done so often in the past. Arms transfers illustrate the hierarchical nature of the inter-national system. The arms race in the northern hemisphere deepens the economic crisis. The direct cost of armaments—the waste of resources that could otherwise be available for development—is immense. But there are also indirect economic costs. The armaments dynamic sets priorities in shifting resources from productive to unproductive branches of industry and thus creates structural malfunctions of economies.

(7) The East–West conflict has a South dimension. Competition and antagonism between the two systems are transferred to the Third World. The major part of the world is considered by the superpowers and its allies as an object of their own national security ambitions and their sphere of influence. Like in a zero sum game, the loss of influence of the other side is considered as an asset and

vice versa. Arms supplies are used as leverage to maintain influence and to create client regimes. Superpower competition is—as has been pointed out—far from being the sole cause of Third World conflict. Third World governments are not simply pawns in a superpower game. Conflicts in the Third World arise often (possibly primarily) out of domestic conflicts, which would not disappear entirely if outside interventions were halted.

(8) The arms business is quite a profitable business. Thousands of jobs are created by arms production. Control of arms transfer and arms production is, of course, resisted by very powerful and influential forces.

A pessimistic outlook

Reviewing past experiences, analysing the obstacles to control arms transfers and looking at the economic and political interests involved the outlook for arms transfer control can only be a pessimistic one. The problem is how to make governments do something they do not want to do and, for the most part, have steadfastly resisted doing—with certain exceptions—for the last forty years. The most effective mechanism in curbing growth rates of the arms traffic was unintentional—acting through constraints on resources in importing countries, that is, high debt and reduction of hard currency reserves. Looking at the different means available it seems several national control measures—that is, unilateral steps of both exporting as well as importing countries—are required to create a favorable climate for international control agreements. Unless such a changed international situation exists there is scarcely any reason to expect a levelling off of the volume of arms transferred. A different international situation that allows for control in arms transfers would require changed attitudes both in exporting and importing countries. Having in mind the experience of the past, these hopes are possibly only wishful thinking.

A reduction of arms transfers to developing countries requires, first of all, change of those situations where weapons are used. Third World conflicts between neighbouring countries as well as domestic tensions would have to be defused by political and economic measures and not be settled by military means.

Second, in the developed world, particularly in the United States and the Soviet Union, the military would have to be restricted to defence; peaceful settlements of disputes would have priority over the projection of power on almost every part of the globe (and beyond). A strict policy of non-intervention would have to be accompanied by an immediate pledge that arms will not be supplied to either side during a state of belligerency.

Notes

1. During the ten year period from 1973 to 1983, when a severe economic crisis of global scale led to stagnation in world trade, arms exports increased from US$13.7 to US$36.6 billion (in current prices). In real terms (in ACDA 1982 Dollars), arms exports increased from ACDA$26.8 to ACDA$35.1 billion, according to US Arms Control and Disarmament Agency, *World Military Expenditures and Arms Transfers* (1985: 19).
2. In the period immediately after World War II, up to 1952–3, US military assistance was quite limited geographically. The major recipients outside the area that came to be known as NATO-Europe were Iran, Philippines, Thailand, Taiwan, Vietnam (through US subsidization of the French colonial war there—which is not, of course, assistance to the Vietnamese) and, to a lesser extent prior to the outbreak of the Korean War, the Republic of Korea. Much smaller amounts were provided to Brazil, Chile, Colombia, Ecuador, Peru, Uruguay, Burma and Indonesia. What one is really talking about is five Asian countries. (Greece and Turkey and the countries in Western Europe, of course, also received sizeable amounts of military aid.) For details see US Department of Defense, *Security Assistance Program. Congressional Presentation* (annual publication).
3. See SIPRI Yearbook (1985) and previous issues for a detailed account of arms production in the Third World.
4. As for CAT, see Salomon, Louscher and Hammond (1981: 200–8); Blechman, Nolan and Platt (1982: 138–54); and Pearson (1981: 25–65). For a general approach to restraint possibilities, see Krause (1981: 189–207).
5. Information on the so-called threshold countries is in SIPRI Yearbook, annual issues.
6. In a Tripartate Declaration of France, United Kingdom, and the United States of 25 May 1950 the principle of restraint is repeated; at the same time, however, it is recognized that the adversaries in the Arab–Israeli conflict need to 'maintain a certain level of armed forces of (sic) assuring their international security and their legitimate self-defense. . . . ' The text is reprinted in Nutting (1967: 178–9).
7. According to US Arms Control and Disarmament Agency (1985: Table II) Latin American arms imports doubled from 1978 to 1982.
8. Krause (1981: 203) mentions the following embargoes: Albania and Bulgaria (1949); China and North Korea (1951); Near East Region

(1956); South Africa (1962); Portugal (1962); and Southern Rhodesia (1965).

9. See *Hearings of the West German Parliament*, Deutscher Bundestag (1984: 231).

10. On Soviet failures, see Centre for Defence Information, 'Soviet Weapons Exports: Russian Roulette in the Third World,' in *Defense Monitor*, **1**, 1979.

11. Quotations from *United Nations Disarmament Yearbooks*, (various volumes); United Nations, Report, Review of the Implementation of the Recommendations and Decisions Adopted by the General Assembly at its Tenth Special Session. Development and International Economic Cooperation, (October 1981: Chapter I and VI). See also Thee (1981).

12. These proposals on new IMF conditions have been put forward by P. Lock in 'Bundestagsausschuss fur wirtschaftliche Zusammenarbeit', unpublished mimeo, pp. 34–7.

13. A legislative proposal to that effect has been initiated in 1985 in the West German parliament by the opposition Social Democratic party.

14. A recent report (one example of a large body of literature) has been published in Sweden, giving detailed data on the need for and consequences of conversion of the Swedish arms industry. See *In Pursuit of Disarmament. Conversion from Military to Civil Production in Sweden*, Report by the Special Expert Inga Thorsson, Stockholm (1984).

Bibliography

Aben, J. and Smith, R. P. (1985), 'Défense et emploi au Royaume-Uni', *L'effort économique de défense: France et Royaume-Uni*, J. Fontanel and R. P. Smith (eds.), *Armes: Defénse et Sécurité* Special Issue, Grenoble, CEDSI, pp. 145–70.

—— (1986), 'Defence and Employment in the UK and France: A Comparative Study', *Peace Defence and Economic Analysis*, F. Blackaby and C. Schmidt (eds.), Oxford, Basil Blackwell.

Albrecht, U., Ernst, D., Lock, P. and Wulf, H. (1974), 'Armaments and Underdevelopment', *Bulletin of Peace Proposals* **2**, pp. 177–80.

Arrow, K.J., Chenery, H.B., Minhas, B.S. and Solow, R.M. (1961), 'Capital Labor Substitution and Economic Efficiency', *Review of Economics and Statistics* **43**, pp. 225–50.

Austin, D. (1984), 'Things Fall Apart', *Africa in the Post-Decolonization Era*, R.E. Bissell and M.S. Radu (eds.), New Brunswick, N.J., Transaction Books.

Ball, N. (1983), 'Defence and Development: A Critique of the Benoit Study', *Economic Development and Cultural Change* **31**, pp. 507–24.

—— (1984), 'Measuring Third World Security Expenditure: A Research Note', *World Development* **12**, pp. 157–64.

—— (1984a), *Third-World Security Expenditure: A Statistical Compendium*, FOA Report C10250-M5, Stockholm, National Defence Research Institute.

Barnet, R. (1984), 'Why Trust the Soviets?', *World Policy Journal* **1**, pp. 461–82.

Bauer, P.T. (1965), 'The Vicious Circle of Poverty', *Weltwirtschaftliches Archiv* **95**, pp. 4–20.

Benoit, E. (1973), *Defence and Economic Growth in Developing Countries*, Lexington, Mass., D. C. Heath and Co. Lexington Books.

—— (1978), 'Growth and Defence in Developing Countries', *Economic Development and Cultural Change* **26**, pp. 271–80.

Bienen, H. (1980), 'African Militaries as Foreign Policy Actors', *International Security* **5**, pp. 168–90.

Blechman, B.M., Nolan, J.E. and Platt, A. (1982), 'Pushing Arms', *Foreign Policy* **46**, pp. 138–54.

Brzezinski, Z.K. (1983), *Power and Principle: Memoires of the National Security Advisor 1977–81*, New York, Farrar, Straus, Gerous.

Brzoska, M. (1983), 'The Military Related External Debt of Third World Countries', *Journal of Peace Research* **20**, pp. 271–7.

—— (1984), 'The Concept of Third World Militarization', *Vierteljahres-berichte der Friedrich-Ebert-Stiftung* **95**, pp. 95–124.

—— and Ohlson, T. (1986), *Arms Production in the Third World*, London, Taylor and Francis.

Centre for Defence Information (1979), 'Soviet Weapons Exports: Russian Roulette in the Third World', *Defense Monitor* **1**.

Chan, S. (1985), 'The Impact of Defence Spending on Economic Perform-ance: A Survey', *Orbis* **29**, pp. 403–34.

Chenery, H. (1979), *Structural Change and Development Policy*, A World Bank Research Publication, New York, Oxford University Press.

—— and Syrquin, M. (1975), *Patterns of Development 1950–1970*, Published for the World Bank, London, Oxford University Press.

Datta-Chaudhuri, M. K. (1979), *Industrialization and Foreign Trade: Korea and the Philippines*, Asian Employment Programme Working Paper, Bangkok, International Labour Organisation.

Deger, S. (1985), 'Human Resources, Government Education Expenditure and Military Burden', *Journal of Developing Areas* **20**, pp. 37–48.

—— (1985a), 'Does Defence Expenditure Mobilise Resources in LDCs?', *Journal of Economic Studies* **12**, pp. 15–29.

—— (1986), 'Economic Development and Defense Expenditure', *Economic Development and Cultural Change* **35**, pp. 179–96.

—— (1986a), *Military Expenditure in Third World Countries: The Economic Effects*, London, Routledge and Kegan Paul.

—— and Sen, S. (1983), 'Military Expenditure, Spin-off and Economic Development', *Journal of Development Economics* **13**, pp. 67–83.

—— and Smith, R. P. (1983), 'Military Expenditure and Growth in Less Developed Countries', *Journal of Conflict Resolution* **27**, pp. 335–53.

Deutscher Bundestag (1984), *Hearings of the West German Parliament*, 10. Wahlperiode, Stenografisches Protokoll der 18. Sitzung des Ausschusses für wirtschaftliche Zusammenarbeit, Anhang zu den Ausführungen des Sachverstandigen W. Geisler.

Eide, A. and Thee, M. (eds.) (1980), *Problems of Contemporary Militarism*, New York, St. Martin's Press.

Faini, R., Arnez, P. and Taylor, L. (1984), 'Defence Spending, Economic Structure and Growth', *Economic Development and Cultural Change* **32**, pp. 487–98.

Fontanel, J. (Grenoble Centre for Security and Defense Studies) (1980), 'Relationship between Military Expenditure and Economic Development', *Study for UN Special Expert Group on Disarmament and Development* **1**, mimeo.

—— Smith, R. P., and Humm, A. (1985), 'La substitution capital travail dans les depenses militaires', *L'effort économique de défense: France et Royaume-Uni*, J. Fontanel and R. P. Smith (eds.), Ares: *Défense et Sécurité* Special Issue, Grenoble, CEDSI, pp. 129–44.

Frederiksen, P. C. and Looney, R.E. (1983), 'Defence Expenditure and

Economic Growth in Developing Countries', *Armed Forces and Society* **9**, pp. 633–46.

Gantzel, K. J. *et al* (1986), *Die Kriege nach dem 2. Weltkrieg bis 1984*, Munich, Weltforum.

Ghosh, P. K. (1984), *Disarmament and Development: A Global Perspective*, Westport, Conn., Greenwood Press.

Griffin, L. J., Wallace, M. and Devine J. (1982), 'The Political Economy of Military Spending: Evidence from the U.S.', *Cambridge Journal of Economics* **6**, pp. 1–14.

Grimmett, R. F. (1982), *Trends in Conventional Arms Transfers to the Third World 1974–1981*, Washington, D.C., Congressional Research Service.

—— (1985), *Trends in Conventional Arms Transfers to the Third World 1977–1984*, Washington, D.C., Congressional Research Service.

Halliday, F. (1983), *The Making of the Second Cold War*, London, Verso.

Harkavy, R. E. (1979), 'The New Geopolitics: Arms Transfers and the Major Powers' Competition', *Arms Transfers in the Modern World*, S. Neuman and R.E. Harkavy (eds.), New York, Praeger, pp. 131–48.

—— (1984), 'The Lessons of Recent Wars: A Comparative Perspective', *Third World Quarterly* **6**, pp. 868–91.

Hartman, T. and Mitchell, J. (1984), *A World Atlas of Military History 1945–1984*, London, Lee Cooper with Secker and Warburg.

Hicks, N. and Kubisch, A. (1984), 'Cutting Government Expenditures in LDCs', *Finance and Development* **21**, pp. 37–9.

Holzman, F. D. (1980), 'Are the Soviets Really Outspending the US on Defense?', *International Security* **4**, pp. 86–104.

Horowitz, I. L. (1982), *Beyond Empire and Revolution: Militarization and Consolidation in the Third World*, New York, Oxford University Press.

Hurwitz, L. (1973), 'Contemporary Approaches to Political Stability', *Comparative Politics* **12**, pp. 449–63.

Independent Commission on International Development Issues (1980), *North-South: A Programme for Survival*, Report of the Brandt Commission, The Hague, IBIDI.

Ingrassia, L. (1985), 'World Weapon Sales Slow and Competition by Suppliers Heats Up', *Wall Street Journal*, May 30 issue, p. 1.

International Institute of Strategic Studies (1978), *The Military Balance 1976–1977*, London, IISS.

—— (1983), *The Military Balance 1983–1984*, London, IISS.

—— (1985), *The Military Balance 1985–1986*, London, IISS.

—— (Annual), *Strategic Survey*, London, IISS.

International Monetary Fund (1985), *Government Finance Statistics Yearbook, Volume IX*, Washington, D.C., IMF.

Jackman, R.W. (1976), 'Politicians in Uniform: Military Governments and Social Change', *American Political Science Review* **70**, pp. 1078–97.

Jackson, R.H. and Rosberg, C.G. (1982), 'Why Africa's Weak States Persist: The Empirical and Juridical in Statehood', *World Politics* **35**, pp. 1–24.

Kemp, G. (1979), 'Arms Transfers and the 'Back-End' Problem in Developing Countries', *Arms Transfers and the Modern World*, S. Neuman and R.E. Harkavy (eds.), New York, Praeger, pp. 264–73.

Kende, I. (1980), 'Local Wars 1945–76', *Problems of Contemporary Militarism*, E. Eide and M. Thee (eds.), London, Croom Helm.

Klare, M. (1983), 'The Unnoticed Arms Trade', *International Security* **8**, pp. 68–90.

Kozyrev, A. (1985), *The Arms Trade: A New Level of Danger*, Moscow, Progress.

Krause, J. (1981), 'Die Beschrankung konventioneller Rustungstransfers in die Dritte Welt', *Moglichkeiten und Methoden Kooperativer Rustungssteuerung*, W. Graf von Baudissin, D.S. Lutz (Hg.), Baden-Baden, Kooperative Rustungssteuerung, pp. 189–207.

—— (1985), *Sowjetische Militaerhilfepolitik gegenueber Entwicklungslaendern*, Baden-Baden, Nomos.

Kravis, I.B. (1984), 'Comparative Studies of National Income and Prices', *Journal of Economic Literature* **22**, pp. 1–39.

—— Heston, A. and Summers, R. (1982), *World Product and Income: International Comparisons of Real Product*, Phase III United Nations International Comparison Project Report, Baltimore, Md., The Johns Hopkins University Press.

Kurien, C. T. (1978), 'The New Development Strategy: An Appraisal', *Economic and Political Weekly* **13**, p. 1264.

Leitenberg, M. (1981), 'Efforts at Reducing Defense Expenditure in the United States', *Public Policy* **4**, pp. 437–71.

Lipset, S.M. (1960), *Political Man: The Social Bases of Politics*, New York, Doubleday.

Lock, P. (1981), 'New International Economic Order and Armaments', *Elements of World Instability*, E. Jahn and Y. Sakamoto (eds.), Frankfurt, Campus.

Looney, R.E. (1987), *The Causes and Consequences of Third World Military Expenditure and Arms Production*, forthcoming.

—— and Frederiksen, P.C. (1985), 'Defence Expenditure, External Public Debt, and Growth in Developing Countries', *Journal of Peace Research* **23**, pp. 329–37.

Loose-Weintraub, E. (1984), 'Spain's New Defence Policy: Arms Production and Exports,' ch. 4, *World Armaments and Disarmament: SIPRI Yearbook 1984*, Stockholm International Peace Research Institute, London, Taylor and Francis, pp. 137–50.

Louscher, D.L. (1977), 'The Rise of Military Sales as a U.S. Foreign Assistance Instrument', *Orbis* **20**, pp. 933–64.

Luckham, R. (1978), 'Militarism and international dependence in disarmament and development', *Disarmament and World Development*, R. Jolly (ed.), Sussex, Institute of Development Studies.

Maizels, A. and Nissanke, M.K. (1986), 'Determinants of Military Expenditures in Developing Countries', *World Development*, **14**, pp. 1125–40.

Marris, R. (1983), *Comparing the Incomes of Nations: A Critique of the ICP Project*, Birkbeck College Discussion Paper 142, London, Economics Department, Birkbeck College.

— (1984), 'Comparing the Incomes of Nations', *Journal of Economic Literature* **22**, pp. 40–57.

McCloskey, D. M. (1983), 'The Rhetoric of Economics', *Journal of Economic Literature* **21**, pp. 481–517.

Mir, P. (1986), 'El complejo militar-industrial espanol', *Mientras Tanto* **25**.

— (1986a), *L'estructura i politica militar-industrial espanyola des de finals dels 70*, Universitat Internacional de la Pau, Barcelona, Sant Cugat.

National Bipartisan Commission on Central America (1984), *Report*, Washington, D.C., US Government Printing Office.

Neuman, S.G. (1985), 'Coproduction, Barter and Countertrade: Offsets in the Arms Market', *Orbis* **29**, pp. 183–213.

Nutting, A. (1967), *No End of a Lesson*, New York, Clarcsen N. Potter.

Organisation for Economic Co-operation and Development (Annual), *Development Co-operation: Efforts and Policies of the Members of the Development Assistance Committee*, Annual Report by the Chairman of the Development Assistance Committee, Paris, OECD.

Palme, O. (1982), *Common Security: A Programme for Disarmament*, The Report of the Independent Commission on Disarmament and Security issues, London, Pan Books.

Pearson, F. S. (1981), 'U.S. Arms Transfer Policy: The Feasibility of Restraint', *Arms Control* **1**, pp. 25–65.

Pesaran, M. H. and Smith, R. P. (1985), 'Evaluation of Macroeconometric Models', *Economic Modelling* **2**, pp. 125–34.

Ralet, O. (1982), *Illegale Wapenhandel*, Berchem, EPO.

Rothstein, R. L. (1977), *The Weak in the World of the Strong*, New York, Columbia University Press.

— (1984), 'Dealing with Disequilibrium: Rising Pressure and Diminishing Resources', *International Journal* **39**, pp. 553–76.

— (1985), *Peaceful Transitions from Authoritarianism*, Report for the Office of the Historian, Washington, D.C., US Department of State.

— (1987), 'The "Security Dilemma" and the 'Poverty Trap' in the Third World', *National Security Expenditures and Development in the Third World*, R. L. West (ed.), forthcoming.

Salomon, M. D., Louscher, D. J. and Hammond, P. Y. (1981), 'Lessons of the Carter Approach to Restraining Arms Transfers', *Survival* **5**, pp. 200–08.

Sen, A. (1981), 'Public Action and the Quality of Life in Developing Countries', *Oxford Bulletin of Economics and Statistics* **43** pp. 287–319.

— (1981a), *Poverty and Famines*, Oxford, Clarendon Press.

— (1983), 'Development: Which Way Now?', *Economic Journal* **93**, pp. 745–62.

— (1985), 'Food, Economics and Entitlements', Elmhirst Lecture, Spain, International Association of Agricultural Economists.

Singh, A. (1979), 'The "Basic Needs" Approach vs the New International Economic Order', *World Development* 7, pp. 598–9.

Sivard, R. L. (1983), *World Military and Social Expenditures 1983*, Leesburg, Virg., World Priorities.

Skjelsbaek, K. (1983), 'Dimensions and Modes of Militarism', *Militarism and Militarization*, E. Holdt and A. Lejins (eds.), SIPRI Conference Papers 3, Stockholm, SIPRI.

Smith, R. P. (1977) 'Military expenditure and capitalism', *Cambridge Journal of Economics*, March, pp. 61–76.

Smith, R. P. (1980), 'The Demand for Military Expenditure', *Economic Journal* 90, pp. 811–20.

—— Humm, A. and Fontanel, J. (1985), 'The Economics of Exporting Arms', *Journal of Peace Research* 22, pp. 239–48.

Snepp, F. (1977), *Decent Interval*, New York, Random House.

Sorley, L. (1983), *Arms Transfers under Nixon*, Lexington, Ken., University of Kentucky Press.

Stockholm International Peace Research Institute (1971), *Arms Trade with the Third World*, Stockholm, Almqvist and Wicksell.

—— (1972), *World Armaments and Disarmament: SIPRI Yearbook 1972*, Stockholm, Almqvist and Wiksell.

—— (1973), *World Armaments and Disarmament: SIPRI Yearbook 1973*, Stockholm, Almqvist and Wicksell.

—— (1979), *World Armaments and Disarmament: SIPRI Yearbook 1979*, London, Taylor and Francis.

—— (1984), *World Armaments and Disarmament: SIPRI Yearbook 1984*, London, Taylor and Francis.

—— (1985), *World Armaments and Disarmament: SIPRI Yearbook 1985*, London, Taylor and Francis.

—— (1986), *World Armaments and Disarmament: SIPRI Yearbook 1986*, Oxford, Oxford University Press.

Subrahmanyam, K. (1986), 'Insecurity of Developing Nations and Regional Security', *Strategic Analysis* 9.

Summers, R. and Heston, A. (1984), 'Improved Comparisons of Real Product and Its Composition 1950–1980', *Review of Income and Wealth* 30, pp. 207–62.

Terhal, P. (1981), 'Guns or Grain: Macro-Economic Costs of Indian Defence, 1960–1970', *Economic and Political Weekly* 16, p. 2001.

Thee, M. (1981), 'The Establishment of an International Disarmament Fund for Development', *Bulletin of Peace Proposals* 1, pp. 53–8.

Thompson, W.S. (1969), *Ghana's Foreign Policy 1957–66: Diplomacy, Ideology and the New State*, Princeton N.J., Princeton University Press.

—— (1978), *Power Projection: A Net Assessment of U.S. and Soviet Capabilities*, New York, National Strategy Information Center.

—— (1981), 'Choosing to Win', *Foreign Policy* 43, p. 78.

Thorsson, I. (1984), *In Pursuit of Disarmament: Conversion from Military to*

Civil Production, Report by the Special Expert, Stockholm.

Tullberg, R. (1985), 'Military-related Debt in Non-oil Developing Countries 1972–82', *World Armaments and Disarmament: SIPRI Yearbook 1985*, Stockholm International Peace Research Institute, London, Taylor and Francis, pp. 445–58.

Ungar, S. J. (1985), 'Africa May Starve, But it Has Arms Aplenty', *Outlook*, September 9 Issue, Washington, D.C., Washington Post.

United Nations (1982), *Handbook of World Development Statistics*, New York, UN

—— Centre for Disarmament (1981), *Reduction of Military Expenditures: Reporting of Military Expenditures*, Study Series 4, New York, UN

—— Conference on Trade and Development (1983), *Handbook of International Trade and Development Statistics*, 1983 Supplement, Geneva, UNCTAD.

—— Department for Disarmament Affairs (1983), *Economic and Social Consequences of the Arms Race and of Military Expenditures*, Study Series 11, New York, UN.

—— General Assembly (1981), *Review of the Implementation of Recommendations and Decisions*, General Assembly Tenth Special Session, New York, UN.

—— General Assembly (1985), *Reduction of Military Budgets: Expenditures in Standardized Form*, Report by the Secretary-General, New York, UN.

US Agency for International Development (1983), *Implementation of Section 620(s) of the Foreign Assistance Act of 1961*, A Report to Congress, Washington, D.C., USAID.

US Arms Control and Disarmament Agency (1984), *World Military Expenditures and Arms Transfers 1972–1982*, ACDA Publication 117, Washington, D.C., ACDA.

—— (1985), *World Military Expenditures and Arms Transfers 1983*, ACDA Publication 123, Washington, D.C., ACDA.

US Congress, House, Committee on Foreign Affairs (1980), *Economic Development versus Military Expenditures*, 96th Congress, 2nd Sess., Report, Washington, D.C., US Government Printing Office.

—— Senate, Committee on Foreign Relations (1984), *National Bipartisan Report on Central America, Hearings, February 7–8*, 99th Congress, 2nd Sess., Washington, D.C., U. S. Government Printing Office.

US Department of Defense (Annual), *Security Assistance Program*, Congressional Presentation, Washington, D.C., US Government Printing Office.

Wallis, K. F. (1979), *Topics in Applied Econometrics*, 2nd edition, Oxford, Basil Blackwell.

Waltz, K. N. (1979), *Theory of International Politics*, Reading, Mass., Addison-Wesley.

Wolpin, M.D. (1973), *Military Aid and Counter-revolution in the Third World*, Lexington, Mass., D. C. Heath and Co. Lexington Books.

—— (1981), *Militarism and Social Revolution in the Third World*, Totowa, N. J., Allanheld, Osmun and Co. Publishers.

—— (1986), *Militarization, Internal Repression and Social Welfare in the Third World*, New York, St. Martin's Press.

World Armies (1983), London, Macmillan.

World Bank (1976), *World Tables 1976*, Baltimore, Md., The Johns Hopkins University Press.

—— (1980), *World Tables 1980*, The Second Edition, Baltimore, Md., The Johns Hopkins University Press.

—— (1982), *World Development Report 1982*, Baltimore, Md., The Johns Hopkins University Press.

—— (1983), *World Tables 1983*, Baltimore, Md., The Johns Hopkins University Press.

—— (1985), *World Development Report 1985*, New York, Oxford University Press.

Author Index

Subject Index